Antoine and Christine van den Assem

I0528769

BORN TO OVERCOME

DESTINED TO WALK IN FAITH AND VICTORY

EQUIP PRESS

Colorado Springs

Library of Congress Control Number: 2025913977

First Edition: 2025
Born to Overcome / Antoine and Christine van den Assem
Print ISBN: 978-1-966923-08-4
eBook ISBN: 978-1-966923-09-1

Excitement, challenge, adventure, romance - Antoine van den Assem's stories of God's working in Europe and Asia in the 1970s and 1980s has it all. We are given a deeper understanding of the truth of Ephesians 6.10– 18: human opposition is never the reality; spiritually oppressive powers are always the backdrop.

Having known Antoine and Chris, their family and their ministry, for more than forty years, I learnt much more from these pages. The world of the 2020s is very different from that of the 1970s, but the same truths endure. Our individual lives may be "nur noch ein Strich in der Landschaft" - just a line in the landscape, but in obedience to God, and by experiencing Jesus' resurrection power we can change our world. Be challenged as you read, but more importantly, make these stories real in your own life.

Anthony Harrop, former senior publishing consultant with the United Bible Societies, spent four decades working with national Bible societies in Asia and Africa. His career in sales, marketing and publishing includes an MBA from MIT. Now retired and living in Reading, United Kingdom, he continues to be active in local church ministry, with a global interest in missions as a consultant and board trustee.

Antoine and Chris van den Assem are great missionaries and apostles of this era. They have a genuine heart for winning the lost for the kingdom of God, especially in Asia. I have closely observed their leadership, and the way they understood the challenges and overcame them absolutely impressed me. It impacted my life to overcome my own challenges. I am sure the reader of this book will be greatly challenged.

Pastor D. H., director of a growing indigenous church planting ministry in South East Asia. Pastor D was discipled and trained by VFA.

BORN TO OVERCOME

"... for everyone born of God
overcomes the world.

This is the victory that has *overcome*
the world, even our faith.

Who is it that *overcomes* the world?

Only the one who believes that
Jesus is the Son of God."

(1 John 5:4–6 NKJV, author's emphasis)

DEDICATION

This book is dedicated to faithful disciples who, many of them at a very young age, left their homelands to become missionaries. Their vision was to reach those who have never heard the message of salvation through the Lord Jesus in unreached places. They laid down their lives and thus learned to overcome.

This book is also dedicated to countless brothers and sisters in Asia who were reached through the dedication of these servants of God. Today they continue to overcome and are bringing forth much lasting fruit.

We thank all the faithful believers in the U.S., Europe and elsewhere who for many years have been tirelessly supporting the ministry of Vision for Asia. Their persevering prayer and sacrificial financial giving remain crucial for the overcoming of many challenges. As this book was about to be completed, one of them—my wife's dear sister—Maria Kay Hostetter died unexpectedly in a tragic car crash. Therefore, we especially dedicate this book to her memory and to her husband, Steve.

We praise God for our five grown children and their wonderful families. Our children had to grow up living in and adjusting to five different countries. We thank them for involuntarily going along with us no matter where we happened to be!

Lastly all honor and glory goes to our Lord Jesus Christ who is the Lion of Judah. It is only because of Him that we overcome.

You are of God, little children, and have
overcome them, because He who is in you
is greater than he who is in the world.
1 John 4: 4 (NKJV, author´s emphasis)

PROLOGUE

Normal life is full of challenges that need to be overcome. But who decides what is "normal" and how are you supposed to overcome? The experiences and lessons learned by two disciples of Christ and described in this book could be termed "not normal." The development of the VFA mission work in Asia took some interesting turns. Partly because these lessons were gained under the extreme circumstance of forsaking all that is familiar to obey a higher call. On the other hand, every true follower of Christ—wherever he is or whatever he is told to do—will live an extraordinary life. For all those born of God there is one very clear challenge to overcome: *the world*. This poses another question. What does "the world" mean for those who desire to be disciples of Christ?

The biblical concept of "world" can be classified into six categories: the physical world, the human world, the moral world, the temporal world, the spiritual world and the coming world. The physical world includes the whole universe, the cosmos, or the creation. There is no doubt that we are living in a fallen world. No matter how hard humanity tries, things have not improved much since Cain killed Abel. In fact, it has gotten worse. Most of human history is a nonstop violent succession of man rising up against man. Instead of overcoming, humanity has been overcome by envy and hatred just as Cain was. Defeated because of perceived superiority, opposing world and religious views, the "wrong" skin color, power struggles, abuse, addiction, corruption, lust, pride . . . you name it. The ages passed and mankind fell ever deeper into the hole dug by their own actions.

Ten generations after the creation of Adam, God saw that the earth was corrupt and filled with violence, and He decided to do away what He had created. God gave a new chance to eight survivors, Noah and his family who overcame in a world flooded by sin. But not much changed and in no time this world was once again taken over by corruption. God then chose Abraham and promised him that through one of his descendants, all the families of the earth would be blessed. Sadly the children of Israel also went their own way. Approximately 1,800 years—or forty-one generations—later, Jesus, the Son of God, Messiah and Savior of the world was born. His origin and the purpose for His coming are well described in the Bible:

> "In the beginning was the Word, and the Word was with God, and the Word was God. He was with God in the beginning. Through him all things were made; without him nothing was made that has been made. In him was life, and that life was the light of all mankind. The light shines in the darkness, and the darkness has not *overcome* it."
> (John 1:1–5 NKJV, author's emphasis)

The word *overcome* in this passage says it all. Darkness will try to overcome the light, but it will not succeed. Light always overcomes darkness. Darkness cannot and will not be able to overcome the presence of light. Jesus, the Son of God and the Light of the World, came to overcome the darkness in this fallen world.

> "The true light that gives light to everyone was coming into the world. He was in the world, and though the world was made through him, the world did not recognize him. He came to that which was his own, but his own did not receive him. Yet to all who did receive him, to those who believed in his name, he gave the right to become children of God— children born not of natural descent, nor of human decision or a husband's will, but born of God."
> (John 1:9–14 NKJV)

Jesus, the Word made flesh came to that which was his own,

but he was not well received. His own rejected Him. Jesus overcame this rejection by obeying God's will for his life. He had to overcome not only rejection, but fear, torture and death. Because He was born of God and without sin He overcame sin, death and Satan. He fulfilled His calling as the Lamb of God taking the sins of this world upon Him. He was delivered over to death but rose up victoriously for our justification.

**"Pilate therefore said to Him, 'Are You a king then?'
Jesus answered, 'You say rightly that I am a king.
For this cause I was born, and for this cause I have
come into the world, that I should bear witness to the
truth. Everyone who is of the truth hears My voice.'"
(John 18:37 NKJV)**

All who did receive Him, to those who believed in His name, He gave the right to become children of God— children born not of natural descent, nor of human decision or a husband's will, but born of God. Like Jesus, those born of God are called to live in this world, bear witness to the truth and help bring in the harvest of righteousness. We are called to be tools of righteousness and holiness, tools in God's own hand to be a blessing to the nations of this world. We may face opposition, but we will also see eternal fruit that remains. The good news is: those born of God who believe that Jesus is the Son of God will overcome the world. By faith. In the past those who obeyed God overcame by their faith. In Hebrews 11 there is a whole list of heroes, both famous as well as those unsung, who all learned to overcome. The definition of faith is "confidence in what we hope for and assurance about what we do not see" (Heb. 1:1). The world was not worthy of these men and women. (v. 38)

**"These things I have spoken to you, that in Me
you may have peace. In the world you will have**

tribulation; but be of good cheer, I have *overcome* the world." (John 16:33 NKJV, author's emphasis)

The seven churches mentioned in Revelation 2 and 3 all faced different challenges, but the promise is given each time to those who overcome!

To him who *overcomes* I will give to eat from the tree of life. (Rev. 2:7 NKJV)

He who *overcomes* shall not be hurt by the second death. (v. 11)

To him who *overcomes* I will give some of the hidden manna to eat.

And I will give him a white stone, and on the stone a new name . . . (v. 17)

And he who *overcomes*, and keeps My works until the end, to him I will give power over the nations. (v. 26)

He who *overcomes* shall be clothed in white garments, and I will not blot out his name from the Book of Life; but I will confess his name before My Father and before His angels. (Rev. 3:5)

He who *overcomes*, I will make him a pillar in the temple of My God, and he shall go out no more.

I will write on him the name of My God and the name of the city of My God, the New Jerusalem And I will write on him My new name. (v. 12)

To him who *overcomes* I will grant to sit with Me on My throne, as I also overcame and sat down with My Father on His throne. (v. 21) (author's emphasis)

CONTENTS

Born to Overcome   iii
   Dedication   v
   Prologue   vii

Jesus People   1
   Chapter 1: Narrow Escapes   3
   Chapter 2: Born from Above   11
   Chapter 3: Born of Spirit and Water   19

Learning to Be a Disciple   31
   Chapter 4: Born to Overcome   33
   Chapter 5: Stronger through Struggle   42
   Chapter 6: The Spiritual Battle   52

Go Therefore   61
   Chapter 7: An Allegory – The History of the Bamboo   63
   Chapter 8: India Calling   68
   Chapter 9: The Circus of God   76

God's Ways Are Higher   79
   Chapter 10: Learning to Wait   81
   Chapter 11: God's Ways Are Higher   88
   Chapter 12: Laying a Foundation   101

India at Last   109
   Chapter 13: Overland to India   111
   Chapter 14: A Bloody Birth   118
   Chapter 15: Making Disciples   121

Overcoming the Strongman   133
   Chapter 16: The Weapons of Our Warfare   135
   Chapter 17: Signs and Miracles   143
   Chapter 18: Discipleship and Discipline   154

Enlarging the Vision for Asia	165
Chapter 19: The Land of Serendib	167
Chapter 20: The Land of the Pure	181
Chapter 21: Favor from the Lord	188
Divine Appointments and Opposition	221
Chapter 22: Divine Appointments	223
Chapter 23: Trouble in Paradise	234
Chapter 24: Land of the Warrior Race	245
Endurance Produces Character	261
Chapter 25: A Sharp Disagreement	263
Chapter 26: Challenging a Giant	271
Chapter 27: The Two Harvests	301
Epilogue	309
Fruit That Remains:1991–2024	311

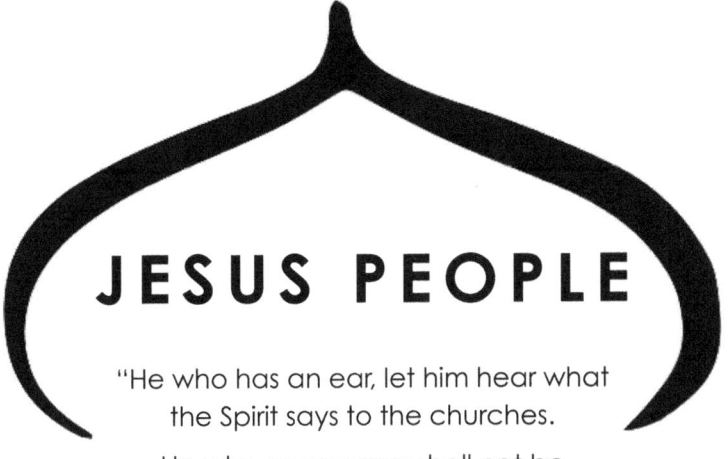

JESUS PEOPLE

"He who has an ear, let him hear what
the Spirit says to the churches.

He who *overcomes* shall not be
hurt by the second death."

(Rev. 2:11 NKJV, author's emphasis)

1
NARROW ESCAPES

My eyes were fixed on the train tracks glistening in the moonlight before me; I stood there waiting. The faint rumbling of a fast-approaching train could be heard in the distance. My decision was made. I was twenty years old and waiting for death. The evening cold, not death, was making me shiver.

Soon it will all be over, I thought. The headlights of the locomotive flared up out of the darkness. The train came speeding my way.

Now, lie down quickly and put your neck on the train track, I ordered myself.

But then something unexpected happened.

"So, do you really think it will all be over when you kill yourself?" A soft but stern voice spoke clearly in my mind. It confused, convicted and totally sidetracked me. Deep in my heart I knew Truth was speaking. I hesitated for a moment. Too late. The train thundered by, twisting me around in its wake. Two red backlights glaring at me like angry demon eyes disappeared in the darkness. I was still alive.

"Why did you do this to me? I am a failure. I can't even kill myself!" I shouted at the Invisible One above. The answer was silence. "Well, if you don't let me kill myself, you show me who you are and why I live!"

It was not the first time I had encountered death.

The sunny Dutch beach was crowded with people sunbathing, playing games, shouting and splashing in the waves of the North Sea. The small two-year-old boy I was at the time could easily get lost in all this commotion. Attracted by the water, I wobbled into it. I immediately fell over backward upon being struck by the first small wave. I vividly remember the ripples of small waves passing right above me in water 50 centimeters deep. Then two big hands ripped through the surface, grabbed me and pulled me out of the water. My father's hands! He had seen me fall and rushed to my rescue. "Am I going to see the angels?" I asked him.

The pain felt like knives being thrust into my abdomen, unbearable for an eight-year-old boy. I finally called for my father. With lights flashing and sirens full blast, the speeding ambulance cut through the traffic in The Hague, Netherlands, rushing me to the Children's Hospital. A case of acute appendicitis was about to blow out the flickering candle of my childhood. It was the middle of summer. My eyes opened slowly. My right arm was tied firmly to a stiff board. A needle was stuck into my arm, which was attached to a weird tube and a plastic bottle filled with liquid hanging over my head. It was hot, I was alone, in pain and terribly thirsty. I was sure I was about to die—if I weren't in hell already. But I did not want to die!

My dear mother had died the previous year after she developed thrombosis from varicose veins. Eight young children—five sisters, two brothers and I—were suddenly left behind, half orphans. My hard-working father, a teacher, bravely kept the family together with the help of a housekeeper and his oldest daughter. Now I was lying in a hospital, very afraid I was going to die just like my mother.

Somehow a certain teacher we had in our Christian elementary school came to mind. She wasn`t very good-looking but she was very sweet! When I get to heaven, she will be the first person I would like to see. She faithfully read us fascinating stories about the adventurous lives and dangerous experiences of missionaries. Like a real superhero, God always seemed to come to their rescue, appearing on the scene right on time. I had already heard and read enough Bible stories to know that Jesus healed the sick, at least in the Bible. My childlike mind paused a moment . . .

A SIMPLE CONCLUSION

I decided to make a deal. If I would offer Jesus to become a missionary, He would then definitely be impressed enough to heal me. And, so I did. Sure enough, He reached down, touched me and healed me. Within a short time I was able to leave the hospital, shining like an angel. Only years later I would read in the Bible what Jesus spoke about childlike faith:

> **"Truly I tell you, anyone who will not receive the kingdom of God like a little child will never enter it." (Mark 10:15 NKJV)**

Later in elementary school I was deeply moved by a very graphic film about African people suffering horrible diseases like Elephantiasis and sleeping sickness. I made up my mind to study hard and become a missionary medical doctor. After all, I had to fulfill my promise to God. I had received a heart of compassion and, henceforth, always sided with the underdogs.

However, the road to hell is paved with good intentions.

My family moved to a newly built suburb of our city where my father found a new wife willing to risk the challenge of raising eight kids who weren't her own. My four older sisters were growing into puberty, and my two younger brothers, our younger sister and I were the normal lively bunch. Unfortunately our new mother lacked the sense of humor that had characterized our own mother and was inherited by all us kids. With a no-nonsense approach she organized the family like a regiment. Everybody was on duty. Grace was obtained by hard work. Love was a scarce commodity. Ours was a world void of desperately needed affection and attention.

Needless to say, we were on a collision course. Nonetheless my parents tried their best to make things work. My father owned one of the first cars in our street, an old French station wagon. He fitted it out with two opposite benches in the back to accommodate a family of ten. As a teacher my father had six weeks of summer holidays. He took great pains to transport us to the dunes, or the beach or to go skating, which was his passion. He even built his own trailer to take us on our yearly holiday, either in the woods or at a beachside campground in the Netherlands.

My brothers and I were not allowed to take friends into our crowded, small-scale Dutch home. So come rain, snow, hail or storm, we always played outside in the swamps, ditches and trees around the construction sites in our new suburb. My two brothers always relied on me to lead and come up with new ideas to defeat boredom. We played "Cowboys and Indians," soccer or fought other boys in the neighborhood. Especially after Christmas, there were fierce battles over discarded Christmas trees which would be collected by each street gang. In the narrow Dutch streets they would be burned in huge, very dangerous bonfires on New Year's Eve. This custom was and still is a big riot in my country. Dutch cities literally go out with a deafening, fiery and prolonged bang on the last day of the year.

CAR CRASH

After elementary school I cycled to high school on the other side of town through rain, wind and snow. The first year was OK, but then I started spacing out, becoming more interested in after-school activities. I was very playful and only studied the minimum, which soon became evident in my grades. My father then put me into the school where he worked as a teacher. One day near a busy intersection, I was walking on the sidewalk and passed by the local cinema featuring *Lawrence of Arabia*.

As I looked in the store window, the sickening sound of screeching tires and crushing steel shook me. Right behind me two cars crashed into one another. One of the cars, a Volkswagen van totally out of control, came speeding up the sidewalk. It smashed into the wall between the two windows just four yards away from me. The driver's door was thrown open by the impact and the unconscious driver fell out onto the pavement right in front of me. Utterly traumatized, I took off and escaped around the back side of the Volkswagen—anything to get away from this unexpected scene of death. Somebody out there was trying to kill me.

The Beatles, with their upbeat music, took the hearts of our young 1970s generation by storm. Long hair and miniskirts were in, parents were out. Love and freedom were in the air. Soon LPs of the Rolling Stones, Pink Floyd, Led Zeppelin and Black Sabbath, Jimmy Hendrix and Janis Joplin were filling my room as well as my heart and mind. My hair grew long, and my morals grew short. My promise to God started to fade away.

The flatboat loaded with crates full of cucumbers and tomatoes moved slowly through the narrow canal. My uncle's worker, who was standing behind the crates in the back, was leaning heavy on a long pole and pushing it into the shallow water to propel the boat forward. During the summer holidays I used to earn pocket money by picking cucumbers and tomatoes at my uncle's commercial greenhouses.

After a long, sweaty day we were heading for the auction market. Standing in the front of the flatboat, I used my own pole to keep the boat on track. Behind me, the cucumbers were stacked three crates high. My head stuck out just above them, so I could communicate with the worker in the back. While approaching a small and very low concrete bridge, I was distracted by a friend passing over the bridge on his bicycle.

"Hey, how are you doing?" I yelled. The front of the boat moved slowly underneath the low bridge. All of a sudden a much louder voice shouted in my head:

"Bow down!"

Instinctively I ducked—just in time. I got the shock of my life. If I had waited a second later, my head would have been severed from my torso by the immovable crates behind me and the hard edge of the concrete bridge in front of me. My whole body shivered and shook as I came out into the sunlight from underneath the dark bridge. Once again narrowly escaping death, I had to wonder . . . who was the Somebody who shouted?

WHO AM I?

Small white crosses as far as I could see covered the ground in front of me. While ambling through a park in the Netherlands, I suddenly found myself in front of a huge military graveyard. Lined up in endless rows, resembling soldiers standing at attention, each cross bore the name of a young foreign soldier. All of them had given their lives to liberate my country from Nazi rule during World War II.

Reading the names and ages, I noticed that many of them were between eighteen- and twenty-five years old when they died. My age. They must have had plans, hopes and visions for life after the war. Their deaths were another testimony to the shocking reality that life could be cut off at any time. It made me think. What about me? What is the reason for my life? How and for what purpose am I going to live this short time on Earth? From that moment onward three questions occupied my mind.

Who am I? Why do I live? Where am I going?

WHY DO I LIVE?

The situation at home got worse as my father battled bouts of manic depression. My four elder sisters all left home as soon as possible. I had already forgotten about my intention to study medicine. Instead, I would have loved to study journalism, but in trying to please my parents I ended up studying horticulture. I was very unmotivated and already on a downward spiral in my life. Instead of studying I ended up goofing off with friends, doing side jobs like decorating shop windows and hitchhiking around Holland and parts of Europe.

When my father asked which kind of new plant was growing in his backyard, my reply was: "A rare type of flower!" In reality I had started growing marijuana or hashish for my own consumption in my father's garden. Back then this was illegal in the Netherlands. However, after famous music idols Jimmy Hendrix and Janis Joplin both died prematurely of an overdose of drugs, my attraction to the "all you need is love" culture started to crumble. I never enjoyed smoking and usually avoided smoking over my lungs, but in order to consume marijuana I had to start doing that. My throat felt like a chimney which kept me from getting too much into doing hashish.

One incident turned me upside down. Some of my "friends" had invited me to join their party in their commune. I entered their marijuana-smoke-and-music-filled room where they were all chilling out. With a mean grin on his face, somebody offered me some tea. Whatever they had put into that tea I will never know. After some time a strange feeling came over me and I started hallucinating. I could barely stand up and staggered out of that room toward the steep stairway.

While trying to go down the narrow steps, demon faces were all around me laughing and grinning and chasing me. A very real, dark and evil fear gripped my soul. I had never believed in the reality of demons or the devil. Now the King of Darkness had busted in mercilessly to blow out whatever candlelight was left in my soul. My self-confidence disappeared completely, and my hands and heart started shaking. A spirit of fear took hold of me, forcing me to stay away from people. Loneliness, restlessness and hopelessness enveloped me like a dark and heavy cloak.

WHERE AM I GOING?

"Vanity of vanities," says the preacher
king Solomon in Ecclesiastes 1:2–3.
"Vanity of vanities! All is vanity. What does man gain
by all the toil at which he toils under the sun?"

And he continues in verse 9:

"What has been is what will be, and what has
been done is what will be done; and there
is nothing new under the sun." (NKJV)

One Sunday I walked into a church and sat all the way in the back in the hope of hearing something that could help me get out of this swamp. The reverend in the pulpit spoke words, but none of them reached my wounded heart and spirit. So I left the way I came.

Life became a heavy burden, and I slipped more and more into darkness and despair. After about a year I started to consider suicide as the only option left to end my suffering. That is when I decided train tracks and a fast train could do that job. But an inner voice from above had stopped me in the last moment. I had been going my own way and ended up in a dead-end street. Where was I going? Deep in my heart I knew there must be a better way, a better truth and a better life.

2
BORN FROM ABOVE

"For the wages of sin is death, but the gift of God is eternal life in Christ Jesus our Lord." (Rom. 6:23 NKJV)

An open Bible was in front of me while I was on my knees in my tiny study room in the city of Utrecht, Netherlands. I had started reading the Bible again. One thing had become clear to me: the wages of sin is death. I knew I was such a sinner and had just tasted death. But how was I to get rid of sin? Who is going to help me overcome temptation, sin and death in my life? Tears started to flow while pouring out my heart in conviction and desperation to an invisible God. It felt like being hemmed in behind and before. "Please answer me!" I sobbed.

THE HAND OF GOD

"You hem me in behind and before, and you lay your hand upon me." (Ps. 139:5 NKJV)

All of a sudden I felt a Presence in my room. Time stood still. A huge warm Hand was slowly laid on my back, and as it touched me a powerful sensation of Peace started to flow through my cold and restless soul. My heavenly Father's Hand! Wave after wave of gentle Peace passing my understanding flooded my wounded inner being. For hours I was bathing in this ocean of Peace. It felt like standing under a warm shower washing away all the dirt. When it finally ebbed away and my strength returned, I knew for sure: God is real. He is alive. He touched me!

Great joy filled my heart. I had to tell somebody and stormed into the room of a fellow student.

"God is real, I just met Him!" I shouted.

In shock he looked at me in bewilderment as he listened to what had happened to me. "You have been smoking too much weed (marijuana)!" he finally concluded, looking into my ecstatic face with its wide-eyed pupils.

The sun went down over the North Sea in an explosion of orange, red and yellow streaks of evening light. My worried parents had picked me up from my study room in Utrecht, and now we were driving along the coast toward my hometown The Hague. I had failed my studies and had no clue what I would do next. Stretched out on the backseat, I watched this spectacular light show.

Once again this supernatural assurance surrounded me and filled my heart with Peace. Somehow I knew there was nothing to worry about. Surely the One who created such beauty—the sun, the moon, day and night—was in perfect control.

JOY-FILLED REBELS

Sometime later one of my sisters attended a special meeting in my hometown where a preacher had shared about New York gangsters being changed into saints. There seemed to be a place in the east of my country where the same was happening, so she tried to rally her brothers and sisters to join her at this youth "happening". We were not much in contact with each other anymore. Each of us had gone his or her own separate, wayward and rebellious way. Amazingly enough, on this day two of my brothers, two of my sisters and I ended up traveling to the "Bron" (the Well). This conference center was in picturesque Dalfsen in the province of Overijssel near the German border. The place was overflowing with mostly young people. Something special was happening!

Immediately I started exploring the area and soon found myself in a most interesting conversation with a twelve-year-old boy. I have always loved kids, but this little guy was very different. Although young, he impressed me with his maturity concerning the things he experienced about knowing God personally. In fact, I felt like the spiritual twelve-year-old—or even younger—while he appeared to be the twenty-year-old. It reminded me of the twelve-year-old Jesus explaining the Scriptures in the temple to baffled, bearded, gray-haired and self-righteous teachers of the law. God did not seem to care much about age but was more concerned with the openness of a person's heart and their hunger for Truth.

In the area surrounding the conference center, people were enthusiastically talking two by two or in small groups; some seemed to be praying. Around a corner I was attracted to rhythmic guitar music and lively singing. A motley crowd of dark-colored, long-haired, Asian-looking young men and women was joyfully singing and dancing to the music.

I was spellbound as I looked into their faces, shining with a heavenly glow. They were Ambonese, descendants from Ambon Island, which is a part of the Maluku Islands of Indonesia. This area had been colonized by the Dutch up until briefly after World War II. They were promised independence by the Dutch, but with Indonesia becoming independent none of their aspirations were fulfilled. Their parents had immigrated to the Netherlands but had kept the love for their homeland alive.

Many of these youngsters were in rebellion against the Dutch government. At one point they even hijacked a train and killed hostages. So far I had only known them as aggressive and unpredictable, dangerous to be around in discos or bars. Now I was flabbergasted to see them so happy and full of genuine love. While talking to some of them they all attributed this phenomenon to meeting Jesus! Wow! I had already met God personally, and now they were telling me I could meet Jesus personally as well.

A STRANGE FORCE

However, things took a strange turn when I noticed one of my younger brothers talking to an elderly man. Tears were streaming from his eyes. I never expected my brother to cry in public! All of a sudden I felt uncomfortable and sensed a strange force trying to pull me away from this place of so much wondrous spiritual activity. The strange force was compelling me to leave at once, but a gentler force was telling me to stay. Being torn between the two, the strange force seemed to get the upper hand.

It was getting late, and I decided to persuade my brothers and sisters to call it a day and leave right away. But then a long-haired but very kind young hippie got in between and started to tell about how he had met the Lord while traveling through the U.S. He very wisely suggested that if we were to leave, we should pray together first. We agreed, and while holding hands, he blessed us and bound the demonic forces that were trying to separate us from Jesus.

After that simple but powerful prayer, I felt like I was nailed to the ground and could not leave. I did not realize it at the time, but I was obviously bound by a demonic influence trying to assert its dominion over my life. Now the gentler force seemed to have won the battle for my soul, and it felt like being carried away by the current of a gently flowing river. We decided to stay and attend the evening meeting overflowing with young people.

After a short time of upbeat songs about God and Jesus, a haggard-looking, skinny man in his forties got up and walked to the front. He started telling us about all the terrible things and immoral sins he had done in his life. He did not seem to be ashamed of baring all these intimacies to this much younger crowd of hairy individuals in front of him. Then he told us how he had met Jesus, who had told him to repent of his sins and get rid of all the garbage in his life by surrendering his life to God. He had done that, was forgiven of his sins and had received a new heart and life. At the end he was telling us that we could experience the same if we were willing to come to the front and repent.

Now the gentle force became more forceful, and I felt a great urge to go forward. I looked around. Nobody was moving. Not able to hold back any longer, I ran to the front. I couldn't care less what others were thinking or doing; I just wanted to get rid of the garbage in my life. Kneeling in the front, I started crying uncontrollably, confessing my sins.

THE FILM OF MY LIFE

Lost in another world, I was unaware of what was happening around me. On an imaginary screen in front of me I was shown the film of my life up to that point. Scene after scene flashed by—all the good and bad things I had ever done or experienced. A pair of measuring scales appeared in front of me. In the right scale were the good things I had done, and in the left were the bad things. It surprised me a bit that God had also kept a record of the few good things I had done. The left scale went down rapidly, and I felt very convicted of my sins. A huge cross appeared with a blood-smeared body hanging on it. With tender and compassionate, loving eyes, Jesus looked down on my broken spirit below. He did not speak a word but that was not necessary. I knew He had forgiven me and accepted me. Unspoken words echoed in my mind: "I did this for you, what are you going to do for Me?!"

"Behold my son, thus speaks the Lord," the elderly man— completely unknown to me—who was praying and speaking over me, halted for a moment. I could not see the Lord. Only this man.

Then he continued, "Behold and know, that there was a time, during which I kept my eye upon you and went after you with my Spirit, a time during which you were very disobedient, a time in which I could not catch you, my son, but my love has caught you, nevertheless. Therefore, my son, I want you to be thankful so your thankfulness will bear fruit. My son, did I not love you with a great love, did I not save you, did I not pull you away from the edge of the abyss, says the Lord?!"

By this time I knew for sure God, and not this man, was speaking to me. My eyes welled up with tears of thankfulness.

"Therefore my son, my Spirit wants to reveal Himself within your inner man in a greater way than before; and therefore, I say to you my son, deliver up to Me everything which is not from God and I will renew you completely. Yes, I will make space in your inner man, and you will be able to become a wonderful blessing, thus speaks the Lord."

Soon I learned the Holy Spirit inspired gift of prophecy had touched my personal life. It could not have been more accurate.

Watching a waterfall splashing into a small brook at the conference grounds made me realize what was happening inside of me. The spiritual change in me felt like rivers of living water flowing out of my belly. I was forgiven of my sins, washed clean by the blood of Jesus and now I had received a new heart. The old things have passed away, a new life has started! A new beginning, but where to start and now where to go? Feeling an urge to get away from people to be alone with God, I walked into a nearby wooded area. There I poured out my heart to my newly found heavenly Father.

"Dear Lord, here I am, what do you want me to do now, how can you use me?"

The answer came promptly and surprised me.

"Do you remember what you promised Me when you were eight

years old?"

Eight years old? How was I supposed to remember what happened twelve years ago? I strained to go back through my memory, clouded by my recent past life.

A GOOD MEMORY

Suddenly it hit me: when I was eight years old, my mother had just died the year before and I was also about to die of acute appendicitis. I did not want to die and had promised God I would become a missionary if He would heal me. God had kept His promise and did heal me, but so far I had not kept my side of the promise. I thought for a moment. Two things struck me. First of all, obviously God has a good memory and had not forgotten my promise to Him. Secondly the amazing fact that God took the promise of an eight-year-old boy so seriously.

Was all this trouble I had gone through and the dead-end street I had gotten stuck in all about God trying to get me to a point to surrender myself to do His will? Of course, and He was perfectly right in doing so.

"Ok Lord, if that is what you want me to be and do, then I want to be a missionary and I will go wherever you want me to go." His next words surprised me even more:

"Then first go home, reconcile with your mother and tell her what has happened to you!"

I had expected something like God telling me to go to Africa, but His no-nonsense answer made sense to me. My weapon had always been my sharp tongue. With a few well-chosen cruel words, I had often purposely hurt others and my stepmother in particular. Death and life are in the power of the tongue. If God had forgiven my sins, I should in return first be willing to forgive my mother and ask her to forgive me.

On the train toward the town of Papendrecht, where my

parents then lived, I felt a great urge to talk to my (mostly young) fellow passengers about the new life I had found in Jesus. My heart was so full of joy that I couldn't hold back.

My stepmother opened the door when I rang the bell. Not wanting to lose much time, I immediately started to share with her what had happened to me and why I came. She was totally overwhelmed and started to cry when I asked her to forgive me. I took her into my arms and then we both cried as we forgave each other. We stood there for quite some time.

All the hatred, hurt and resentment were washed away by those tears. Words and acts of life had replaced words and acts of death. From then on I was able to accept and honor her as my mother and our relationship improved dramatically over the years.

3
BORN OF SPIRIT
AND WATER

My burning desire to share the message of the gospel to any-body who would listen was limited to some extent by the spirit of the fear of man, which was still lurking in the background. After pouring out this burden to God, my heavenly Father gave me a good idea: read every Bible verse that has to do with the subject of fear.

"You have not received a spirit of fear, but of power, of love and of a sound mind." (2 Tim. 1:7 NKJV)

It became one of my favorite Scriptures. Memorizing and proclaiming these words of life became my medicine and weapon against this unseen enemy of my soul. This proved to be a very effective strategy to overcome fear, and within a year I was free of this fear. But God had much more in mind for my spiritual well-being.

School holidays were still on, and my two brothers and I had decided to do what Jesus told his disciples. Go and preach the gospel to all men, beginning in Jerusalem, which for us in Holland meant the city of Apeldoorn, where our aunt lived. We needed a base from where we could operate for ten days, but we did not tell our aunt what we were up to.

Descending upon her home, we started out with hours of intensive prayer in her living room. We knew without God we would not be able to save anyone. Crying out loud with tears, we prayed for the salvation of our fellow youth in that town. Our poor aunt did not dare to show up or interfere and must have wondered what in the world was going on with her nephews.

All fired up, we went to the main walking street where we just sat down on the ground and started to sing songs about Jesus to the bewilderment of the mostly older people walking by. However, some young folks stopped and listened. After a couple of songs one of my brothers would stand up and share briefly what God had done in his life. I had made up my mind that I would never stand up and share publicly in front of strangers staring at me. Talking to people personally was my specialty.

We sang more songs. Suddenly my brother stood up, pointed to me, and announced to the crowd: "Now my brother Antoine will share with you how Jesus changed his life!"

My heart sank as I looked at him with unbelief and despair. How could he do this to me?! All these curious eyes were boring into me expecting me to say something. I started to shake. But I knew there was no turning back. So I stood up reluctantly. Strangely enough, from that moment a powerful assurance flooded my being. Words I had not thought about started pouring out of my mouth with such boldness it surprised me as well as those who listened. In fact, I could not have stopped even if I had wanted to stop speaking.

Wow! This was not me but God speaking through me and helping me to overcome the fear of men. The result of this move of God through such simple young men was quite amazing. At least ten young boys and girls—including one drug addict—gave their lives to Jesus!

POWER FROM ON HIGH

An elderly gentleman had watched our street meeting and invited us to join his Bible study taking place that evening. Hungry for more of Jesus, we decided to take part. The theme of that evening happened to be "The Baptism in the Holy Spirit." After a time of fellowship this brother in the Lord gave a short, but very clear teaching from the Bible about the gifts of the Holy Spirit and how to receive them.

Previously I had already met a young Christian who had claimed to be able to speak in "another" tongue or language through the Holy Spirit. The fact that I had only heard him speak and constantly repeat the same two strange words had not convinced me that he was speaking in an unknown language. In high school I had studied English, German and French—and, of course, Dutch. Any language consists of many words and not just two. Eagerly we listened, read the Bible ourselves and soaked up this exciting news about how the Holy Spirit could work through us.

"You shall receive power when the Holy Spirit has come upon you; and you shall be my witnesses in Jerusalem and in all Judea and Samaria and to the end of the earth." (Acts 1:8 NKJV)

Jesus promised this to his disciples. They had already received a new heart and Jesus promised them power to be His witnesses through the outpouring of the Holy Spirit upon their lives. We now heard and understood that we could also receive this Holy Spirit. At the end of the Bible study the pastor wisely suggested that he was willing to lay hands on us to receive the Holy Spirit, but that if we wanted, we could just pray ourselves. We consulted among each other and decided to ask God directly. If God would baptize us with His Holy Spirit without this pastor praying for us, we could be sure we really received it from Him and not from a man.

We thanked the pastor and left to find a place all by ourselves. We found a small public garden lighted by the last sun rays of that late summer evening. A warm breeze rustled gently through the leaves of the trees. All three of us knelt down on the soft grass. Pregnant with expectation, we started to pray and cry out loudly to God. We did not have to wait for long.

The fire of God's warm and tender love embraced us, filling us with joy and laughter as each of us started speaking in different unknown languages, praising and worshiping our Creator. We could not stop it anymore and tears of gratefulness filled my eyes. When a stranger happened to walk by I suddenly jumped up and ran to him with a well-meaning, "Jesus loves you!" Startled and obviously not yet in need of so much love, he took off at once for a safer location.

From now on I was sure I had received the Holy Spirit enabling me to preach the good news to all near and far with a new and fresh anointing and authority.

BEGINNING A NEW LIFE

While trying to help young drug addicts kick their habit, an odd but very dedicated Christian couple from the Dutch backwoods experienced a setback. One of the addicts died of an overdose of heroine at their rehabilitation center in The Hague. A Dutch journalist picked up the story and named them "Jesus People" after the revival among young people already taking place in the U.S.

Indeed, not only drug addicts but many high school students and other youth started to join this couple's Bible study and evangelistic street meetings. Fed up with materialism, young people were searching for spiritual answers in their quest for direction and the meaning of life. "One Way Jesus" based on Jesus's statement, "I am the Way, the Truth and the Life" became their battle cry. Their numbers and zeal were growing week by week and soon "Jesus People" bases were popping up in many other towns in the Netherlands.

One of these towns was Dordrecht, a small city surrounded

by rivers and with a remarkable evangelical history. On July 15 and 16, 1572, representatives of most cities in the Netherlands met in Dordrecht in a building named Het Hof (The Court), where they appointed Wilhelm of Orange their leader and declared their independence from Catholic Spain. This gathering marked the beginning of the Eighty Years' War—the Dutch war of independence. In1618 and1619 the important Dordrecht Synod of the two Reformed churches in the Netherlands took place in Dordrecht in order to discuss the "Statenvertaling," the first translation of the Bible into the Dutch language. In 1632 Dutch Mennonites held a Synod in Dordrecht, during which the "Dordrechter Bekenntnis"—a Christian statement of faith—was formulated. In 1972 the Jesus People (JP) were reviving this godly heritage in Dordrecht and preached the good old gospel to all who wanted to listen.

The city of Papendrecht, where my parents lived, was located opposite of Dordrecht on the other side of the river "Oude Maas." In order to visit the JP base in Dordrecht we had to cross the river by ferry. They met in a tiny, rented shop building situated along one of the canals in the center of the city.

Crammed on top of each other, these long-haired Jesus People fervently sang their songs accompanied by enthusiastic guitarists and tambourine swaying youth. They held Bible studies and boldly conducted regular street meetings reaching even more youth all needing salvation.

When some told their Calvinist parents about their newfound faith, they were met with anger. How could they dare claim they were now sure of their salvation! Their parents' belief in God's predestination forbade them from believing that one could be sure about salvation. Only God could decide that matter. One could never be sure about salvation, and it was sinful and proud in their eyes to say so. Despite facing strong opposition from their parents these young believers continued to join the meetings.

A DILEMMA

Born into a Dutch Reformed family, I was already baptized as an infant. Surely my parents meant it well as they were simply following the teaching of their church denomination. However, I did not have any peace about waiting any longer to be baptized as an adult. I was lost and had been found by my Savior Jesus Christ, and now it was my turn to say "yes" by taking another step of obedience. Baptism by immersion was not all accepted by my grandfather, whom I loved. My grandfather direly predicted it would cause his premature death if my siblings and I would be baptized again.

Was it OK to obey God at the expense of my grandfather's death? Several times I postponed my baptism until I finally lost all my peace. The thought came to me that if God wanted me to obey, He probably could keep my grandfather from dying. So after six months of waiting, I was baptized in a swimming pool in The Hague along with more than thirty other young people. I jumped out of the water for joy, leaving my old life behind and ready to live a new life only to please my Savior Jesus. My grandfather ultimately died, but not due to my baptism.

Child baptism is not clearly mentioned in the Bible. Jesus himself was baptized by immersion. Jesus blessed the children, and his disciples did not baptize babies. All who were baptized were first told to repent of their sins. Babies are not yet aware of their sins.

The practice of "baptizing"—or rather sprinkling—babies may have its roots in ancient Germanic tribal cultural beliefs. Germanic tribes would not consider a baby a living being until the father had personally accepted it by first putting it on his lap. Until this happened the family could "set the baby out" if it was not wanted, particularly if it was deformed or a twin. But if the newborn was taken upon the father's lap, it was sprinkled with water for purification, given a name and, at last, a gift. Only after that it was recognized to be a person and accepted into the tribe. Apart from the setting-out part this old practice is quite a beautiful picture of what God does to us when we are born again.

When we repent of our sins we are accepted by the Father in heaven, who takes us on His lap where we find comfort and acceptance. He then cleanses us by His blood from our sins and by the water of baptism. We will receive a new name in heaven, but first we receive a present—the gift of the Holy Spirit—who enables us to obey God and do His will. Could it be that the idea of sprinkling babies originated from this old custom?

School had started again, and I prayed about whether to continue to study or serve the Lord full time. I did not have peace about studying and felt led to join the staff at the JP base in Dordrecht. Enveloped and surrounded day and night by an overwhelming presence of God's love and peace, I started out on this new chapter in my life. After all the loneliness and the many years of emptiness, living without knowing Jesus, this constant sense of God's warming love was balsam for my soul.

The Holy Spirit was very real but also very strict with me. Previously I had been quite talkative, but suddenly I was not able to speak unless I felt urged by the Holy Spirit to say something useful. God was teaching me to control my tongue and use it only when He needed me. This lesson of learning to overcome this weakness later proved to be very useful for God's plan for my life. How would I be able to learn to hear God's voice unless I would shut my mouth and listen first? So surrounded by a most bizarre bunch of ex-drug addicts, former hippies and students, I felt perfectly at peace in the will of God for my life.

FORTY THOUSAND VOLTS

At first we all lived by faith in God's provision, but soon our leadership decided anyone who was not studying should find some job to help pay for the cost of living. We ended up looking for part-time jobs so we could use the rest of the time to preach the gospel. A former speed-freak would drive me on the back of his motorcycle to work the night shift together in an engine oil factory.

Since I had never been a person who liked to stay up late at night this proved to be quite a challenge. I had to fight an overwhelming urge to sleep while working nonstop to keep up with a conveyor belt of never-ending empty oil cans needing to be filled. It was very stressful. We could only sleep in the morning because in early afternoon the first visitors would descend upon our JP base.

All our evenings were full of either prayer or Bible study meetings and ministry to young people. On weekends we had street meetings and evening meetings for new seekers.

Opposition to all this sincere spiritual activity was bound to come. Dutch people like to drink beer and on weekends some drank too much and roamed around our city late at night shouting, fighting or throwing up. The "Jesus loves you" sign and other slogans written all over our shop window inevitably drew their attention as they passed by in a stupor. Then the mocking started while they banged on our door and even ended up breaking windows while we were trying to sleep. We had to barricade our windows with wooden panels. This scenario was repeated each weekend and sometimes also during the week.

It was nerve-racking and terrifying, and I came to the point where I was about to give up. "Lord," I cried out one night, "I thought my troubles would be over when I started to follow you and now I am drowning in troubles. I can't take this anymore!" The answer came in a very unexpected way.

All of a sudden an enormous sensation of power hit me. It felt like forty thousand volts were surging through my body for at least ten minutes without burning or hurting me. As if God without words was saying: *"Here I am, this is my power, so why are you afraid. What can mortal man do to you?"* Well, I got the message, and from then on I was able to overcome my fear and cope with the situation. Who can be against me when such a powerful God is for me?

Once a month the different JP groups from various cities in the Netherlands would meet for a weekend in The Hague. This was usually a good time of fellowship, worship and teaching.

Holy Supper was celebrated, during which the elders would pray for and prophesy over each person present. Secretly I hoped to receive something like, "My son, I want to transform you into a second Billy Graham" as a word from the Lord. Instead of that, the person praying for me only came up with, "My son, I want you to read your Bible more often!"

At first I was a bit disappointed, but then I realized it was true. In my zeal to preach the gospel I had neglected my daily personal Bible study. So I decided to overcome that habit and be more disciplined. From then on I started to pray and read my Bible at 5 a.m. each morning. And when we draw near to God, God draws near to us.

"Like a city whose walls are broken through is a person who lacks self-control." (Prov. 25:28 NKJV)

A DISTURBING DREAM

One night I had a dream I will never forget. It started out with a huge ocean liner moored at the dock in a harbor about to leave for a long overseas journey. The ship was packed with people who were waving goodbye to those on the quay. Standing amid them, I felt a bit lost because none of those on board were related to me. All of a sudden the back side of the ship went down and the front went up. The ship was sinking, and panic broke out as people were trying desperately to get off by jumping overboard. Shocked by this scene I ran forward and grabbed the first hand I saw and pulled a person out of the water, then another one and many more. Looking over my shoulder, I noticed that none of those standing on the quay did anything to try to help those who needed salvation. So I kept on pulling people out of the water until I was completely exhausted.

Then the dream ended.

This disturbed me deeply. For a long time I was pondering

what God was trying to tell me.

The next night I fell asleep and dreamed the same dream once again. When I woke up I was still reeling from the impact of that dream. One question stood out in my mind: why did I dream this two times?

While praying about this the Lord told me to randomly open my Bible. By that time I had already become a systematic reader of the Bible. Two chapters a day; simultaneously, one in the Old Testament and then one in the New Testament. I was not used to opening my Bible and reading it randomly. But I obeyed and with closed eyes opened my Bible. When I opened my eyes, at once I saw the following Scripture:

> **"And the dream was repeated to Pharaoh twice because the thing is *established by God*, and *God will shortly bring it to pass*." (Gen. 41:32 NKJV, author's emphasis)**

I felt goose bumps all over my body as I realized what these words really meant in the context of my double dream. The ocean liner is the world. The people on it and on the quay are the world's population going its own way. The ocean liner suddenly sinking is the end of the world. The people dying and crying for help are those lost without knowing salvation in Jesus. God was telling me that the time for the end of this world is clearly fixed by God and that this end will come soon!

In the dream I was the only one helping to save people from destruction. God was clearly telling me there is now no more time to lose. You are living in the last days. Get busy with the things that concern Me; save the lost! Do not look around or wonder why others are standing idle. Get going yourself and others will follow! This dream burned itself into my conscience and memory and has kept me going ever since. It has helped me overcome many challenges, disappointments and difficulties.

"For God so *loved* the world that he *gave* his
one and only Son, that whoever *believes* in him
shall not *perish* but *have* eternal life. For God
did not *send* his Son into the world to *condemn*
the world, but to *save* the world through him."
(John 3:16–17 NKJV, author's emphasis)

God, our heavenly Father, is only motivated by love to save the lost and not by a desire to condemn them and let them perish. That's why He gave His only Son and sent Him to save those who are already lost in sin, darkness, hatred, bondage, sickness and death. From then on these eight verbs mentioned by the Lord Jesus above: **to love, to give, to believe, not to perish, to have, to send, not to condemn and to save** became the most important verbs in my life, formulating and stimulating my daily motivation and purpose in life.

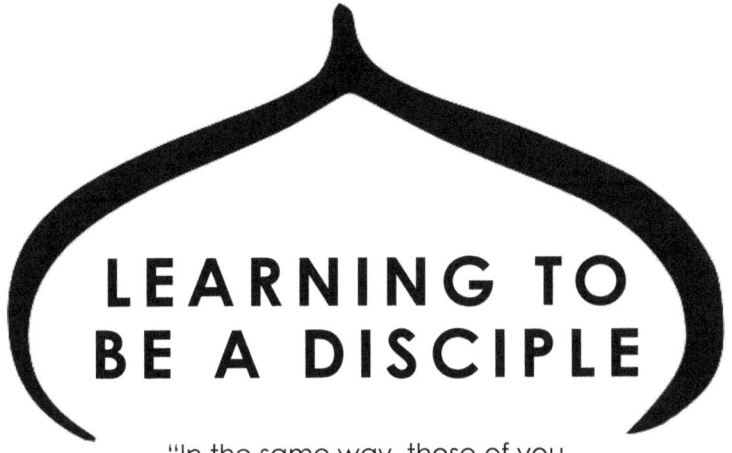

LEARNING TO BE A DISCIPLE

"In the same way, those of you
who do not give up everything you
have cannot be my disciples."

(Luke 14:33 NKJV)

4
BORN TO OVERCOME

"Stop shouting 'the blood of Jesus!'" One of two young drunken attackers screamed these words at one of my teammates, as he was beating him. Another one was holding a chair trying to bust it over my head. The two of them had entered our meeting room in Dordrecht, opened the fridge and were throwing eggs and other items all over the room. Of course we tried to stop them, but since we were now nonviolent Christians, we would not hit back.

I was taller than my attacker and while praying in the Spirit I just held the chair in the air, so he could not hit me. Another teammate was in his bedroom and told to stay there and just pray. For a good reason. He was a huge, blond-haired, almost six-and-a-half-foot-tall hulk of a guy who looked like a Viking warrior. Before his salvation he had been on drugs. Once in Amsterdam it had taken ten policemen to wrestle him down to arrest him. Jesus had changed him completely, and he was a now a very kind and gentle person. Yet I was afraid he could be tempted to use his enormous physical strength to squash our violent visitors.

"The blood of Jesus, there is power in the blood of Jesus!"

My much smaller teammate, who had been a former speed freak, kept on shouting and proclaiming these words even louder. And it worked! All of a sudden the attackers left the meeting room in a great hurry. Amazingly, the next day they came back and even apologized for their behavior, asking us why we did not hit them back. So we had a great opportunity to share the message of forgiveness through Jesus with them. Most importantly the lesson we learned was that the way to overcome is not by human power or might but by the power of the blood of Jesus!

One day some Scandinavian missionaries happened to pass by one of our JP evangelistic street meetings in The Hague. They were thrilled to see the zeal of these young people who were sharing their faith so publicly. For many years they had worked hard evangelizing in the city of Antwerp in the Flemish (very similar to Dutch) speaking part of Belgium.

Sadly, without much result, and they were about to give up. God spoke to them to invite the JP to come to Belgium. They contacted our leadership and offered them their mission base, a house in Mortsel, a suburb of Antwerp, for a year free of rent. The condition was for them to send a team of young people to evangelize in Belgium. Our leadership agreed, and to the great surprise of these missionaries, within a few weeks a considerable number of young people came to Christ.

During our regular JP weekends all the different outposts would meet for teaching and encouragement. Soon we were joined by many young kids from Belgium with their red, henna-colored long hair and their unmistakable soft-spoken Flemish accent.

CALLED TO THE LAND OF TINTIN

Sometime after I was called in by the JP leadership in The Hague.

"We need you to go to Antwerp in Belgium to lead the outpost in Mortsel. The work there is growing, and we are reaching out into other towns, so we need more workers," they told me.

"What? Why me?" I answered in shock.

Saved only less than a year, I was certain they were making a big mistake and tried desperately to convince them to look for someone else. How was I supposed to teach new disciples in a foreign country when I was a very young and inexperienced disciple of Christ myself?

There was no way out.

"You won't be there all by yourself; we will come from time to time to teach and help you out," they said, trying to still my fear and insecurity. They gave me some time to pray about my decision.

I turned to God. "Lord, is it really necessary for me to do this?" I begged.

It felt like a young eagle was being pushed out of its safe nest to learn to fly on its own. The answer was yes and through a gentle urging of the Holy Spirit God assured me that I would not be there alone. He would go and be there with me and catch me when I was about to fall. Reluctantly I went, and sure enough my insecurities were soon overcome. Learning to fly carried by the wind of the Holy Spirit into a foreign land, it was to be my first experience as a missionary.

The history of Belgium extends before the founding of the modern state of that name in 1830, a history intertwined with those of its neighbors: the Netherlands, Germany and Luxembourg. Due to its strategic location and the many armies fighting on its soil, since the Thirty Years' War (1618–1648), World War I (1914–1918) and World War II (1939–1945) Belgium has often been called the "battlefield of Europe". Belgium's modern shape can be partly traced back at least as far as the "Seventeen Provinces within the Burgundian Netherlands. The Eighty Years' War (1568–1648) led to the split between a northern Dutch Republic and the southern Netherlands from which Belgium and Luxembourg developed.

The French Revolutionary wars led to Belgium becoming part of France in 1795, bringing the end to the semi-independence of areas which had belonged to the Catholic church. After the defeat of the French in 1814, a new United Kingdom of the Netherlands was created, which eventually split one more time during the Belgium Revolution of 1830–1839, giving birth to three modern nations: Belgium, the Netherlands and Luxembourg.

The ports and textile industry of Belgium were important back into the Middle Ages, and modern Belgium was one of the first countries to experience an Industrial Revolution. Belgian culture involves the Dutch-speaking Flemish and the French-speaking Walloons as well as some German speaking areas. The Flemish draw intensively from both the English-speaking culture (which dominates sciences, professional life and most news media) and the Netherlands; whereas French-speakers focus on cultural life in France, and less outside.

Jews who have formed a component of Flemish culture—in particular that of Antwerp—for more than five hundred years, have their own culture. Belgium has numerous well-known cartoonists, such as Hergé (The Adventures of Tintin), Peyo (The Smurfs), Franquin (Spirou and Fantasio, Marsupilami, Gaston) and Morris (Lucky Luke).

All these factors combined molded the Flemish people we worked with into very interesting people. Their laid-back style of life, their great but very polite sense of humor and their generally cautious much humbler attitude was quite different from my boisterous and outgoing Dutch culture. But it made them easy to love and accept them just the way they were.

CULTURAL CLASH

In general the Dutch mistakenly tend to feel superior to Belgians. It became my goal to overcome this tendency by laying down my life and to humble myself. Not to try to compare my own culture with theirs. Rather love and accept them as Jesus would have loved them if He would have been there instead of me. The true shepherd lays down his life for the sheep. The biggest mistake a missionary can make is to constantly compare the culture of the people he or she is trying to reach with his own culture at home. This attitude is counterproductive and leads to much frustration and irritation.

True Christlike love lays down its own life and culture and covers a multitude of sins and cultural differences. In Belgium, window shutters in all homes went down at nightfall, which made me feel shut out from their lives. Why so? Because in the Netherlands no one uses window shutters or even curtains. Day and night you can walk by Dutch homes and, if needed, enjoy the sight of people living inside those homes. Nobody bothers or cares. That was one of the smaller cultural differences I had to learn to overcome.

Our base in Mortsel was a big house with many rooms and a big garden in the back. Some team members were accommodated at the base. About ten to twenty-five mostly young people would come to our home several times a week in the evening for fellowship and Bible study. Since I was expected to lead these events, I had to study my Bible hard to come up with enough new spiritual food to feed these hungry sheep. This caused me to have deeper fellowship with Jesus.

A young Christian myself, I was mostly only one week ahead of those I was trying to teach. Leading worship, playing the guitar, preaching, ministering, counseling and praying for seekers kept me busy. During the day we evangelized in Antwerp mostly among drug addicts, or we were invited to Catholic retreats to share our testimony with hundreds of young people.

A FREEDOM FIGHTER
FINDS FREEDOM

In the beginning I ministered full time, and it was very encouraging to see how God provided for us. A Christian entrepreneur and inventor who visited our meetings occasionally was very blessed by our ministry. He invited me to work part time for him. My job was to help him to fill countless electronic fuel-saving devices with tar. He had invented them and didn't want anyone to figure out how it worked. He also paid for the printing of hundreds of Bibles, which we distributed among the many new contacts we made.

A round-faced, bearded young guy with curly black hair often attended our evening meetings without giving his life to Jesus. He was very interested and would try to argue with me as much as he could about why we should not believe in God. He had been involved in a radical movement in Belgium. Their aim was to create a new state for Dutch-speaking Flandern separate from French-speaking Wallonia by use of violence. They would not shrink back from using explosives or weapons to further their cause. After many weeks I got tired of answering his provocative questions.

"You have asked me many questions over and over again, and some I just cannot answer," I said.

"Why don't you ask Jesus yourself directly?"

Bewildered, he looked at me in surprise. He paused for a long time.

"Yes, why not?!" He finally countered with a smile on his face and slowly bowed his head.

I put my hand on his head and helped him to pray his first prayer. God really touched him because he changed dramatically and became one of our closest coworkers.

OVERCOMING THE FLESH

It was only natural for a young man like me to start having problems in the flesh again. Before I was born from God's Spirit I had never touched a girl in an unclean way but I battled unclean thoughts and behavior. I knew this was wrong and it never satisfied me. The desire men and women have to be loved and to belong to somebody are God-given by the One who created us male and female. The sexual desires are an important part created by our heavenly Father and are meant for pleasure and procreation.

However there is a safe and proper time, place and relationship to truly enjoy all of this: marriage. This is the relationship between one man and one woman for life based on true love and an unconditional commitment. To give in to sexual desires without this safe environment will never satisfy men or women. So now I had to learn to overcome old habits.

God has destined us to rule over sin and to be overcomers and that includes this area of life.

"If you do what is right, will you not be accepted? But if you do not do what is right, sin is crouching at your door; it desires to have you, but you must rule over it" (Gen. 4:7 NKJV)

"Therefore do not let sin reign in your mortal body so that you obey its evil desires." (Rom. 6:12 NKJV)

"Oh, Lord fill my heart with your love every day,
so I really can be full of your power every day,
break my heart, give me tears,
so the devil disappears,
make me new, take my hand,
lead me to the promised land."

Over and over again we sang and repeated the words of this simple song. Our Belgium disciples and I were trying out our first all-night prayer and worship session. We could not imagine being able to watch and pray for so long. But in the middle of the night when I took my guitar, the Lord gave me this song. It was a powerful prayer for personal change and helped us to overcome our natural need for sleep.

The Holy Spirit came upon us, and with tears we sang and

prayed in Spirit and in truth without ceasing. When morning finally broke, we felt cleansed and refreshed and it was as if we had only prayed a couple of hours. The Lord was teaching us a powerful truth which helped to transform my prayer life. Prayer and worship are never meant to be in competition with or to be separate. Worship helps open the door to pray in Spirit and in truth.

"Yet a time is coming and has now come when the true worshipers will worship the Father in the Spirit and in truth, for they are the kind of worshipers the Father seeks. God is spirit, and his worshipers must worship in the Spirit and in truth." (John 4:23–24 NKJV)

THE KNIFE AND THE NAME OF JESUS

One evening I was ministering alone to a young Belgian man who often came to our house. He had lots of problems and was taking illegal drugs. Over and over again I had tried to convince him of his need to confess and turn away from his sins and cry out to God for help to overcome his addiction. All of a sudden, in the middle of our conversation, a dark shadow flashed over his face. His eyes narrowed and his strong body tensed as he whipped out a knife to stab it into my body. For a split second I froze in fear. Then the presence and authority of the Holy Spirit came over me just as fast.

"In the name of Jesus, I command you demon of murder to leave!" I heard myself shout.

His hand froze and the knife dropped to the ground. His body started to shake uncontrollably as he broke out in tears asking me to forgive him for what he had intended to do to me. We both sat there for a long time as I tried to explain what had happened to him and reassured him that I had forgiven him. I had just learned a new lesson: how to overcome demonic power in the name of Jesus.

More than forty years later he wrote me a card:

"I continue to be thankful for God bringing you into my life. Your patience, meekness of heart and forgiving spirit saved my life at that time."

"I have given you authority to trample on snakes and scorpions and to overcome all the power of the enemy; nothing will harm you." (Luke 10:19 NKJV)

5

STRONGER THROUGH STRUGGLE

The following personal prophecy in our monthly meetings in The Hague strengthened me:

"My child, I have seen your zeal for Me, behold you will go through many struggles, but know that this is meant to harden you. I have a great task for you." My first missionary experience to the land of Tintin was short-lived because I was soon asked to help develop the JP base in the Dutch city of Rotterdam. The Port of Rotterdam is currently the biggest port in Europe and the sixth biggest in the world by annual cargo output. Located 2 to 6 meters below sea level, the city has an ongoing struggle against the water. Historically and economically it has struggled to stay on the cutting edge of business in an ever-changing world.

No event in Rotterdam history left a deeper scar in the society and city development than the Nazi German invasion in May 1940. On May 14, 1940, the inner city and the 17th century port were completely destroyed by a bombardment. Approximately nine hundred people died, and eighty thousand citizens became homeless. Five years of oppression followed.

Later during the war, the city suffered from bombings by Allied Forces in October 1941 and March 1943. The citizens of Rotterdam were left with a "city without a heart." However, the struggle to do a "city heart transplantation" resulted in a Rotterdam with the most modern city center in the Netherlands.

One day I noticed the coat of arms of Rotterdam with two lions holding the coat of arms and the words "Sterker door Strijd" (Stronger through Struggle). I sensed these words were to be prophetic for the time I would spend there. Our JP base was situated in a rundown four-room apartment. It had a tiny dining room and a small kitchen and was located at the busiest cross-section in town in an old housing block that had not been destroyed by the bombing.

Right around the corner was a brothel and the city center was within walking distance. But winning souls for Jesus, not comfort, was our highest goal. All our team members were very motivated young people working a job or still studying. One of the girls worked half time and cooked the evening meal for the whole team of about six people. The bigger room at ground level served as a meeting, prayer, church and ministry room. Everyone shared in paying the rent and living expenses. There was no shower, so we had to visit a bathing house and a place to do our laundry once a week.

Ministry, such as prayer, church meetings, house-to-house visiting, personal ministry and evangelistic meetings took place in the evening and on weekends. There was always a lot going on with people going in and out until late at night. Recreation and time out were rare.

RESIST THE DEVIL

One day our main base in The Hague sent us a young man who had been addicted to alcohol from an early age. He grew up in a family in which alcohol addiction was rampant. He was a very sad person but occasionally he could become quite aggressive. He was put up in my room and would often take his aggression out on me by threatening me. This caused a lot of tension in my life. I did not realize it at the time, but God was allowing this situation to teach me that our fight is not against flesh and blood. Ours is a fight against the powers of darkness which we cannot see but are real forces of darkness trying to oppose the plans and work of God.

One Saturday morning I was about to wake up after a good sleep. Suddenly something jumped on me. A strange force squeezed my throat tightly. At first I panicked and felt paralyzed, unable to move. Then I quickly realized something demonic was taking place. With all my strength I tried to shout and rebuke "in the name of Jesus" whatever had come over me. Unable to utter one word the only way left was to shout in my mind: "There is power in the blood of Jesus!"

In that very moment the vicious grip on my throat was released. Something jumped off my body. Believe it or not, when I rose out of my bed I caught a glimpse of a tiny dwarf-like demon figure grinning apologetically while hurriedly making his way out of my room. Very irritated and mad at the devil for daring to try to kill me, I vowed before God to preach the gospel even more than ever before. The reformer Martin Luther, awakened by the devil during the night, supposedly courageously defended himself against Satan by throwing an inkwell at him. In my case, mentioning the blood of Jesus was more than sufficient.

Soon after, the young alcoholic left our house as well.

> **"Submit yourselves, then, to God. Resist the devil and he will flee from you." (James 4:7 NKJV)**

THE TORNADO

The warning came over loudspeakers fixed on motorcars driving hectically all over the city. "Attention! Attention! A monstrous tornado is fast approaching our city! Flee for your lives!" Masses of panic-stricken people ran and tried to find shelter wherever they could. I found myself amid this turmoil, and I decided to run away as fast as I could out and away from the city. When I finally reached the outskirts of town I was already completely out of breath, but shear fear kept me running into a nearby forest.

Stumbling over roots and being scratched by low twigs, I

finally collapsed and fell to the ground. "Now I am finally safe," I gasped while my head sank down on the soft moss. All of a sudden a thunderous roar broke the silence. Looking back in great fright, I saw the tornado was about to hit right where I was. I woke up, drenched in sweat.

Immediately I realized this was a dream from God. Often I had been fearful with a tendency to expect the worst in hard situations. Running away from hardship seemed to be a good solution. God was revealing an important truth through this dream: stop running away, stand firm, face the problem and expect a miracle from God. Overcome fear by faith!

"But we do not belong to those who shrink back and are destroyed, but to those who have faith and are saved." (Heb. 10:39 NKJV)

THE GROOM IS TAKEN AWAY

I had not thought much about fasting until one day during my daily Bible reading, I came upon a Scripture which drew my attention:

**"Then John's disciples came and asked him, 'How is it that we and the Pharisees fast often, but your disciples do not fast?' Jesus answered, 'How can the guests of the bridegroom mourn while he is with them? The time will come when the bridegroom will be taken from them; then they will fast.'"
(Matt. 9:14–15 NKJV)**

The Holy Spirit asked me: "Today, is the groom taken away or not?"

My answer was: "Yes, of course, Jesus is now seated at the right hand of God."

The Holy Spirit continued: "Then you should also fast, if you desire to be a disciple of Jesus!" Wow, that was quite logical and clear advice. Immediately my fleshly nature rebelled, because as far as I understood, fasting meant not to eat at all for some time. When you are twenty-two years old, you need your food.

"Why fast and for how long?" I countered.

"In this spiritual battle you do not fight against flesh and blood but against powers of this dark world!"

Hunger, headache, nausea, tiredness all banded together to discourage me from fasting again after the first day I tried it. But I had promised God and made up my mind to fast one whole day per week. So as the weeks went by, each Thursday, the battle to overcome the craving of my weak flesh and to obey the willingness of my spirit started all over again. Dutch people drink a lot of coffee. The absence of caffeine during my fasting caused severe headaches. The answer was to reduce my caffeine intake the day before fasting and to refrain from drinking coffee on the day of fasting. This strategy—as well as drinking more water— helped me to overcome these headaches.

Reading about the life of Rees Howells in England was very encouraging. On Dec. 26, 1934, Rees Howells received a vision from the Holy Spirit in the middle of the night. It was 3 a.m. and the Lord began to call him into faith for world evangelism and the completion of the Great Commission. "The world became our parish, and we were led to be responsible to intercede for countries and nations." Rees had said. Rees was a man of prayer and fasting.

While working hard in a mine, he and others fasted for ten days against an invasion of Hitler's army in England. I was well-informed about World War II and had always wondered why Hitler had not given orders to invade England. After the defeat and miraculous evacuation of more than three hundred thousand British, French and some Dutch soldiers at Dunkirk,

England was at its lowest point. Hitler's generals fumed, but Hitler hesitated. Until it was too late. God answered the prayers of Rees and others as they prayed and fasted. If England had been conquered by the Nazis, victory in the battle to eventually overcome them would have been very difficult without England as a starting point for Allied Forces.

A NARROW ESCAPE

For days on end I was heavily burdened by a great urgency to pray. This was the first time I experienced travailing prayer. For no apparent reason I could not do anything but pray incessantly in the Spirit. During work or breaks, during mealtimes, ministry times or at night my spirit was constantly enveloped by nonstop Holy Spirit agony for something or somebody. Travail is hard work and can be compared to childbirth. Any mother can tell you there is intense pain and agony involved in childbirth. Travail is a form of intense intercession that is initiated by the Holy Spirit. In travailing prayer, an individual or group is gripped with that which grips the heart of God.

So what was gripping the heart of God in my case?

Since this condition didn`t let up, I decided to fast a day or two because a breakthrough needed to come. Then, suddenly, the sense of urgency ebbed away and was replaced by an overwhelming sense of peace and a certainty of victory. The next day I found out what had happened. One of my brothers had a problem with manic depression, a psychological condition where a person can be in a very elated and extremely positive mood. This can change overnight into a severe condition of feeling hopelessly down. My brother was a good-looking guy, and in his manic condition could be very convincing.

One day he applied for a management position in a big firm and was accepted. However, after one week it became clear he was not the desired candidate after all. This time he wanted to travel abroad by airplane. Since he did not have the airfare, his grand idea was to hide himself in the luggage compartment of the airplane, which he somehow managed to do. An airport employee found him in time so he was saved from an ordeal that would have killed him. He was found the day I felt my prayer burden lift! When we make ourselves available, the Holy Spirit will help us to overcome in prayer on behalf of others in situations unknown to us.

"In the same way, the Spirit helps us in our weakness. We do not know what we ought to pray for, but the Spirit himself intercedes for us through wordless groans." (Rom. 8:26 NKJV)

THE LITTLE RED SEED

From the beginning, our team in Rotterdam strongly emphasized prayer and we spent much time interceding for other nations in Europe, such as France and Spain. At that time France was practically void of the true gospel, and Spain was still ruled by the dictator Franco. We prayed hard for God to pour out his Holy Spirit upon these nations and for a change to take place. Some of us spoke French and were able to preach the good news about Jesus to young French tourists visiting the Netherlands. Finally in 1975, after the death of Franco, the country of Spain gradually became a freer country.

We rejoiced in this answer to our prayers. It encouraged us to focus on prayer and in practical ways for other countries such as Cambodia, where from 1975 onward, Pol Pot's murderous Communist regime was slaughtering 2 million people in the most brutal and vicious ways. The port of Rotterdam was frequented by sailors from all over the world. One of our target groups was sailors from Communist Red China—in those days a completely closed nation. They could never walk the streets of Rotterdam alone. They were only allowed to walk in groups of ten to fifteen sailors led by one Chinese government official watching over them. A little red booklet crammed with Communist indoctrination written by their dictator Mao Tse-Tung was compulsory literature for all Chinese.

Our strategy was simple. We acquired many little red Gospels of John in Chinese. When a group of Chinese sailors walked by like ducks in a line, one of us would approach their leader and keep him busy and sidetracked for a short time. The rest walked by each of the other sailors with a nice smile on our face. Then, without saying a word, each of us quickly pressed a little red gospel booklet into the hands of a sailor. The advantage of surprise did the trick. Because they were small and red, most sailors accepted the booklet and quickly hid them in their pockets without their leader noticing it. This way we made the Word of God accessible to many unreached Chinese. Only Heaven can tell how much lasting fruit this little red heavenly Seed ultimately brought forth.

CONSCIENTIOUS OBJECTOR

Because I had dropped my studies, I received a letter from the Dutch government that I was to be drafted into the army for a year-and-a-half. Before I met Jesus in a personal way, I had actually looked forward to joining the army. The possibility of getting a truck driving license at the government's expense was one of the advantages. However, my mindset had changed completely, and now I could not imagine having to learn to use a gun to kill a so-called enemy. I would rather seek and save people than seek and destroy them for whatever national interest came along.

So I refused to be drafted. The only option was to become a conscientious objector. In those days this was a lengthy and difficult process. It started with waiting for more than a year for an appointment to appear before a committee comprised of military officials, a reverend, a psychologist, a doctor, etc. One had to come up with quite a solid argument to be eligible and accepted as a conscientious objector.

I prayed hard about it and asked the Lord to show me what I was supposed to say. The answer was quite simple: "Tell them you are already in an army, the Lord's army, and involved in a spiritual battle."

The problem I had to overcome was how to convince non-spiritual people of a spiritual reality. "Search for key verses in the Bible which have to do with the spiritual battle for the salvation of men and women," was His reply. I liked this strategy: a soldier for Jesus versus a soldier of the world. The Word of God versus the word of the world. On the day I was to appear before the committee I was ready with some fiery solid biblical arguments which raised some eyebrows.

I told them briefly how God had changed my life and how I was busy saving youth bound by Satan through addiction to sin, alcohol and drugs, by the power of the name of Jesus. The Scripture mentioned below was the main foundation of my argument. After various questions, all testing my motives, I was told the session was over. In the end I was indeed approved and allowed to be an official conscientious objector. This meant that instead of military service a year-and-a-half, I had to work for a social institution for two years on a low-paid budget. At the time I was already working in the laboratory of a university hospital opposite our mission base on behalf of an employment agency. So I simply asked to switch employers and make the hospital my employer instead.

This request was granted, which meant that I could stay and work in the same place and keep on ministering with the same JP base in Rotterdam for the next two years.

"For our struggle is not against flesh and blood, but against the rulers, against the authorities, against the powers of this dark world and against the spiritual forces of evil in the heavenly realms."
(Eph. 6:12 NKJV)

6
THE SPIRITUAL
BATTLE

The week we all spent in The Hague to hear an older, experienced, spirit-filled Dutch missionary share about his life and teach about the reality of the spiritual world was very helpful. Apart from some amazing signs and wonders that he had experienced, the most helpful in preparing me for my future were his practical insights. Over the years he had gained experience about the spiritual battle going on in this world and how much Satan's agents—called demons—are involved in this war.

In general people in the Western hemisphere, and even many Christians, tend to downplay or downright deny the existence of Satan and demons. I had been one of them. The God of this world has successfully blinded our eyes through humanism, unbelief and materialism. No one can overcome in a battle without knowing who his enemy is and the strategies he uses.

The idea of one-third of the angels falling from heaven is found in Revelation 12:4:

**"Its tail (Satan's) swept a third of the stars (angels)
out of the sky and flung them to the earth."
(NKJV, author's emphasis)**

It is clear angels have existed since the beginning of creation. Sometime prior to Genesis 3, Satan (then a leading angel) rebelled against God and was judged. Many other angels rebelled with him, and became the fallen angels or demons mentioned throughout the Bible. Since the number of angels is "innumerable" (Heb. 12:22), one-third includes a vast number of demons who have rebelled against God. Fortunately two thirds of the innumerable angels did not rebel and are serving God's servants here on Earth.

As a Christian it always feels good to be part of a majority and not a minority. At the beginning of his ministry, Jesus was led by the Holy Spirit into the desert and was tempted by Satan. Jesus overcame and withstood these temptations by using the Word of God against the lies of Satan. Casting out evil spirits or demons by the Finger of God, which is the Holy Spirit, was an important part of Jesus` ministry. Demons know who Jesus is.

> "When he saw Jesus, he cried out and fell at his feet, shouting at the top of his voice, 'What do you want with me, Jesus, Son of the Most High God? I beg you, don't torture me!'" (Luke 8:28 NKJV)

Several kinds of demons are mentioned in the Bible such as unclean spirits, evil spirits, spirits of weakness, deaf and dumb spirits, etc. Our dear missionary friend opened my eyes for the fact that demons can cause many problems in the lives of people through sin, fear, doubt, unbelief, addictions, lies, cursing, uncleanness, abuse, self-pity, pride, murder, etc. Not all are demon-possessed, but many people are tortured by these evil spirits in certain areas of their lives. Thus, they are unable to overcome until they are set free by the power of the Holy Spirit in the name of Jesus.

A WISE AND DISCERNING HEART

> "At Gibeon the Lord appeared to Solomon during night in a dream, and God said, 'Ask for whatever you want me to give you.' Solomon answered, 'You have shown great kindness to your servant, my father David, because he was faithful to you and righteous and upright in heart. You have continued this great kindness to him and have given him a

> son to sit on his throne this very day. Now, Lord my
> God, you have made your servant king in place of
> my father David. But I am only a little child and do
> not know how to carry out my duties. Your servant
> is here among the people you have chosen, a
> great people, too numerous to count or number.
> So give your servant a discerning heart to govern
> your people and to distinguish between right and
> wrong. For who is able to govern this great people
> of yours?' The Lord was pleased that Solomon
> had asked for this. So God said to him, 'Since you
> have asked for this and not for long life or wealth
> for yourself, nor have asked for the death of your
> enemies but for discernment in administering justice,
> I will do what you have asked. I will give you a wise
> and discerning heart, so that there will never have
> been anyone like you, nor will there ever be.'"
> (1 Kings 3:5–12 NKJV)

King Solomon was still a young man like me and his request for a wise and discerning heart and God's favorable answer greatly appealed to me. Which great work and responsibility was awaiting me? How much wisdom and discernment would I need to fulfill that task? This realization forced me upon my knees, and I never regretted asking God for my portion of His divine wisdom and discernment. It helped me to overcome and carry out the work which lay ahead of me.

"WHERE ARE THE GIRLS?!"

A deep male voice growled late at night. The door at our base was always closed after 11 p.m. After all we were living in an unsafe area. Just around the corner was a brothel frequented by sailors from all over the world. Somebody had left the door open. Our team members including the girls were already in bed. I rushed down the stairs. A heavy set, muscular and fully drunk sailor had mistaken our house for the brothel he wanted to visit. His stature filled the narrow entrance as he staggered towards the bottom of the stairs.

"Where are the girls?!" he sputtered with a slurred voice while starting to make his way up the stairs.

Physically I was no match for him. I stood there frozen for a moment. I was responsible for the safety of the girls upstairs. First fright but then holy anger welled up in me as I suddenly heard myself shout with great authority:

"You unclean demon, I bind you and cast you out in the name of Jesus Christ!!"

The effect of those words was quite amazing. This huge hulk of a lusty, violent man suddenly changed into a harmless sheep. He stood there like a deflated balloon.

"And now you leave this house at once," I spoke sternly as I laid my hand on his shoulder and quickly guided him out the door. I made sure it was securely shut behind him. My legs started to shake after I realized what had just happened. Once again God had proved that the authority He had vested in his Son Jesus Christ was available to His mortal children in their struggle to overcome the powers of darkness.

"Then Jesus came to them and said, 'All authority in heaven and on earth has been given to me.'" (Matt. 28:18 NKJV)

FALLING IN LOVE

How do you fall in love? By letting yourself fall. During this freefall you tend to lose all sense of reality. So how do you overcome this challenge? By pulling the safety line. It happened to me, and it started to bother and distract me. I had no idea whether the girl was in love with me. I had never talked to her and only knew her from seeing her in the monthly meetings in The Hague.

Nonetheless my fantasies started to overtake this reality. Deep in my heart I knew this was not yet my time to get into a relationship. I knew I was being prepared and trained to leave my country to work in God's harvest fields abroad. So how could I be sure this girl I longed for would be willing to go with me? I had not yet proved to myself that I was able to overcome the challenges that lay ahead of me. I pulled the safety line by writing her a letter stating that I was in love with her and wanted to know what she thought about that. She politely wrote back that she was not open to a relationship. With a jolt, my parachute unfolded and I floated safely back to reality.

"Do you believe I can provide you with the woman who will be suitable for you and the ministry I am calling you to?" the Lord spoke to me during my prayer time.

I bowed my head and surrendered, "OK Lord, I will trust you, but I have one request: if this woman meant for me is not yet saved, then please save her now and keep her for me!"

About ten years later I found that this prayer was answered in a wonderful way. During all the years of waiting, God's grace helped me to overcome having problems in the flesh.

NO GARBAGE CANS

My colleagues and superiors at my job in the laboratory of the university hospital were from all walks of life. They ranged from a Portuguese cleaning lady who barely spoke Dutch, to a professor. Since I knew I would not spend the rest of my life at this job, I had asked the Lord for opportunities to share the gospel with each one of them.

During coffee breaks one colleague at my department habitually ended up talking about subjects with a heavy sexual content. After some time this started to greatly irritate me, especially since no one would say anything about it. His mouth was literally overflowing with filth.

"A good man brings good things out of the good stored up in his heart, and an evil man brings evil things out of the evil stored up in his heart. For the mouth speaks what the heart is full of." (Luke 6:45 NKJV)

After praying about it, the Lord gave me a good idea. One of my jobs was to empty the garbage cans. The next time we met for our coffee break, when my colleague had just started out on his old ritual, I interrupted him.

"I always enjoy drinking coffee with all of you guys, but you know that I am a Christian and do not appreciate having to listen to filth all the time. I am sorry, but my ears are not garbage cans, so please be so kind and find another subject to talk about in my presence," I said.

For a moment there was a great silence. Then with an apologetic smile flashing over his face he agreed and never uttered a single filthy word after that in my presence. Everybody in the room seemed to be relieved and the atmosphere during our coffee breaks became much more enjoyable. As a disciple of Christ you have to overcome the darkness and be bold, but at the same you should stay friendly towards those who are overcome by that same darkness!

My desire to share the good news of Jesus Christ at least one time with each person in my department at the hospital was answered in quite a tragic way. The fiancé of one coworker in that department was among those killed in a tragic train accident in Rotterdam. Everyone was overcome by great despair and sadness. For an entire week the Lord opened opportunities for me to bring comfort and encouragement to each person in our department and let them know the real purpose and meaning of life on Earth.

READY TO GO

My alternate service as a conscientious objector was almost over and so was my time at the hospital. Even the professor tried to convince me to stay when he heard that I was going to leave. When he called me into his office, I was able to explain why God wanted me to go abroad. He became the last person in our department to hear the message of salvation. A new chapter was about to start. All four years in Rotterdam I had been praying and waiting for God to show me His will. It was not a matter of whether I was to go but only of when and where to go as a missionary.

During that time the Lord had encouraged me through His Word but also through prophecies such as these spoken out over my life by beloved brothers and sisters during special prayer times: "Behold my child, so speaks the Lord, I see that you serve me with an upright heart. I shall bless you my child. I shall increase your knowledge. Yes, my child, you shall become a strong and sturdy tree, my child, a tree with many leaves and a lot of fruit, a tree with sturdy roots growing deep into the soil. A tree, my son, which cannot easily be uprooted" (The Hague, 1973).

"My child, I have placed you here, and I have seen your hard work and everything you have done for me unseen by others. I love you very much. Do not be afraid of the way I am performing my will in your life, because many things are still hidden for your eyes and you cannot yet understand them. You are a pleasant fragrance before My Presence. I want you now to learn to live by the day, because I have great plans for you." (Rotterdam, June 2, 1976)

During the past four years I had learned how to lead others to Christ, how to be a disciple myself and how to make others into disciples of Christ. I had learned some lessons on how to overcome and to how pray and fast for the salvation of souls, for my country and for nations around the world. God had also already spoken to me about the practical need to learn English, which I did. In Rotterdam, God had brought me to live together with like-minded brothers and sisters who also had a burden to go out as missionaries wherever God wanted them to go.

In my spirit I now sensed a holy restlessness and expectancy for what was about to come. I had started to pray fervently for God to show me where He wanted me to go. One of our sisters had left us to join a Bible school in England. One day she sent me an innocent-looking, little red booklet named "The History of the Bamboo." This booklet hit me like a rock. It not only showed me the country where I was to go but also served as a blueprint for how God was going to transform me into a blessing to that nation and many other nations afterwards.

GO THEREFORE

"*He who overcomes* and who keeps my works until the end, I will give him power over the nations, and he shall rule them with a rod of iron, as when earthen pots are broken in pieces, even as I myself have received power from my Father, and I will give him the morning star. He who has an ear, let him hear what the Spirit says to the churches."

(Rev. 2:26–28 NKJV, author's emphasis)

7

AN ALLEGORY[1] –
THE HISTORY OF THE BAMBOO

On the mountain hills of the province Kucheng[2] in India, the most valuable trees are usually marked with the name of their owner. The water, which flows from springs located on the mountain tops, is transported to the villages through pipes made from bamboo tree trunks that are carefully fitted into one another.

On the slope of a cool hill amid other trees stood a majestic tree; its dark-colored trunk and splendid branches gently swaying in the evening breeze. Amongst a soft rustling in the leaves was heard:

"You admire my beauty, my stately trunk and my lovely branches—and yet I cannot boast in anything. All I own I owe to the watchful love of my Master. He planted me on this fertile hill where my roots could grow deep and reach out into the hidden springs. To drink continuously from their living water to draw nutrition, freshness, beauty and strength for my whole being. Do you see those trees on the other side? Notice how meager and how shriveled up they look? Their roots were not yet able to reach out to the hidden waters. Since I found the hidden waters, I have never lacked anything. Did you notice the letters carved into my trunk? Take a close look—they have been carved into my being. The treatment was painful. At the time I wondered why I had to suffer so much, but it was the hand of my Master Himself, handling the knife. When the work was done I recognized, while sobbing with unspeakable joy, that it was His own

---

[1]   *Leven en Getuigenis (Life and Witness)*. Ede, Netherlands: Lektuur-fonds Arnhemseweg 57, n.d.

[2]   Kucheng is not in India, but in China. Obviously, God had His own way of showing His way for me.

name that He carved into my trunk. Then I understood with unshakable certainty, that He loved me and wanted everyone to know I belonged to Him. I am so proud to have such a Master."

While the tree was telling us about his Master, I looked around and behold . . . there was the Master Himself! He looked at His tree with tender love and great yearning while holding a razor-sharp ax in His hand.

"I need you," He said. "Are you perfectly willing to give yourself over to Me?"

"Master," the tree answered, "I belong completely to you, but how can you use me?"

"I need you to bring my living waters to dry and arid places without water," the Master continued.

"But Master, how can I be useful that way? I can continue to be rooted in your living springs and use the waters for my own upkeep. I can stretch out my branches heavenwards and be satisfied with fresh dew and become beautiful and strong. I rejoice about my beauty and strength which come from you as well, and I tell everybody that you are a Master full of mercy. But how can I bring water to others?"

With a wonderfully gentle voice, the Master replied: "I can use you, my tree, if you are prepared to let Me have My way. It will be necessary to hew you down, cut off your branches and leave you naked and with your leaves striped off on the ground. Then I will tear you loose from your land of birth, which you love so dearly—and from your brethren, the other trees, in order to take you all alone very far away to mountain slopes. There, nobody will speak to you in a loving way in a place where only grass, bushes and thistles grow. Yes, and there I will have to use terrible steel tools to take out all dividers in your heart, to hollow out a free passageway through which my living water can flow.

You are ready to die, you told Me; yes, my precious tree, you will die, but My life-bringing water shall flow freely and incessantly through you. From now on, no one shall look at you and admire your freshness and splendor. However, there will be very many people who will bend down to quench their thirst from the river of living water, which will reach them unhampered because of you. They may not pay you any attention, but will they not bless your Master who has given them living water through you? Are you ready for this, my tree?"

I held my breath to be able to hear the answer.

"My Master," replied the tree. "All I am and all I have comes from You! If You really need me, I am prepared to joyfully give You my life. And because I need to die, so You can pass Your living waters on to others, I do agree. I belong to You! Take me, my Master, and use me according to Your will."

The countenance of the Master became even more tender. Yet he took the sharp ax, and with powerful blows, he caused the beautiful tree to crash to the ground. The tree did not rebel; no, he surrendered to every blow and whispered softly:

"My Master, may Your will be done."

The Master continued axing down the tree until the trunk was separated from its roots. Then the beauty of the tree—his splendid tree crown of heavy branches—was lost forever. Yes, there he lay, naked and leafless. But the expression of love radiating from the countenance of the Master increased even more as He took what was left of the tree on His shoulder. He carried it very far away over the mountains while his mourning friends, the other trees, remained behind. Yet the tree, out of love for his Master, allowed all of this and whispered softly:

"My Master, may Your will be done."

Arriving at a lonely forsaken place, the Master briefly halted and once again His hand took the razor-sharp ax and thrust it with a blow into the heart of the tree. Through it he wanted to dig a canal for His living water, because only through the heart of the hewed down tree could it flow without hindrance to the dried out, thirsty areas. Yet the tree did not resist and whispered again with a broken heart: "My Master, may Your will be done."

The Master's heart was filled with love. His countenance was filled with tender compassion as he continued His painful blows, not holding back. Working the sharply polished blade tirelessly, he removed all dividers. The heart of the tree lay completely open from one side to the other. Then the heart of the Master was satisfied. He picked him up and carried him tenderly away, broken and full of pain, to a place that he had not yet noticed. There welled up a spring of living, crystal-clear water. Then the stream of life flowed through the heart of the tree, from one side to the other, through the canal, which was carved out through terrible wounds. It was a gentle and silent stream, entering him, flowing through and out of him—continually, incessantly. And the Master smiled satisfied.

Then the Master went out to choose other trees. Some of them shrank back for fear of suffering. Others surrendered joyfully to Him, saying: "Master, we entrust ourselves to you, deal with us as you wish."

Then He let them go, one after the other, along the same painful way. To lay them down so their ends would fit into one another. Each time a new tree was laid down, the fresh and clear living water from the same spring flowed through the broken heart. This way, the pipeline became longer and longer until it reached the unfruitful land at last. Men, women and children, exhausted and thirsty, came to quench their thirst, hastening away afterwards to tell others the good news: "The living water has finally come! The long drought is finally over! Come and drink!"

They came from all directions to quench their thirst and to receive New Life. The Master saw it, and his heart was filled with joy. Then the Master walked up to his tree and asked him full of love, "My tree, do you now regret your loneliness and suffering? Was the price too high, the price that you paid to bring the living water to the world?"

The tree answered, "No, my Master, thousands upon a thousand times no! Even if I had ten thousand lives I would be prepared to give them all to you in order to know the blessing, now known to me, to be able to contribute to your happiness."

8
INDIA CALLING

Staring at the booklet, I slowly laid it down. My eyes filled with tears as my heart was stirred and lost in emotion. This was a message straight from my heavenly Father, and it could not have been clearer. He did not force me to lay down my life but tenderly asked me for my permission to use and mold it for His glory and divine purpose tailored for my life. The only answer I could give was: *"Yes, Lord, here I am. If India is where you want me to go, then show me the way to go, and I will follow you there."*

"Then I heard the voice of the Lord saying, 'Whom shall I send? And who will go for us?' And I said, 'Here am I. Send me!'" (Isa. 6:8 NKJV)

From that moment onward things started to roll. Confirmation after confirmation came from many unexpected corners and each time it had to do with India. My knowledge about India was quite limited, but I knew it was a densely populated, mostly poor country with many gods and very hot. I had never liked hot weather. My freckled skin was not made for the sun, and I usually returned from a visit to the beach looking as red as an overripe tomato. The only time I had been in a hot climate was one summer when I hitchhiked to Italy with a friend and my sister before I gave my life to Jesus. To cool down I drank bottle after bottle of ice-cold lemonade, which made me terribly sick to my stomach. So as soon as I could I was on my way back to my dear Holland and kissed the green grass upon arrival. Nevertheless, my yes was yes—now there was no way back and I did not want to disobey. The Lord comforted me and gave me confidence to overcome this challenge with the following Scripture:

"The Lord watches over you–- the Lord is your shade
at your right hand; the sun will not harm you by
day, nor the moon by night." (Ps. 121:5–6 NKJV)

A MYSTERIOUS MAGAZINE

Strange things started to happen. To this day I do not know how an English mission magazine featuring a group of young Jesus People in the U.S. happened to be lying around in our living room. When I glanced through it my eye immediately fell upon the page where it reported how they had sent out a small team to India for evangelization. They were young, dedicated, spirit-filled disciples of Jesus. Again, India! Could this be the way the Lord had for me to go to India?

Sometime before, I had attended a mission conference in my country. Although the meetings were great and encouraging, I had returned quite disappointed. The only workers these mission agencies seemed to be asking for were doctors and nurses. What about evangelists and apostles? At one mission stand—to my great joy—I met a former classmate who was also serving Jesus. He asked me to join their mission organization. When I asked whether I would be allowed to use the gifts of the Holy Spirit if I joined them, he sheepishly told me no.

I felt an urge to write a letter to the address mentioned in that magazine. God had called me to go to India to preach the gospel, I told them, and requested that they let me know how I could join them. After one month no answer came, so I wrote again. No answer. Lord, how can this be? Again I wrote, and again only silence. I started to get desperate. I decided to write one more last time. Finally I received an answer in which there was an apology for answering so late. They told me if I wished to join their group, I could join their team in Sweden. *Sweden?* I thought. *Is not India in the opposite direction?*

I received the following prophetic answer: "My child, I love you very much. I have already given you much, and I will give you much more. Stay in Me. I will give you much wisdom for the people around you. Fear not, my child, I will go with you" (Rotterdam, June 28, 1976). My uncertain future was now in God's hand. He knew the way. I had to trust Him for each step of the way and not give in to fear.

TURN ON THE TV!

The last two weeks in my native country the Netherlands were spent at the home of my dear parents. I needed time to be alone and desired to spend some time in fasting to ask the Lord for one last confirmation for the way ahead of me. At the same time I wanted to honor my parents by spending some time with them. Who knew when and where I would see them again? A cute, brown Dachshund puppy was their new acquisition. I arrived just in time to teach it how to behave and obey human beings. For many years Dobbie became a great blessing to my parents.

One evening, after my parents had gone to bed, I was praying in their living room. All of a sudden I heard an inner voice say, "Turn on the TV!" I had not watched any television for the past five years, so I was sure this was the voice of the devil trying to distract me from praying. Once again this voice urged me even more strongly, "Turn on the TV!" I finally took a chance and decided to obey.

When I randomly flipped on the TV, it took me straight to a documentary on the streets in Bombay, India. It was nighttime and obviously very hot. While slowly driving by in a rikshaw, a camera man held his camera very low to the ground. On the screen I saw endless crowded rows of men and women sleeping side by side on the sidewalks. I was shocked. Suddenly I heard soft music and then the prophetic words of a heavenly song, (not coming from the TV) "The day is short, and the night is coming in which no one can work!" I broke down with tears of compassion and thankfulness, sobbing for a long, long time. God had spoken, and I needed no more confirmations.

"As long as it is day, we must do the works of him who sent me. Night is coming, when no one can work." (John 9:4 NKJV)

Before I was set to leave my country, I had asked God for two confirmations: First of all, for someone to take my place in the team—so the JP ministry I left would go on unhindered. Secondly, that I would be sent to the mission field with the blessing of the JP leadership. A suitable replacement was found just in time. And on the day I was blessed and sent out by the elders, our JP leader, not knowing about my travel plans, gave me the following prophetic word from the Lord:

"The Lord shows me a ship, the lines are thrown and the ship sails away. And the Lord says: 'Behold my child, in the same way I am taking you away from this quay, yes, my child, I Myself am going to take over the steering wheel of your life. I will take you to many places. Therefore, entrust your life to Me, my son, and do not hesitate to listen and obey time and time again. You will receive many treasures in your life that you will bring to many coasts, because I Myself will fill you with a message. My son, know that I will provide, and I will help and give what you need, because behold, my son, I have pleasure in you; I have seen you and rejoice in you. My Spirit will go with you to show you the way, thus says the Lord.'" (Rotterdam, January 26, 1977)

SWEDISH INVASION

My brother and his wife accompanied me to the ferry in Amsterdam, which was to take me straight to Goteborg, Sweden. The prophecy of my Dutch JP leader literally came to pass. We hugged and said goodbye. As I walked over the ramp toward the ferry, I left everything known, loved and familiar behind to enter into an unknown and unfamiliar future. It felt like being emptied out and torn apart. While closing the berth door behind me, I dropped on my bed and started praying. My heart felt sad and anxious. The ferry sounded its horn and, with a shudder, left the quay. Soon we were on our way on to the North Sea, where waves caused the ferry to sway gently, like a huge crib.

The Holy Spirit comforted me: "You are now hidden under My wings; I will go before you and I will give you rest." The Lord had taken over the steering wheel of my life. I was about to enter upon a zig-zag course.

"Swedish Invasion" was the unfortunate name my new missions organization—Christ is the Answer (CITA)—had chosen for an evangelistic campaign in Sweden. Up to that point no foreign army had ever invaded Sweden, so this name was an affront even to Christian Swedes and very counterproductive. The original purpose of this "invasion" had been to raise new workers and funds through local churches for the CITA teams in Italy—and especially to fund a new team going overland to India. However, very few churches opened their doors for the CITA team.

By the time I arrived to join them in Goteborg, the team had shrunk to just a few American members who were trying to hold the fort in vain. It was the winter of January 1977, with lots of snow. It was freezing cold, and we had hardly any food to eat. Whether we liked it or not we were forced to fast and pray, which we did. There were very few opportunities to minister, so within a month after my arrival the decision was made to dissolve the fledgling team in Sweden and for all to return to the main team based in Italy. Who were these committed young disciples I had just joined, and how and where did this move among young people come from?

ONE DIVINE MOMENT

Radical students in many parts of the U.S. and Europe were rising up against the status quo with burning, destroying property, rock throwing and other forms of violence and rebellion. During one Divine moment, on the cold winter day of February 3, 1970, a heavenly Visitation occurred quite unexpectedly in a small school named Asbury College in Wilmore, Kentucky.[3]

For some time before that day, a small group of students had been getting up a half an hour earlier each morning for prayer, Bible study and other ministry activities. Various groups had also been meeting at different times to pray for spiritual awakening. A spirit of expectancy had been building up on the campus. A few students had received prophetic words that a great outpouring of the Holy Spirit was at hand.

The Hughes Auditorium at Asbury College filled up that morning with more than a thousand students for the usual 10 a.m. chapel service. The program did not follow its customary worship pattern. The dean of the college, who was the scheduled speaker, did not feel impressed to preach. Instead, he felt led to have the students participate in a testimony meeting.

After he shared his own testimony, several students quickly arose and started to give fervent personal testimonies, reflecting deep heart searching. Soon a mass of students moved forward

---

[3]   Coleman, Robert E., and David J. Gyertson. *One Divine Moment: The account of the Asbury Revival of 1970*. Wilmore, KY: First Fruits Press, 2013.

making heartfelt confessions of all kinds of sins and shortcomings. There was no room for all who wanted to come forward. There were outbursts of joy when students experienced relief through forgiveness of their sins. Spontaneous songs of praise sounded forth. God was moving upon His people. The presence of God became so real that all other interests seemed unimportant. The bell sounded for classes to begin but went unheeded.

Students and faculty members alike started to melt down in the refining fire of God's presence. For more than 185 hours, this redeeming fire burned unabated, gently drawing not only students but local church members and nonbelievers as well. Local churches canceled their regular services, and up to 1,600 people crammed day after day and night after night in the Hughes Auditorium.

The news of this God-initiated revival started to spread to other colleges and churches all over the U.S. On weekends students from Asbury College swarmed out to other cities where they were invited to share their testimonies. Wherever they went, the same cleansing fire started to burn. People from all walks of life—but especially young people, students and hippies alike—started to turn away from sin and evil. Praying and weeping with deep emotion, many made their hearts right with the living God and heavenly Father.

Soon, this fire started to spread to other nations far and wide. The Netherlands was one of them, and God had graciously touched me as well. This revival was of Divine origin by a sovereign and merciful God, cleansing the churches and society through the genuine witness of simple, mostly young, people. Called "Jesus People" or "the Jesus Movement," a generation of committed young people and leadership were raised up to stand up for God and His eternal purposes. New forms of worship and praise, and a heart for evangelization and missions, were especially at the core of this movement.

Without realizing who they were at the time, I had already met some of them when the JP band "The Sheep" visited our home base in The Hague sometime in 1973. To my embarrassment, I was asked to translate for them while these long-haired brothers shared wild stories of their old lives and how they found true salvation in Christ Jesus. That had been one of those moments when I had to learn to obey, overcoming my fear of failure. Little did I know at that time how much and how soon I would have to translate in various languages.

9
THE CIRCUS
OF GOD

Ten adults and two toddlers sat uncomfortably on the hard, wooden floor in the back of a closed van. We were on an eight-hour trip from Belgium—where we had met up with some new team members arriving from the U.S.—to the team somewhere in Italy. When we finally arrived, I found myself in the middle of a "Circolo di Dio" (Circus of God) as the Italians lovingly used to call the Cristo E La Risposta (Christ is the Answer) evangelistic tent ministry.

It had all started in the U.S. with tent evangelization, and in Italy the same strategy was used. The Big Top—as the huge circus tent was called—was the core of the evangelistic meetings which were mostly held in the evening. The tent was located on an empty lot near the town, surrounded by a number of antiquated trucks, vehicles and smaller tents. They were used as dormitories for a few couples, the single ladies, the kitchen, wash and shower rooms and workshops. The single men were accommodated behind the stage under the Big Top. About fifty brothers and sisters from various nations such as the U.S., Canada, El Salvador, Germany and many Italians worked together to keep this circus for Christ moving across Italy.

When the team first moved to Italy, it was predicted that they would probably starve to death. Italy was not considered a wealthy nation, and Italian born-again Christians were few and quite poor. The opposite happened. These precious Italian brothers and sisters behaved very much like the churches of Macedonia mentioned in the Bible:

"In the midst of a very severe trial, their overflowing joy and their extreme poverty welled up in rich generosity." (2 Cor. 8:2 NKJV)

After the rejection of rich Christians in Sweden, I was now experiencing the abounding riches of the liberality of Italian Christians living in deep poverty. In return for the "chibo spirituale" (spiritual food) these "servi di Dio" (servants of God) from far away had come to bring them, they brought pasta, vegetables and all kinds of food to our team kitchen in abundance each day. After the Sunday church meetings in local churches, our team members were usually invited to eat in Italian homes.

The first time in front of a plate of delicious spaghetti with meat sauce, the friendly host repeated "Fratello, manchi di piu!" (Brother, eat more!) I ate as much as I could. Soon I found out this was just the beginning and only the first of a four-course meal. A meat dish, a vegetable dish and a dessert were still to be overcome. The only way to process that much food was to take an extensive nap or siesta afterwards. Welcome to Italian culture.

It is hard to describe Italy. You must experience it. During the next two years I had this privilege. Politically, Italy has been able to set a record. Since 1945 roughly sixty-six different governments have tried to rule this country. Italians love to talk and argue, so I guess over the years their politicians had plenty of opportunities. The first time I entered a Plaza, the public square in the middle of a small Italian town where we were going to evangelize, it was full of wildly gesticulating people shouting at each other. To me it looked and sounded like a riot was about to breakout. My buddy helped me understand that this was not a riot but the way Italians communicate while having a good time.

Italians do, in fact, have two languages: the vocal language and the body language. Hardly anyone spoke English, so I tried my best to learn at least some of both languages. It was my desire to share the good news with them if I was to be there. Some of the verbs I learned from a grammar book. My best teachers, however, were the Italians I met on the streets. "Come se chiamo questo?" (How do you call this?) was my standard question to learn new words. Plenty of helpful, friendly Italians were eager to give an answer to a curious "Olandese."

Spiritually, Italy was always a Catholic nation, especially in 1977. After all, the Pope resides in the Vatican, a religious state of its own, in Rome. Between 1970 and 1980 secular Italians managed to push through liberal laws on divorce and abortion. Devout Catholics, on the other hand, would not give in to this worldly way of thinking, but they also would not accept true revival. Some of the older Italian brothers told me of the opposition they had suffered from the Catholic church because they were born again and filled with the Spirit of God and had left the Catholic church. These "Pentecostali" (Pentecostals) were sometimes persecuted in various ways.

GOD'S WAYS ARE HIGHER

"He who overcomes shall be clad thus in white garments, and I will not blot his name out of the book of life; I will confess his name before my Father and before his angels. He who has an ear, let him hear what the Spirit says to the churches."

(Rev. 3:5–6 NKJV, author's emphasis)

10
LEARNING TO WAIT

Before being allowed to go to India, my leadership had advised me to stay with the team in Italy for some time. The reason was to come to know the way they worked and for them to see if I would be fit to go to a country like India. This meant learning to wait and making the best of the situation. Living under a tent basically meant that apart from being shielded from sun and rain, I was practically living outside and exposed to whatever weather came along. We traveled from town to town all over Italy to preach the good news. The heat in Italy can become quite unbearable and inescapable, which was a good preparation for learning to overcome the even greater heat awaiting me in India.

During winter the temperatures in higher elevations could be very low. The only places to enjoy a bit of comfort were my outdoor sleeping bag and by the fire in one of the tents for those who woke up early to read their Bibles. While waiting upon God and learning many new things, I kept up my own lifestyle of seeking God early at 5 a.m. and fasting once a week on Thursdays. To my surprise there were very few team members with a similar lifestyle. By then I had already learned not to look upon what others did or did not do. My aim was to seek and to please the One who sent me, and not men.

Traveling and living in a circus tent was quite labor intensive. Setting up the tent could be quite dangerous. The huge canvas tent roof was held up by tall steel poles that needed to be raised slowly to standing positions by a steel cable pulled by a truck. After an evangelistic tent campaign was over, the reverse procedure took place. One day ten of us were standing in a line with our hands reaching up to help lower a tent pole to the ground. All of a sudden the steel cable snapped. The pole dropped to the ground. Most of us were able to jump aside in the nick of time, but one sister standing behind me did not. The full weight of the pole pinned her leg to the ground. While lifting the pole, we feared the worst. However, she got up totally unharmed! We all stood there in disbelief, overwhelmed by this amazing miracle of supernatural divine protection.

> "The angel of the LORD encamps around those who fear him and delivers them." (Ps. 34:7 NKJV)

THE "MAN CHILD"

Our tent ministry took us all over Italy. On the island of Sicily, which is a part of Italy, we set up our tent in cities like Syracuse. Here, the apostle Paul had stayed for three days on his way to Rome and Catania. We were not far away from Mount Etna, at 3,327 meters (10,915 feet)—the most active volcanic mountain in Europe. While doing night guard duty around our campgrounds, I saw the glowing stream of burning lava, like a fiery snake sneaking down against the darkness of the sky.

After a daily body meeting—a time of team worship, prayer, a short teaching and the coordination of daily team activities—I was usually part of the street evangelization team. At times I was asked to help mend the aging canvas of the tents in constant need of repair. This helped me identify with my great example, the apostle Paul in the Bible, who was a tentmaker by trade.

On Sundays we would divide up in small teams to share our testimonies and preach in local churches whose members participated in our revival meetings during the week. Sicilianos are small of stature but very kind and warmhearted people. Once we entered the church, we men were greeted by the brothers with three customary kisses on the cheek: a "bacio a destra," a "bacio a finistra" and a "bacio a destra"—a kiss on the right cheek, the left one and again on the right one. The only problem was that these mostly poor peasants did not shave very well. After being kissed by all thirty men present, the skin of your cheeks felt like a lawn mower had just passed over it.

After the meeting we were usually asked to pray for the needs of the believers. One lady walked up to me with what appeared to be a baby wrapped underneath a shawl on her arms.

"Shall I pray for your baby," I asked.

"Si, fratello," (Yes, brother) she replied.

When she opened the shawl, I got a real shock. There in front of me was the face of a twenty-five-year-old man with a body the size of a baby! My heart was filled with compassion as I looked into the sad and desperate eyes of the mother. I scraped up the little faith that I had and prayed for that "man child." Nothing happened. Now it was my turn to become desperate.

"Lord, why don't you answer our prayer?"

I received an unexpected answer: "My son, I am showing you this for a reason. What you see is the sad spiritual condition of many of my believers worldwide. Many confess to be Christians, but they have not been taught to be disciples and stopped growing spiritually at a very young age. They may know me and my saving power for twenty-five years or more, but spiritually they remain babies. Go and teach them to be my disciples and to obey my Word and help them grow into spiritual maturity."

This exceptional experience stuck with me, and I shared this in many situations to help believers understand the need for true discipleship and growth into spiritual maturity. In writing to Galatian believers, the apostle Paul exclaimed like a loving and caring parent:

"My dear children, for whom I am again in the pains of childbirth until Christ is formed in you!"
(Gal. 4:19 NKJV)

In his letter to the Ephesian church the apostle Paul explained how this problem of spiritual immaturity can be overcome:

"And his gifts were that some should be apostles, some prophets, some evangelists, some pastors and teachers, *to equip the saints for* the work of ministry, for *building up the body of Christ*, until *we all* attain to the unity of the faith and of the knowledge of the Son of God, *to mature manhood*, to the measure of the stature of the fullness of Christ; *so that we may no longer be children*, tossed to and fro and carried about with every wind of doctrine, by the cunning of men, by their craftiness in deceitful wiles. Rather, speaking the truth in love, *we are to grow up in every way to him* who is the head, into Christ, from whom the *whole* body, joined and knit together by *every* joint with which it is supplied, when *each* part is working properly, *makes bodily growth* and upbuilds itself in love." (Eph. 4:11–16 RSV, author's emphasis)

This God-ordained and Holy Spirit-inspired, fivefold ministry is made up of:

1. Apostles,
2. Prophets,
3. Evangelists,
4. Pastors,
5. Teachers.

It is the unshakable foundation for a healthy environment in which new believers will be equipped to thrive and grow up into spiritual maturity.

HIDDEN SIN

On the way back from a meeting, our team passed over a hill after which we were normally able to see the tent. We rubbed our eyes and could hardly believe what we saw: the tent was gone! Coming closer we could see that the tent laid flat on the ground like a deflated balloon. What had happened? While we were gone, an unexpected gust of wind had hit the tent. It was filled with air, torn loose from its tent pins and was lifted up along with the huge tent poles. Then it slowly descended, giving those inside just enough time to get out from under it. Miraculously no one was hurt, and the tent itself suffered very little damage!

It was easy to blame this occurrence on Satan and his opposition to our team's evangelistic activities. To the credit of our team's leadership, the situation was not just left at that. During our next daily body meeting the whole team was asked to go on their knees, search their hearts and confess any hidden sin. The Holy Spirit came upon us all, convicting us of sin, righteousness and judgment. Sins, both big and small, were confessed. Forgiveness was pronounced. Hearts and the spiritual atmosphere were cleansed. The ministry could continue with renewed blessing and vigor.

The concept of hidden sin and its devastating effect on a person, his family and the community at large is very evident in the story of Achan and his hidden sin after the conquest of Jericho.

The battle of Jericho was a glorious and quite miraculous event. After encircling the city one time for six days and seven times on the seventh day, the trumpets sounded, the people shouted and the thick and sturdy walls of Jericho came tumbling down. The Israelites just had to run in and take the city. However, they were told not to take any of the spoil devoted to God for themselves. Achan did not obey this command and hid a mantle, silver and gold underneath his tent for his own use. The next time the army of Israelites was defeated at the small city of Ai. When Joshua and his people were discouraged, God spoke:

"The Lord said to Joshua, 'Stand up! What are you doing down on your face? Israel has sinned; they have violated my covenant, which I commanded them to

> keep. They have taken some of the devoted things; they
> have stolen, they have lied, they have put them with
> their own possessions. That is why the Israelites cannot
> stand against their enemies; they turn their backs and
> run because they have been made liable to destruction.
> I will not be with you anymore unless you destroy
> whatever among you is devoted to destruction.'"
> (Josh. 7:10–12 NKJV)

Eventually Achan confessed his hidden sin after he was exposed, and he and his family paid for it dearly with their lives. Sin was atoned for. The next battle for Ai was won. Any hidden personal sin will always hinder and limit God's blessing not only for one individual but also for his family and community. The way to overcome is by honest confession and repentance of any hidden sin. Renewed victory for yourself, your family and community will be the result.

TRIAL OF FAITH

> "Until the time that his word came; the word
> of the Lord tried him." (Ps. 105:19 NKJV)

Nobody likes to wait. We all would like to see quick results. Our eternal heavenly Father does not think or move according to our impatient terms or hectic time schedules. My time in Italy was a time of waiting and the trial of my faith. To overcome such times, it helps to spend time reading God's Word and edifying books. God spoke very clearly and confirmed His way of working in my life while reading from Oswald Chambers book, *My Utmost for His Highest*[4]:

---

4   Chambers, O., & Reimann, J. (1995). *My Utmost for His Highest: Selections for Every Day*. Discovery House Publishers.

"I reckon on you for extreme service, with no complaining on your part and no explanation on mine."

During my time in Gela, Italy, in 1978, a sermon I read explained this principle:

"Let us see how God prepares a person for a great work. Joseph was sent to Egypt to be a deliverer for the seed of Abraham. 'He sent a man before them . . . he was laid in iron' (Ps. 105:17). A helpless slave, bound by a chain he could not free himself from—on his way to the throne. Yet far more trying than the bondage and the humility of it all was the conflict in his soul resulting from his love for the Word. Until he received that which God had promised him, the Word of God tried him.

"This trial by the Word comes to all servants who seek to walk in truth. The trial by the Word lasts only until God's set time to bless comes. There is a trial of faith and the more you love God's Word, the more severe your trial will be! We have become so preoccupied in proving God that we have not prepared our hearts for the great tests of life whereby God proves man. Could it be that the great trial you are now facing, the burden you now carry, is actually God at work proving you? God left him, to try him, that he might know all that was in his heart.

"Often while in the righteous pursuit of God's work, the steward of the Lord finds himself apparently forsaken, tried to the limits of endurance and left all alone to battle the forces of hell.

"Every man or woman God has ever blessed has been proved in the same manner."[5]

"God left him . . . to test him . . ."
(2 Chron. 32:31 NKJV)

---

[5] https://bibleportal.com Wilkerson, David. "When God Proves Man," n.d.

11
GOD'S WAYS
ARE HIGHER

"For as the heavens are higher than the earth,
so are my ways higher than your ways and my
thoughts than your thoughts." (Isa. 55:9 NKJV)

Each year during summer our Italian team would break up into smaller teams, which then went on outreach in neighboring countries like Spain, Portugal, France or Germany. Each team needed at least one person who knew the local language to help translate in churches or during evangelization in those countries. An American team member, who had studied in Munich, Germany, had been the translator for the German team. However, he left the ministry, so there was no one to translate. I was about to learn that God's ways are indeed higher than my ways and His thoughts way beyond my thoughts!

A RELUCTANT TRANSLATOR

One day the American team leader approached me with an unexpected proposal:

"We need a translator for the German team. We think you are the right person for the job."

"What?" I replied. "I am not a German, and I have only been to Germany once for one day as a child. How can you expect me to translate there?"

"Well, your Dutch language is similar to German, right?" he argued sheepishly.

Only Americans could come up with such an idea, I thought.

During my school days I was required to learn four languages: Dutch, English, French and German. I learned the grammar of these languages, but unlike the Dutch, English and French languages, there were few opportunities to put my German into practice. Dutch and German are similar languages, but German grammar is quite difficult. I could not imagine embarrassing myself standing in front of a congregation, or during street meetings in Germany trying to translate from English into broken German.

I tried to explain all these facts. It did not help much. "Just pray about it and let me know," he replied, leaving me behind with my bewildered thoughts. Pray I did, and I had great faith for the Lord to bring another person into our team to do the job of translating in Germany. As the months slipped by, soon only one month was left before the outreach team for Germany was supposed to leave. No substitute had showed up. Becoming increasingly more nervous and restless, I became quite desperate in my prayers.

"You had better start learning to translate into German!" This time it was not the voice of my leader but the soft, stern voice of the Holy Spirit. There was now no way out. Sermons and testimonies during meetings under our revival tent, the Big Top, were usually translated from English into Italian. The only way to learn to translate was to translate for myself whatever I heard while listening to a sermon as it was being translated into Italian. When I heard an English word or term that I did not know in German, I would write it down. Scriptures used during the sermon I looked up and read in an old German Bible. During free time I grabbed an English-German dictionary to look up the German words unknown to me and memorized them. This way my knowledge of German—and Christian terminology in German—slowly improved. There was little time left.

The team's antiquated German passenger bus, adorned with some sort of semi-legal, American international license plate, allowed us passage through international European borders. With squeaking brakes, it slowly and painstakingly wound its way up and down the breathtaking alpine mountain roads. Our team of about ten members had left the sweltering summer heat of Italy behind on our way to our evangelistic outreach in Germany. For sure, to some extent, I was looking forward to the much cooler climate in northern Europe. However, the Damocles sword of having to translate into German still hanging over my head did little to make me feel comfortable.

"Why are the people in Germany always amused and smiling when you translate for me? I'm not telling any jokes!" my American team leader finally desperately asked.

He was a man of few and quite simple words who used short sentences while preaching. This was very helpful for me as I tried to translate as well as I could in the few small charismatic churches we visited in the German state of Bavaria.

"I don't know," I replied, "but aren't you glad that these serious Germans are feeling a bit happy?"

Only much later a kind German brother finally took me aside to tell me why they were so amused. I had been learning my German by using a very old Lutheran Bible. My choice and pronunciation of German words was the equivalent of what would happen if I were speaking in a King James Bible version of English in the U.S. The gospel out of the mouth of an American preacher was translated into German with a heavy Dutch accent. Above and beyond that, my Martin Luther German was bound to cause unexpected amusement for the German listeners.

After that brother gave me a more modern German version of the Bible, the listeners finally became more serious again. The leading of the Holy Spirit may take us to places we do not wish go. Sometimes it causes us to have to do things we do not wish to do. When we surrender our will to the Lord we will learn to overcome our natural reluctance. Slowly it started to dawn on me that going to Germany might be one of the higher ways of God. After all, I did not really want to go, but it was as if Someone else was leading me to go where I did not want. But, why Germany?

"Very truly I tell you, when you were younger you dressed yourself and went where you wanted; but when you are old you will stretch out your hands, and someone else will dress you and lead you where you do not want to go."
(John 21:18 NKJV)

A BROKEN, HUNGRY, DIVIDED BUT PROSPEROUS NATION

In 1945, at the end of World War II, Germany and all other countries involved were left with 50 million dead—both military and civilians—including the extinction of 6 million Jews. The economy and infrastructure of Germany, as well as the rest of Europe, was in shambles. Allied forces divided Germany into an eastern section—controlled by Communists—and a western section, controlled by capitalist influence. For the next two years until 1947, the entire population was on the brink of starvation. The Allies had agreed for German reparations to be paid through the dismantling of German industry and transferring all manufacturing equipment, machinery, machine tools, all railroad cars, locomotives and ships to the Allies. Also, all gold, silver and platinum and all foreign currency held by any person or institution in Germany was confiscated. All patents and research data relevant to military application and processes were taken over and the German population was subjected to forced labor.

However, something had to be done to avoid repeating a vicious cycle of social upheaval and radical political movement. In June 1947, in a twelve-minute speech to Harvard University graduates, U.S. foreign minister Marshall proclaimed: "It would be neither fitting nor efficacious for this government to undertake to draw up unilaterally a program designed to place Europe on its feet economically. This is the business of the Europeans. The initiative, I think, must come from Europe. The role of this country (U.S.) should consist of friendly aid in the drafting of a European program and of later support of such a program so far as it may be practical for us to do so. The program should be a joint one, agreed to by a number, if not all European nations."[6]

The American congress endorsed the Foreign Assistance Act, and the European Recovery Program—or Marshall Plan—came into effect on April 3, 1948, allowing aid for the next four years. Annually, this aid had to be applied for and approved. Until 1952 these services amounted totally up to 14 billion dollars. The greater part, amounting to 9.3 billion dollars were subsidies, the rest mostly loans and "conditional aid." The subsidies were paid in dollars to be able to import goods and capital. These subsidies did not have to be paid back. However, each government had to pay the equivalent of subsidies received into a special fund (Equivalent Currency Fund). Ninety-five percent of these special funds were then used to stimulate national rebuilding. Eastern Europe was also offered this kind of help, but Russia forbade the countries under its influence to accept capitalist aid or ideas.

As a result of this wise plan, twenty years of rapid economic growth, the so called "Wirtschaftswunder" (Economic Miracle) took place in the whole of Europe, but especially in Germany. Germans are a hardworking, well-organized and disciplined people. Most of them just wanted to leave the shame of defeat and the ugly shadows of a senseless and cruel war behind to concentrate on a better future. The Nuremberg Trials resulted in the death penalty or long-term prison sentences for several Nazi leaders, but

---

6   "Marshall Plan." Wikipedia, March 10, 2025. https://en.wikipedia.org/wiki/Marshall_Plan.

it proved next to impossible to punish or prove the guilt of the majority of former Nazis. The majority suddenly claimed that they never knew about what really happened. They were innocent and quite unaware of Hitler's insane and destructive ideologies. Until the end of the seventies, many of them continued their lives and were put into places of responsibility in the fast-growing economic, educational and governmental sectors of the German society.

Apart from war reparations paid to many countries until 2005, Germany has paid—primarily to Jewish survivors—about 63 billion Euros (equivalent to approximately 87.9 billion Euros in 2022) in compensation overall for Nazi crimes since an agreement was signed in 1952.

During Nazi rule from 1933–1945, in general, the church in Germany in most cases opted to give in and go along with the inhuman policies of the Nazi government. Instead of standing up and suffering for the Truth, they believed their lies and ended up cooperating—and thus denying their Savior Jesus Christ. It was not uncommon to see the Nazi Swastika sign instead of the cross exhibited at the altars of churches. The required so called "Hitlergruss" (Hitler greeting) "Heil Hitler" (Salvation Hitler) itself meant raising your right arm and hand in giving honor to a mere man. Hitler and some of his henchmen committed suicide after his planned Thousand Year reign ended in total destruction after only twelve years.

Fortunately, some members of the "Confessing Church," a group of evangelical Christians stood up against this tidal wave of anti-Christian thought. But they paid dearly for it with their lives. Bold Pastor Paul Schneider, who refused to be silenced, proclaimed the gospel from his isolation cell in prison and was killed in 1939 in the Buchenwald concentration camp by lethal injection. Only a few days before the end of the war, Hitler personally ordered the execution by hanging of theologian

Dietrich Bonhoefer in the Flossenburg concentration camp. This happened because of Bonhoefer's involvement in plots to kill Hitler. Some Catholic clergy also suffered because of their stand against Hitler. On the other hand, among others, high clergy in the Vatican in Rome helped many high-level Nazi criminals escape via so called "rat lines" to South America where they were presumed safe from prosecution.

By the time I arrived in Germany in 1977 there were most-wanted posters in search of Red Army Fraction (RAF) terrorists all over the country. During the seventies and eighties the RAF was a small group of sixty to eighty leftist extremists responsible for the murder of up to thirty-four executives in politics, business and administration including their drivers. Policemen, custom officials and some American soldiers were also killed. They robbed banks, took hostages and carried out bomb attacks. The boss of a German brother and his wife, who later often hosted us, was shot pointblank in his bathroom by one member of the RAF. Ultimately, twenty-four RAF members and sympathizers were killed, some of them by suicide or hunger strikes.

A tiny, fragmented and struggling Free Church and Pentecostal movement was growing toward more unity and growth during these heady days of the seventies and eighties. The upcoming charismatic movement also resulted in the birth of free and spirit-filled churches all over Germany. There was a great need to channel the positive German attitudes of hard work, discipline, organization and endurance into a movement to further the gospel in countries unreached with the gospel. After all, there had been great moves of God in Germany's past.

The reformer Martin Luther stood up to some of the heresies of his Catholic church. He translated the Bible into German, enabling the common man to read the Word of God for themselves. Then there was Count von Zinzendorf and the Moravians in Herrnhut who started one of the first prayer and mission movements. God could do it again.

A PERSON FORGIVEN
MUCH LOVES MUCH

"Therefore, I tell you, her many sins have been forgiven—as her great love has shown. But whoever has been forgiven little loves little." (Luke 7:47 NKJV)

Small Pentecostal churches or charismatic meetings were sparsely scattered in various parts of Bavaria in the south of Germany. As a translator one of my jobs was to contact the pastors and arrange meetings for our outreach team in cities and towns such as Passau, Regensburg, Straubing and Munich. Staying in church buildings or with hospitable local believers, we would spend one to two weeks in each place. After breakfast each day, we had prayer and worship meetings before we would go out for evangelistic street meetings the rest of the day. Those interested were invited to come to our evangelistic evening meetings in the local church.

From my Dutch background I still had some apprehension toward older Germans. After all my country had suffered badly during World War II, and my generation was not particularly fond of "Moffen" as Germans were disparagingly called. However, in a Pentecostal church in Regensburg, I came to know an older German brother. He became my friend because he spread an amazing aura of love and friendliness whenever he was around. In church he prayed and worshipped wholeheartedly, and he was very gifted in sharing very accurate and prophetic words of encouragement for those around him. One day I asked him how he had come to know the Lord Jesus Christ.

"Do you really want to know?!" he asked.

"Yes, why not?" I replied.

His life story first shocked me. During the war he had been a member of the "Schutzstaffel" Protection Squads (SS), the infamous ruthless elite guard of Hitler. The SS was a national socialistic organization that Hitler used as an instrument to rule and suppress. Already in 1934, their responsibility was the operation and administration of concentration camps, and from 1941, also of extermination camps. The SS was mainly involved in the planning and implementation of the Holocaust (extermination of the Jewish race) and other genocides such as of the Sinti and Roma gypsy people groups.

In order to forget the horrible things he had done and seen, he had turned to heavy consumption of alcohol which continued after the war was over. One day he encountered Christians who invited him to attend their church. In one of their meetings the Holy Spirit convicted him of sin, righteousness and judgment. At first it was hard for him to believe that God could forgive him. Finally, he truly understood what the Jew Jesus, the Son of God, had done for him on the cross—how He was able to reach out to and soften even the hardest heart and forgive even the biggest sin. He broke down and asked God to forgive him and help him start a new life.

"God has forgiven me so much, and I am so thankful for so much undeserved grace; that's why I love Jesus with all of my heart," he ended up saying, while his loving eyes met my teary eyes.

It took my breath away. Now it was my turn to search my heart and turn away from unforgiveness. Here I stood in front of a former burning stick snatched from the fire.

"The LORD said to Satan, 'The LORD rebuke you, Satan! The LORD, who has chosen Jerusalem, rebuke you! Is not this man a burning stick snatched from the fire?'" (Zech. 3:2 NKJV)

Who was I to keep holding a grudge deep in my heart against the German people if God was able to redeem and accept such a great sinner? How could I try to preach the gospel to Germans if I had not really forgiven them and was not able to see them the way God saw them? The great change in the life of such an evil person was obvious. Never in my life had I ever met a Christian with so much love and compassion. He had been forgiven much and therefore showed much love. In comparison, many Christians I knew, including myself, had been forgiven much less and showed only little love. I stretched my arms out to him and embraced him. In that very moment God helped me to overcome the prejudice and self-righteousness deep down in my heart. We stood there for quite some time. Words were not needed. Love never fails.

PAST AND PRESENT PERSECUTION

Passau, a town in Lower Bavaria, Germany, is also known as the Dreiflüssestadt (City of Three Rivers) because the Danube is joined there by the Inn from the south and the Ilz from the north. Towering over this confluence of three rivers is the Passau Castle where Anabaptists were persecuted and imprisoned between 1535 and 1540 because of their convictions. Anabaptists were the first Christians who rejected child baptism and propagated adult baptism based on a personal decision to follow Christ. Their "Ausbund" songbook contains fifty-one hymns composed by Anabaptists imprisoned in the dungeon of the Passau Castle where many of these men and women of faith of the past were martyred. The Ausbund is still used today by the conservative Amish in the U.S.

An energetic, young, bold Pentecostal pastor and man of faith of the present invited our team to evangelize in Passau. Despite persecution he shepherded a tiny congregation of only ten members including his own young family. Even nowadays in mostly religious Bavaria, free churches are considered sects by some of the state-sponsored Catholic and Lutheran denominations. Our dear brother was not at all intimidated by this resistance.

Once he was invited to participate in a Catholic charismatic Bible study group led by a Catholic theology professor and attended by others from various denominations. The theme and discussion was about Nicodemus and Renewal. The young pastor was the only one representing the Pentecostal church. After various standpoints had been discussed, the professor suggested:

"Let's give the Pentecostal pastor a chance to share his opinion."

Having waited anxiously for that chance our dear brother came straight to the point:

"You all have been starting from the wrong vantage point. Without true repentance and a change of heart there can never be a spiritual renewal!"

As he went on to share more about how even religious Nicodemus needed to be born anew from God's Spirit, he was soon drowned out by very excited and loud opposition to his explanations. The overheated crowd only calmed down after the professor intervened. To their great surprise he told everybody that this Pentecostal pastor was a representative of the "Urgemeinde" (original church), where believers experienced the gifts of the Holy Spirit and spoke in new tongues—and that they should listen to him carefully. After the meeting, when everyone was gone, the professor fell on his knees in front of the pastor requesting him to pray for him to receive the baptism in the Holy Spirit!

This pastor was very excited to see our team go out on the streets of Passau to preach the good news. Bavarian onlookers were taken by surprise by the way this motivated crew of young foreigners were singing about Jesus and testifying publicly of their newfound faith. For most of them Jesus should be worshipped in a church building depicted while still suffering on a cross.

Some of them became openly hostile and tried to disturb the meetings. We realized all too soon that a spiritual battle for the religious souls of these men and women was going on. Satan has nothing against religions, even Christian religion, as long as it keeps seekers away from the redeeming power of the simple message offered by Jesus. By the sacrifice of His own blood on the cross He purchased for God men and women from every nation, tribe, people and language. Whenever this Truth is preached, the father of lies will try to stop the messenger. But the true messenger is called to overcome this opposition by the power of the blood of Jesus, which is the price paid for the salvation of every man and woman.

"And they sang a new song, saying 'You are worthy to take the scroll and to open its seals, because you were slain, and with your blood you purchased for God persons from every tribe and language and people and nation.'" (Rev. 5:9 NKJV)

THE BURNING BUS

"Wake up, you must wake up now!" A strong sense of pending evil caused me to wake up out of a deep sleep in the middle of the night. After long days of praying, singing, preaching, translating and sharing the gospel outside on the streets in the rain, wind or sunshine we all would be very tired in the evening. We usually dropped into our beds for a sound sleep. In Passau the men in our team slept in their own sleeping bags on mattresses in the tiny church building. The women slept in the home of believers nearby. Our team bus was parked on the opposite side of the street where the church was located.

"Get up, open the curtains and look what is happening outside!" a strong inner voice urged me to take action. Jumping up to the window I tore the curtains aside. Smoke rose out of our bus! Immediately I woke up our team leader: "The bus is burning!"

"Whaa . . . aat?!" he mumbled. Only half awake he staggered towards the window. "Oh nooo . . . !"

Putting on our clothes as fast as we could, we rushed bare-foot outside to the bus. The door of the bus was open. We ran inside, grabbed a fire extinguisher and put out the fire that was just getting started. If we had come ten minutes later it would have been too late. Shocked and out of breath we wondered how this could have happened. Later on we found out that the bus had been left unlocked. At night a drunken man had entered the bus and fell asleep while smoking a cigarette. By the time we came he was gone but had done nothing to stop the fire. We were very thankful the Lord had warned us in time, so the evil plan of our adversary was thwarted and overcome by the angel of the Lord guarding us. Our only means of transport was saved from the fire, and we were able to travel on to preach the gospel.

"For he will command his angels concerning you to guard you in all your ways." (Ps. 91:11 NKJV)

12
LAYING A
FOUNDATION

The higher a building is going to be, the deeper the foundation must be. At first I did not realize it but my time spent in Germany was the higher way God used to lay a strong, deep and solid foundation for future ministry in Asia. Already in Italy I had been asked to accompany and learn from a team leader who went ahead of the team to arrange the next evangelistic campaign in another city. It involved contacting and bringing together pastors from various denominations and getting permissions from local officials. In Germany apart from translating my responsibility was to contact pastors, arrange our meetings and places to stay and keep in contact afterwards. The Lord opened doors all over Germany, and I came to know and could build up relationships with many wonderful pastors and believers.

Our dear pastor friend in Passau, Bavaria, introduced me to his father, who lived in the small town of Grasellenbach in the state of Hessen in the middle of Germany. He and his wife became my most important contact. This brother had suffered from polio as a child, so he limped on one side. During World War II he was a young man who was not drafted into the army because of this handicap. An outspoken and impulsive person like him could get into a lot of trouble during those days. He ended up in one of the worst Gestapo (secret police) prisons. At that time he was still a nominal believer. When they threatened to beat him during interrogation, he heard an inner voice saying: "Lammesnatur behalten!" (Stay like a lamb!) He did and miraculously got out of that prison because of the intervention of a high military official related to him.

Along with many others, he and his wife were told by his

Nazi government to take over a farm in occupied Poland after the owners were chased out. By the end of the war it was the Germans turn to run. The deadly Soviet counteroffensive was in full swing. Hitler ordered his Hitlerjugend (Hitler youth) teenagers, old men and even physically incapacitated people to fight until death for a lost cause. Not willing to fight, this brother deserted with others at the risk of his life. Meanwhile, his wife and their toddlers were fleeing from the Russians known to humiliate, rape and kill German women in their frenzy to take revenge.

Slowly starving, she was unable to breastfeed her twin babies. On the way, one of the twins died as well as one other child. After the war this couple gave their lives to Jesus. These heart-wrenching experiences motivated them to get involved in our ministry. God had brought me into their lives as a replacement for their lost children, and they adopted me as their son and became my German parents. Later on their home became a home away from home and a place of rest from my endless travels. Here, I found true friendship whenever I needed it.

> "Then Peter spoke up, 'We have left
> everything to follow you!'
> 'Truly I tell you,' Jesus replied, 'no one who has
> left home or brothers or sisters or mother or father
> or children or fields for me and the gospel will
> fail to receive a hundred times as much in this
> present age: homes, brothers, sisters, mothers,
> children and fields—along with persecutions—
> and in the age to come eternal life.'"
> (Mark 10, 28–30 NKJV)

ANGELIC NAVIGATION

Our relationship became the foundation for a fruitful network of faithful, praying and giving contacts with brothers and sisters in home groups, fellowships and churches all over Germany, also in the Netherlands. During the fall of that same year the American leader of our new ministry in India came over to Germany for a month to share the vision for India. My job was to organize all of his meetings and translate for him. Finally, I was getting involved with India even without ever having been there! When he arrived at the Frankfort Airport he was accompanied by an Indian businessman whom he had met on the plane. The first thing I ever did for an Indian was to drag his huge and very heavy suitcase across the airport. God was teaching me a lesson: preaching to Indians would mean serving them first.

Traveling and translating all over Germany as well as in the surrounding countries was a very intense and tedious job. It involved night and day translation of each and every regular and ministry conversation and sermon, back and forth into German, English and Dutch. About three weeks in September were needed to arrange the thirty meetings we spoke in during the following month of October. First the team leader from India would show slides about the ministry. He was a fiery speaker, but—helpfully for me—he then preached the same sermon in every meeting. After some time, I had his sermon memorized and found myself translating it even during my dreams at night. We were traveling nonstop, staying at a different place each night. People were moved by these meetings and showed a lot of interest. Especially in Germany, people were giving generously.

Those were the days without today's satellite navigation. We were stuck with plain old country and city maps, or in need of meeting somebody who knew the way. Finding the location of each new meeting and getting there in time was a major stress, especially for me. Arriving late for a meeting in a big German city, we were driving in circles desperately trying to find the way.

"Jesus, help us!" I prayed.

"Folge mir nach!" (Follow me!) Somebody knocked on our

window. A young guy on a bicycle had suddenly popped up out of nowhere motioning us to follow him, shouting over his shoulder: "I will show you the way!"

Before we were able to tell him where we were going, he already took off ahead of our car.

How did *he* know our destination!? There was no time to think so we followed him, taking a couple of right and left turns. All of a sudden he stopped. We verified the street sign. It was the right street and the address we were looking for! Rolling down our car window, I wanted to thank him. I looked around. I could not believe my eyes. He was nowhere to be found. I got goosebumps all over me. God had sent an angel on a bicycle to show the way. Quite fitting for a Dutchman.

SO ABRAM WENT

**Now the Lord said to Abram,
"Go from your country, your people and
your father's household to the land I will
show you . . ." (Gen. 12:1 NKJV)**

**"So Abram went, as the Lord had told him; and Lot
went with him, Abram was seventy-five years old
when he departed from Harran." (Gen. 12:4 NKJV)**

God told Abram that He would make him into a great nation, and bless him and make his name great, so that he would be a blessing and that by him all the families of the earth would be blessed. Abram was not a young man when God told him to go and leave Harran. He was seventy-five years old! God told him to go, and he went as God told him even though he was so old. This always impressed and encouraged me a lot. Although much younger, I had also left my country in obedience to God's calling to go to a country, India, where I had never been.

Getting there would take longer than I had expected. Building a lasting foundation takes time! Before I went to India I first spent the time from January 1977 till December 1979—almost three years—in Italy and Germany being molded into a useful tool in God's hand. During each year, a total of eight months were spent traveling and evangelizing from city to city with our "Circus of God" in Italy and then four months in Germany. Each summer the outreach team for which I translated would spend two months in Germany, and each fall I would return alone from Italy to Germany for another two months. I was there to prepare for and hold meetings with the team leader from India, again translating. My impatient nature was tested to the limit by all this waiting but at least there was enough to do and plenty of challenges to overcome.

MELCHIZEDEK

Praise and worship had been an important part of my time spent in the Netherlands, and it was also a very effective tool for our ministry in Italy and Germany. Apart from translating, I would always sing and play the guitar in our street and church meetings in cities all over Germany. In Italy we also used guitars during street meetings, but during the evangelistic tent meetings in the evening, our own international band Melchizedek—made up of musically gifted team members—took to the stage. This band, their songs and music in Italian and English were very popular with the Italian audience. In any Christian meeting, praise and worship are very important to touch and soften the hearts of men and women in order to open them for the Word of God and the working of the Holy Spirit. However, things are not always the way they appear to be.

One day our team leader came up to me,

"Antoine, we need you for another task."

My first thought was, "Oh no, here we go again!" The last time I was approached this way I ended up in Germany.

"What's up now?" I asked.

"We have a serious problem with our band Melchizedek," he told me. "There is internal strife and disunity among the band members and since you are a spiritually minded person with leadership experience, we want you to deal with this problem."

This job put me into quite an awkward position. As an outsider I was asked to deal with a bunch of strong-headed musicians. The first thing I did was pray for wisdom about how to overcome this challenge.

"Then Melchizedek king of Salem brought out bread and wine. He was priest of God Most High, and he blessed Abram, saying, 'Blessed be Abram by God Most High, Creator of heaven and earth. And praise be to God Most High, who delivered your enemies into your hand.'" (Gen. 14:18–20 NIV)

". . . Without father or mother, without genealogy, without beginning of days or end of life, resembling the Son of God, he remains a priest forever." (Heb. 7:3 NIV)

Melchizedek means "King of Righteousness" and he brought blessing to Abram. Our Savior King Jesus is high priest forever after the order of Melchizedek. The use of such a name for a band meant great responsibility and accountability. Obviously, in their midst the enemy had succeeded in sowing strife instead of peace and disunity instead of righteousness. Consequently, the Melchizedek band was not able to be a blessing.

When we came together to address the problem, I pointed this out and asked them first whether they prayed together before band practice. They did not. Here lies the problem, I explained.

When musical gifts are to be used for God's purpose of worship in Spirit and in Truth, they cannot become a spiritual blessing when there is a lack of truth, unity and prayer. Melchizedek brought out bread and wine, which was a fore shadow of the ultimate sacrifice of the body and the blood of Jesus, the seed of Abram, which sets us free from sin.

In the garden of Gethsemane, while in great distress before he was betrayed and crucified, Jesus begged his disciples three times to stand with him in prayer. They could not do it because they were too overcome by sleep and concerned only about themselves. Jesus was left to fight an unimaginable spiritual battle for the souls of men and women all by himself. Pouring out his troubled soul to his Father in Heaven while sweating blood, he was heard because of his godly fear.

". . . who, in the days of His flesh, when He had offered up prayers and supplications, with vehement cries and tears to Him who was able to save Him from death, and was heard because of His godly fear, though He was a Son, yet He learned obedience by the things which He suffered. And having been perfected, He became the author of eternal salvation to all who obey Him, called by God as High Priest 'according to the order of Melchizedek.'" (Heb. 5:7–10 NKJV)

In the days of his flesh, Jesus, the eternal Word of God, became flesh. Therefore, He is able to identify with our days in the flesh today and have mercy upon our weaknesses and failures. We as sons and daughters of God will learn obedience as well through what we suffer. When we, like Jesus, offer up prayers and supplications with loud cries and tears, our Father in heaven will hear us and save us. In the end, by God's grace, the Melchizedek band members overcame their differences through confession, love, forgiveness and fervent prayer. They became a blessing and a source of salvation once again for the Italian nation.

A FINAL TEST

Our teams in Italy were growing and many young men and women from various nations were joining. Some, as they were traveling around the world, met our team on the streets. They decided to give up their own plans and joined us after they experienced salvation and saw how we were preaching the gospel. A door opened for ministry in the Philippines, and, in response, a team was formed to be sent to that country. The leader of that team approached me to ask me to pray about becoming a part of that team.

The Philippines were located in Asia and a lot closer to India than Italy. Could this be my next step or was this a test? What would happen if I refused this offer? A prolonged stay in Italy? I was highly tempted because I did not want to stay in Europe any longer as eager as I was to go to India. I became restless. After praying about it for some time I did not feel any peace and decided to stay in Italy until the next team would be sent to India—no matter how long that would take. It turned out to be the right decision.

INDIA AT LAST

"He who *overcomes*, I will make him
a pillar in the temple of My God, and
he shall go out no more. And I will
write on him the name of My God
and the name of the city of My God,
the New Jerusalem, which comes
down out of heaven from My God.
And I will write on him My new name."
(Rev. 3:12 NKJV, author's emphasis)

13
OVERLAND
TO INDIA

Clouds of dust and diesel fumes surrounded us for many days. Our old rickety vans were crammed with a very motivated team of new and quite young missionaries and their gear. They shook, rumbled and swerved along trying to avoid countless potholes. We were on the way through former communist Yugoslavia, Greece, Turkey, Iran, Afghanistan and Pakistan.

Destination: India at last.

It was November 1979, and I was part of that team. Finally. It had first taken another month of meetings and translating in Germany to raise funds for the trip. More preparation time was spent in Italy to get the team together and the two vehicles ready for this overland trip to India. Now we were on the way! A small team of the Jezus Kinderen (Jesus Children), from another JP group in the Netherlands, had asked to accompany our team with their own vehicle. They were planning to start their own ministry upon arrival in India. Our vans were much slower than their four-wheel-drive Land Rover. After entering Turkey they changed their plans and decided to go on at their own pace with our approval. We regretted this afterwards.

"You come, follow us!" shouted a Turkish policeman.

There was no explanation. Making good progress driving through Turkey, we had almost completed two-thirds of the way when we suddenly heard the loud siren behind us. His police car overtook our vehicles, and they frantically motioned us to stop. We had no idea what they wanted from us. From a former experience in Turkey, our team leader had learned not to resist or irritate the Turkish police. We followed the police car toward a small town off the main road. The gate slammed shut behind us after we arrived at the compound of a police station. We were all arrested, but why?

Communication was difficult. From what we understood, they were accusing us of trying to convert Turkish Muslims. As a team we had made a rule not to evangelize openly in the Muslim countries on the way to India, so we were not guilty. Our arguments fell on deaf ears. We were told to drive to Ankara to stand before a judge. Now the situation was getting serious. The team started praying hard for God to intervene and help us overcome in this situation. Since our vehicles did not have enough fuel to drive that far, we insisted on our right to contact our embassy first.

We went to the only place in town where we could make a phone call. While trying to contact the American embassy in Ankara, two men walked in dressed in military attire. Surprised to find foreigners, they asked us why we were there. We explained our situation. They were friendly and told us they would help. And they did. We never found out what they did. At that time in Turkey the military had more power than the police. After we returned from our phone call the police acted very different. Our military "angels" must have used their authority to get us out of there.

Relieved and very thankful for this answer to prayer, we hurried out of the compound. As we approached the main road, the Land Rover of the Jezus Kinderen just happened to come by at the same time. They waved happily at us and stopped for a conversation. With great excitement they told us about their exploits. On the way they had stopped in various towns to pull out their guitars and hold evangelistic street meetings! Now it was our turn to get excited. The police had arrested us for something these crazy Dutchmen had done. Hearing our story and what could have happened to them doused their enthusiasm somewhat. We went our separate ways and warned them the situation could be worse in Iran, Afghanistan or Pakistan, the next countries we would have to pass through on our way to India.

DARK CLOUDS

Trying to avoid getting my tired head busted against the window from all the shaking, I thought back over the way God had spoken to me about the tree and the things to come while I was still in the Netherlands:

"Master," the tree answered. "I belong completely to you, but how could you use me?"

The Master continued, "I need you to bring my living waters to dry and arid places without water."

"But Master, how could I be useful that way?"

With a wonderful, gentle voice the Master replied: "I can use you, my tree, if you are prepared to let Me have My way. It will be necessary to hew you down, cut off your branches and leave you naked and stripped of your leaves on the ground— then I will tear you lose from your land of birth, which you love so dearly and from your brethren, the other trees, in order to take you all alone very far away to mountain slopes, where nobody will speak to you in a loving way, to a place where only grass, bushes and thistles grow.

"Yes, and there I will have to use terrible steel tools to take out all dividers in your heart, to hollow out a free passageway through which my living water can flow."

Then the Master went out to choose other trees. Some of them shrank back for fear of suffering; but others surrendered joyfully to Him, saying: "Master, we entrust ourselves to you, deal with us as you wish." Then He let them go, one after the other, along the same painful way. To lay them down so their ends would fit into one another. Each time a new tree was laid down, the fresh and clear living water from the same spring flowed through the broken heart. This way the pipeline became longer and longer until, at last, it reached the unfruitful land. Men and women and small children, exhausted and thirsty for such a long time, came to quench their thirst, hastening away afterwards to tell others the good news:

"The living water has finally come!"

After a long process of being hollowed out, of testing, of trials and pain, these prophetic words proved to be so true and were so real now. Together, with other hollowed out trees, we were now being laid trunk to trunk to form a pipeline to bring the living water to a dry and unfruitful land where people were waiting to quench their thirst. After leaving the relatively green and lush Turkey behind, we entered Iran which was much drier and mostly void of vegetation. Both were Muslim countries, but in Iran the men and especially the women still dressed in Western style. But this was about to change dramatically.

In the middle of Tehran, the bustling capital of Iran, our vehicles were parked on an empty lot surrounded by high-rise concrete apartment blocks. I rolled out my sleeping bag on the uneven ground right outside the bus for a night under the stars. The penetrating Islamic call to prayer resounded eerily from mosques all over the city. Everything was so new and different to me. Although we were only passing through Iran, I kept thinking about the millions of people living in that country. Were there any Christians in Iran, and who was going to tell these Muslims about Jesus?

About ten months earlier on February 1, 1979, Ayatollah Khomeini had returned to Iran in triumph after fifteen years of exile. The more western-minded Shah Mohammad Reza Pahlavi of Iran and his family had fled the country two weeks before. Jubilant Iranian revolutionaries were eager to establish a fundamentalist Islamic government under Khomeini's leadership. Dark clouds were now gathering on Iran's horizon. Shortly after we passed through Iran in December 1979, a new Iranian constitution was approved, naming Khomeini as Iran's political and religious leader for life. Under his rule, Iranian women were ultimately denied equal rights and required to wear a veil. Western culture was banned, and traditional Islamic law and its often-brutal punishments were reinstated. In suppressing opposition, Khomeini proved even more ruthless than the Shah, and thousands of political dissidents and many Christians were executed during his rule. This pattern of oppression continued for the following three decades and even after his death. Eventually this darkness would cause Iranians to question their religious beliefs and start longing for the Light of the World, and I, along with many others, would be involved in the harvest of their souls!

RED FLAGS

We followed the so-called "Hippie Trail,"—the overland route to India used by hippies and young adults seeking adventure, cheap drugs and a new meaning of life in the 1960s and 1970s. Finally our vehicles passed the Islam Qala-Taybad border crossing between Iran and Afghanistan. It was my first time to enter this wild land. We were soon to find out it would be the last time, not only for us, but for the seventy thousand hippies yearly visiting Afghanistan. Very dark clouds were also gathering over Afghanistan. In April 1978, Afghanistan's centrist government, headed by Mohammad Daoud Khan, was overthrown by left-wing military officers and power was thereafter shared by two Afghan Marxist-Leninist political groups. The new government, which had little popular support, forged close ties with the Soviet Union. They launched ruthless purges of all domestic opposition and began extensive land and social reforms that were bitterly resented by the devoutly Muslim and largely anti-Communist population.

Surrounded by antiquated horse buggies throwing up clouds

of dust, wildly driven by bearded, turbaned men, we entered the city of Herat in western Afghanistan. We had left civilization. It looked surreal and felt like being in an ancient film. Time had stood still in this part of the world. We took a break to have some breakfast and drink tea at one of the many tiny, dimly lit, smoke-filled restaurants. Barely visible, men huddled together wrapped up in thin, dark-colored blankets seated cross-legged on short, sturdy tables covered with Persian carpets. Most were sipping tea or smoking hashish. Outside, the few women present moved around like ghosts in mostly black burkas covering their entire bodies.

Kaboom, kaboom, kaboom . . . Our journey continued on the narrow, two-lane main road from Herat via Kandahar to Kabul. It was made of endless rows of sturdy concrete slabs. Passing over these slabs, we were accompanied by the rhythmic but very monotonous thud of our tires hitting the cracks between each slab. After Kandahar we had to cross mountainous terrain on very steep and winding roads overlooking deep-brown-colored valleys below. Occasionally a green patch of land with a few square, flat-roofed mud houses indicated the presence of water and people in this arid land.

Our drivers took turns driving night and day with few stops in between. Red flags hung from tall poles in most of the small towns we passed through.

"Do you know what these red flags stand for?" I asked a friendly bearded Afghan elementary school teacher whom I met in one of the villages along the way.

He paused a moment. "Red is the color of our new government," he answered in broken English.

"Red is the color of the Communists. They don't believe in God and won't allow you to believe in God," I explained.

He looked a bit surprised. Soon after we left, the Soviet army invaded Afghanistan at the end of December 1979 to help their beleaguered local Communist allies. I always wondered what this teacher must have gone through. Waves of war, untold suffering and misery would wash relentlessly over Afghanistan for the next forty or more years.

Chicken Street in Kabul, Afghanistan's capital, was one of the most popular places for hippies to meet. Walking through this famous street we saw row after row of dead plucked chickens, hanging upside down, waiting to be bought by hungry customers. After sipping green tea we were soon on the road again to Pakistan, our vehicles slowly winding down the Khyber Pass, a mountain pass in the Khyber Pakhtunkwa province of Pakistan on the border with the Nangarhar province of Afghanistan.

This pass was a vital part of the ancient Silk Road and had a long lasting important cultural, economic, and geopolitical significance for Eurasian trade. Throughout history, it has been an important trade route between Central Asia and the Indian subcontinent and was of vital strategic military importance for the various states that came to control it. Historically, invasions of the Indian subcontinent have come predominantly through this Khyber Pass; the mighty armies of the Persian kings Cyrus and Darius I, the Mongolian emperor Genghis Khan, the Greek king and conqueror Alexander the Great, as well as Muslim and British armies in later times.

14
A BLOODY BIRTH

Our caravan, or "company of travelers," descended into the hot plains of the Indian continent to start our own "invasion." Crossing the Pakistan border without difficulties, we passed through tribal territory toward the city of Peshawar where, in the past, camel caravans would stop to take a well-deserved break while travelling the Silk Road. One day in the future this dusty and dangerous city would be a home for my young family as we ministered to Afghan refugees fleeing war. The advantage of traveling overland was the possibility to adjust slowly to all the new cultures, religions and climates. This was the best way to come to know the countries we encountered on our way.

Pakistan was the fourth Muslim country we traveled through on our way to India. After 150 years of British rule, British India was divided into two countries: India—a mostly Hindu nation—and Pakistan, a Muslim dominated country. Pakistan's founder Mohammad Ali Jinnah and his All-India Muslim League party had first demanded autonomy for Muslim-majority areas in the undivided India. Only later he settled for a separate country for Muslims. Jinnah believed that Hindus and Muslims could not continue to live together, as they were distinctly different "nations." The partition and bloody birth of these two nations took place in 1947, sparking riots and deadly communal violence across the region—and led to one of the largest human migrations in history.

Muslims who were scattered across India, and the Hindus and Sikhs who were in Pakistan, all desperately tried to make it to the other side of the border. As people fled their homes, a wave of deadly violence was unleashed. Hindu and Muslim neighbors turned on each other, claiming the lives of at least a million people across the Indian subcontinent. People who a year before would have attended each other's wedding parties were murdering one another and raping each other's daughters. Trains loaded with the slain would arrive at train stations in cities like Lahore, in the new nation of Pakistan and vice versa in Amritsar, India. The birth of these two nations turned into incredibly bloody and vicious scenes of mass murder causing deep wounds and resentment between them.

In India, Mahatma "the great soul" Gandhi had taken a leading role in spearheading his campaign for independence from Britain. He had hailed the partition of the subcontinent into the separate independent states of India and Pakistan as "the noblest act of the British nation." He was, however, horrified by the violence that broke out between Hindus, Muslims and Sikhs—and the eviction of thousands from their homes. This twentieth century's most famous apostle of nonviolence himself met a violent end. In 1948 he was assassinated by Hindu radicals who opposed his nonviolent views.

India and Pakistan ended up fighting three wars, the first one in 1947–1948. India and Pakistan contested Kashmir—a Muslim-majority kingdom ruled by a Hindu Maharaja—even before their independence from Britain. But the dispute escalated after Kashmir ruler Hari Singh acceded Kashmir to India in return for New Delhi's help to ward off attacks by an army of Pakistani tribesmen. This situation led to the first full-blown war over Kashmir. A United Nations-brokered ceasefire line effectively partitioned Kashmir. Both sides control parts of the erstwhile kingdom but claim it in its entirety until today. Despite several attempts to solve the Kashmir dispute and de-escalate tensions, the two neighbors fought their second Indo-Pakistan war over the contested region in 1965. The brief war ended with yet another United Nations-mandated ceasefire. Both sides returned to their previous positions.

India and Pakistan fought their third war in 1971, this time over East Pakistan. The conflict ended in a defeat for Pakistan and the formation of Bangladesh. Following Pakistan's surrender in the 1971 war, Indian Prime Minister Indira Gandhi and Pakistani leader Zulfikar Ali Bhutto met and signed an agreement in the Indian hill town of Simla in 1972. The ceasefire line in Kashmir is designated as the Line of Control (LoC) and the two parties agreed to resolve the dispute through negotiations.

15
MAKING DISCIPLES

"Therefore *go* and *make disciples* of *all* nations, baptizing them in the name of the Father and of the Son and of the Holy Spirit, and teaching them to obey everything I have commanded you. And surely I am with you always, to the very end of the age." (Matt. 28:19–20 NKJV, author's emphasis)

Against the historical backdrop of these two enemy nations, our teams started our endeavors to make disciples in both countries. They had to learn to overcome countless challenges. The two teams that had driven overland in the two previous years had tried to apply for Indian residence visas through a dome-building project in South India. The mills of the Indian government were grinding slowly. Only after one year they discovered our team was still there without valid visas. They were told to leave the country at once and were forced to go to Bangladesh, where they tried to do the same applying for their project under the name Christ is the Answer. In a Muslim country this name did not come across so well, so their application was of course rejected.

They decided to forget about doing projects. The team's name was changed to International Gospel Singers (IGS), and they started an evangelistic traveling ministry. The focus was narrowed to North India, as by now they realized that in South India there were already many Christians. North India was and still is a much more needy—and in many parts—largely unreached harvest field. India has 2,717 people groups. More than seven hundred languages are spoken in India. India has no national language because the Indian constitution has not given the status of national language to any language. Twenty-two languages are given official acknowledgment and support. Almost every state in India has its own language and script. In 1979 when our team came to India, the Indian population amounted to 670 million people. Today there are more than 1.4 billion people and ninety percent of the people groups are still unreached. So, this was and still is a huge challenge for the church worldwide.

IGS had already recruited two young, male south Indian disciples during their time in South India. These brothers now returned and joined the IGS team which started evangelistic open-air meetings in North India wherever the door was opened for them. After every meeting, more young men or women over eighteen years of age would decide to join the team. They would always be paired with a more experienced foreign or Indian team member to disciple them into mature Christians. In any given town, contact was made with the small Christian community. In collaboration with one or more local pastors, those who shared our vision, a suitable ground for the public meetings was located and permissions were obtained. A simple stage was constructed. Lights for the stage and for the grounds were put up. Large, thin carpets were spread out in front of the stage for those invited to sit on—men on one side, women on the other side, according to Indian culture.

Working and living side by side with Indian brothers and

sisters day and night was the ideal way to make disciples. After all, this is the way our Lord Jesus did it. For only three short years He taught twelve disciples by His example, sharing His life, His ministry, His sorrows and His victories closely with those He had chosen to follow Him. These disciples were mostly simple and spiritually quite weak people. Jesus showed great patience, forbearance and love while teaching them the principles of how to overcome. He prepared them for the challenges facing them and for the task which lay before. Jesus delegated His authority and responsibility by allowing them to do what He did. Afterward, Jesus made atonement for the sins of the world by dying on a cross. Then He rose from the dead. He revealed himself alive in His heavenly body not to the world but to his disciples. After giving final instructions, He ascended back to His home in heaven.

"But you will receive power when the Holy Spirit comes on you; and you will be my witnesses in Jerusalem, and in all Judea and Samaria, and to the ends of the earth." (Acts 1:8 NKJV)

Soon these weak disciples were empowered by the outpouring of the Holy Spirit and went out fearlessly and boldly to tell the world about the good news. The church grew spiritually and multiplied because these disciples followed Jesus' example and made many disciples. Only the one who is a true disciple himself will be able to make more disciples. The weakness of the church today is the lack of emphasis on discipleship. Without teaching about and living out discipleship, the church soon turns into a place of entertainment and complacency. We are not called to be Christians by name only. This needy world needs disciples and followers of Christ who live, minister and overcome the way He did when He was here on this earth.

The team was divided into small groups which held prayer and Bible studies in the mornings. During the afternoons they would go out two by two to evangelize or hang posters in the towns and nearby villages inviting people for the evening meetings, which would last one or two weeks depending on the situation. Each evening meeting started with the worship band playing songs in English and Hindi—one of the main languages and understood by most Indians in North India. This proved to be a very effective strategy.

From one thousand to forty thousand people would attend these evangelistic meetings all over the north of India. Night after night through prevailing prayer, worship, team members' testimonies and short sermons, the presence and power of the Holy Spirit increased. The forces of spiritual darkness had to flee and men, women and children were convicted of their sins, received forgiveness of their sins and gave their hearts to Jesus. Thousands upon thousands were saved, healed miraculously or delivered from demon possession. Many precious Indians decided to follow Jesus the Light of the world. Countless lives were transformed and believers discipled. During the following years, God used them to bring the Living Water and His good news to their families, friends, colleagues and those who were thirsty for the Truth all over India.

THE DAY OF SMALL BEGINNINGS

Arriving in India to join this team in December 1979, during the much cooler time of the year, was not too bad of a start for me. My first impression was: people. People were not hard to find. In fact, India is people. People everywhere, all over the place, all the time, night and day crowding around going about their noisy business. If you love people, India is the place to be. Jesus left heaven and came to Earth to seek and to save people. We had left Europe to do the same. Our vehicle finally ground to a halt at our destination in the city of Poona (Pune) in the state of Maharashtra in India, where our team had organized an evangelistic meeting.

Ten thousand kilometers of nonstop driving were behind us. I rolled out my sleeping bag on the dusty, hard concrete floor of an unfurnished and dismal three-story apartment where the men's team was located. Closing my eyes, I tried to finally come to some rest. The sound of the diesel engine of a moving vehicle continued to drone in my head no matter how much I tried to shake it off. So far away from home, I felt suddenly very lonely and quite empty. Restless thoughts chased each other: "So, what now? Who are you and who do you think you are? What difference are you going to make in this massive, overpopulated religious country full of Hindus, Muslims, Sikhs and Buddhists?!" Satan, the accuser of the brethren, pounded me with negative thoughts right at the start of my time in India, trying to make me despise the day of small beginnings.

> **"Who dares despise the day of small things, since the seven eyes of the Lord that range throughout the earth will rejoice when they see the chosen capstone in the hand of Zerubbabel?" (Zech. 4:10 NKJV)**

Surely my physical circumstances were quite humbling on

this day of small beginnings. How could I dare to despise this day of small things? God's eyes are on the sparrow, how much more His eye was upon me far away in this distant land of India where He himself told me to go? His eyes saw the chosen capstone in the hand of Zerubbabel and His eyes saw the chosen capstone in my hand as well. The meaning of capstone is the top stone of a structure or wall—or the crowning achievement or final stroke! As with Zerubbabel, in God's eyes, I was a top stone and my situation a crowning achievement! These thoughts greatly comforted and strengthened me. Instead of giving in to those discouraging thoughts I decided once again to overcome by submitting myself unconditionally to God and resist those lies of the devil. Soon the devil fled, and I finally fell asleep. It was the day of small things but the beginning of a very eventful chapter in my life.

"But He gives us more grace. This is why it says: 'God opposes the proud, but gives grace to the humble. Submit yourselves to God. Resist the devil and he will flee from you.'" (James 4:6–7 NKJV)

THE CRUCIFIXION

"Away with him, crucify him!" From the darkness at the back of the dusty and dimly lit meeting grounds, densely packed with curious Indians, an angry mob slowly emerged. Led by fierce-looking Roman soldiers on unruly, neighing horses and soldiers on foot, they pushed and shoved a bloodied figure wearing a crown of nasty thorns in front of them. He stumbled forward.

"Crucify him, he is not worthy to live on this earth!" The whip of a soldier cracked down with force on the back of the miserable man clad in a red, blood-stained robe. The heavy wooden cross he carried swung to the right almost causing him to fall.

"Forward you fool, don't waste our time, faster!"

Thousands of startled Indians sitting cross-legged on the ground on both sides of the aisle watched in shock. The cross-bearer dragged himself forward toward the stage. Buckling down under the cross, he dropped it, falling next to it. A soldier started kicking him. Another one grabbed him by his shoulders and pulled him up again, tearing the robe off his back. For a moment he stood there naked and trembling all over his bruised body, dressed merely in a loincloth. They swung him around with his back toward the crowd. One . . . , two . . . , three!! Another soldier began to whip him slowly but hard and mercilessly. Bloody red stripes appeared all over his pale back. Cries of dismay rose up from among the watching Indians. *Why did this man have to suffer so much pain? What evil did he do to go through so much suffering?*

Dragging his broken body, they dumped it roughly on the cross. With loud bangs, rusty nails were seemingly driven through his bleeding hands and feet. His body being nailed to the cross tightened in excruciating pain. No screams or cries for mercy could be heard from his stiffly tightened lips. He seemed to bear the pain like a lamb led to the slaughter. While the soldiers jeered and the mob cursed, a small company of women and a young man standing nearby could be heard crying and sobbing softly. Strong soldiers heaved the cross. With a loud thud, it sank deep into the hole made in advance for this purpose. Upon impact, his half-naked, battered body cringed and shook wildly. Cruel nails kept him from falling forward. High and lifted up, he could now clearly be seen by the deeply shaken Indian crowd. A superscription was written over him:

THE KING OF THE JEWS

While soldiers parted his raiment, and were casting lots over it, the mob continued mocking him.

"He saved others; let him save himself, if he be Christ, the chosen of God!"

"If you are the Son of God, show us and come down from the cross!"

"If you are the king of the Jews, save yourself," a soldier shouted.

There was a short silence. All of a sudden a loud and clear voice could be heard coming from the cross:

"Father, forgive them; for they don't know what they are doing."

A wave of awe rushed through the Indian spectators. They had never heard of such a thing.

How could this man ask for forgiveness for those torturing and killing him?! A bit later His voice was heard again:

"My God, My God, why have You forsaken Me?"

Forsaken by all, even by His God and loved by none? Many sympathizers in the crowd were able to identify with those words. They had tried so many different gods who could not show them any love.

"I . . . am . . . thirsty . . ." came the broken cry from his parched lips.

The soldiers mocked him, coming to him offering vinegar on a sponge, which he refused. After some time he spoke again:

"Father, into your hands I commit my spirit."

"It is finished!" he cried with a loud voice. His head fell forward on his chest as he uttered these final words and breathed his last breath.

A great silence fell over the whole meeting grounds, broken only by the exclamation of the Centurion high on his horse:

"Truly, this was the Son of God!"

A soldier pierced his side with a spear to make sure he was dead. Blood rushed down his thigh. They took his lifeless body down from the cross, into the arms of one of the soldiers, who carried him slowly back through the aisle. Crying and sobbing could be heard. Over loudspeakers, the whole scene was explained clearly to the crowd in English and Hindi. A short evangelistic message was preached. While the worship team sang softly in the background, an altar call was made. The strong presence of the Holy Spirit moved hundreds of men, women and children forward. They were led to confess their sins, to receive forgiveness of their sins and to experience spiritual and physical healing. Freedom from utter darkness resulted in abundant joy and peace for so many parched souls. Hallelujah, the Living Water had finally come!

In each new evangelistic campaign in India, this crucifixion drama proved to be an extremely effective tool. It explained the message of salvation visibly to these people, many of whom never heard about Jesus before. Being quite tall and skinny, I was often asked to play the role of Jesus in this drama in many evangelistic open-air meetings all over India. However, every time I had to act out the role of Jesus, I had to overcome my reluctance to go through this drama all over again.

Who was I, an average sinner saved from his sin, to even try to portray the supreme sacrifice of my sinless Savior Jesus Christ? For me it was not just a drama but a spiritual weapon to open the eyes of the blind. Trying to feel a bit like Jesus must have felt, I always fasted on the day that I acted out the crucifixion. It made me feel weaker and caused greater dependence upon the Holy Spirit to move among the spectators. Even though I was asked to do it twice on two different days during an open-air meeting, I always refused. My reason was the fact that this drama only had a tremendous impact on new spectators when they saw it the first time. They did not yet know what to expect, but the second time it would become more of a spectacle—of which I felt Jesus was undeserving.

There was some real suffering involved, even in just acting out the role of Jesus. One of our American brothers, a heavily built former marine and Vietnam war veteran, was chosen to be one of the soldiers. One time, while I was lying on the ground next to the cross, he was supposed to act as if he was kicking me in the chest. He must have gotten a bit over excited because he kicked my chest so hard I ended up with a bruised rib. That was quite painful and took about a year to heal.

On another occasion, while carrying the cross down the aisle, a former Sadhu (Hindu holy man) played the part of one of the Indian Roman soldiers. He got a little too much into his role of lashing my back with a dry whip. I halted, turned around and told him to stop.

"Are you trying to kill me before I die on the cross?" I hissed between my teeth. Unlike Jesus, I got quite upset and was about to throw down the cross. There was only one thing that kept me from doing that. A bit later on, while "nailed" to the cross, I would have to speak the words, "Father, forgive them for they do not know what they are doing!"

After some time I found it quite difficult to do this much longer.

Our diet was quite simple: we were very poor, and we only ate rice and dal (lentils), sometimes chapattis (unleavened flat bread). In between, I was able to somehow supplement this diet with peanuts, salty biscuits and tea. On top of that, the constant heat reduced my appetite. I became very skinny, more bone than flesh. It was not so easy to do the drama—and very humiliating hanging half naked on a cross in front of tens of thousands of Indians.

I considered no longer playing the part of Jesus. *Who wants to see a white half naked skinny man dressed only in a loincloth hanging from a cross? I thought.*

"Lord let this cup pass by me," I prayed. The answer came in the form of a short letter from an Indian pastor who had once seen this drama.

"Dear brother Antoine, we are all so touched by this wonderful crucifixion drama. If you ever consider giving up playing the role of Jesus, please don't, for it is such a blessing to India!" *Lord, not my will but your will shall be done.* Discipleship means renouncing yourself for His sake.

OVERCOMING THE STRONGMAN

"He who has an ear, let him hear what
the Spirit says to the churches. To *him who
overcomes* I will give some of the hidden
manna to eat. And I will give him a white
stone, and on the stone a name written which
no one knows except him who receives it."

(Rev. 2:17 NKJV, author's emphasis)

16
THE WEAPONS OF
OUR WARFARE

"When we leave the church in India alone, it will die out by itself; if we put pressure on the church of India it will arise like a lion and overcome the land." To my great surprise, I read this statement in an Indian newspaper not long after I came to India. These amazing words were spoken by Jawaharlal Nehru, India's first and longest-serving prime minister from 1947–1964. It almost sounded like a prophecy very much like the one Caiaphas, in his capacity as high priest over Israel, unintentionally spoke out concerning the real reason for Jesus' death:

"You do not realize that it is better for you that one man die for the people than that the whole nation perish." (John 11:50 NKJV)

Could it be that God had allowed Nehru to pronounce these profound prophetic words in his capacity as the first ruler over this vast Indian nation? I thought so, and it confirmed to me a truth proved over and over again during twenty centuries of Christianity. Persecution of Christ's church has most often resulted in the church rising up in power. A lukewarm church at ease with the world has always lost its appeal and power and usually ends up on the brink of extinction.

Our team's open-air meetings and other evangelistic activities did not go unnoticed by opposing forces—especially smaller open-air meetings in the unreached countryside. In states like Gujarat and Rajasthan in India we were sometimes met with violent opposition. Fanatic religious mobs broke the tube lights on the meeting grounds or stormed the stage to destroy equipment and harm the team members. It is easier said than done when trying to keep one's calm under such circumstances. While leading some of these outreaches, it was becoming hard for me not to give in to that fear. Fear is one of strongman Satan's most effective tools to silence those who dare to speak up for the Truth.

But how to overcome this fear? Only by faith in Someone stronger than Satan and his whole army of demons or unholy spirits. This is Jesus Christ, who told us He would not leave us alone but send us the one and only Holy Spirit after He ascended into heaven.

SATAN IS UNDER HIS FEET

"The God of peace will soon crush Satan under your feet. The grace of our Lord Jesus Christ be with you." (Rom. 16:20 NKJV)

Gradually and steadily this fear started to undermine my faith and joy in preaching the good news. It was an underlying feeling of anxiety and anticipation of something bad about to happen. We were foreigners and not really expected to do what we were doing. Several times we were questioned by the Indian authorities. Our argument was that we were invited by Indian Christians to conduct these meetings, which was true. We told them we could not help it when non-Christians such as Hindus, Muslims or Sikhs chose to participate in our meetings out of curiosity. The Lord gave me much wisdom to answer one of these officials.

"After all, India is the biggest democracy in the world," I argued. "In such a democracy there is freedom for people to question existing views and express their opinions, right?"

"Yes, yes!" the Indian government official proudly answered, while furiously shaking his head from left to right. "We are the biggest democracy in the world, and we encourage freedom of speech," he said. "You can go ahead." I was somewhat relieved. "But," he continued, "I still have to send a report about you all to my superiors in New Delhi."

"Oh no," I thought. "Lord, please blind their eyes, so we may continue the work you have called us to do," I prayed.

In Jaipur, the capital of the state of Rajasthan, in preparation for an evangelistic outreach, I was asked to minister in a small church. Preaching my heart out as usual, I prayed afterward for those who needed salvation or prayer for healing. Last in the line of those who came forward was an old Indian lady. *She must be a poor widow looking for some comfort or expecting to be healed from some sort of sickness*, I thought. She had not come forward for prayer. Instead, she told me about her life and shared a vision that totally transformed my life.

Slowly, she simply narrated how God had used her to preach the gospel while going from village to village and door to door. Amazing miracles had happened as she prayed for people she met. The sick were healed, the blind received sight, the lame walked and demons were cast out. Wow, what a blessing to hear all of this! Such an old lady being used so mightily by God! Now she was preaching to me, and I became the listener. All of a sudden she lowered her voice and while grabbing my hand gently she almost whispered:

"You know, once I had a vision. Would you like to hear about it?"

"Yes, of course," I replied.

"Well, in this vision I saw the whole map of India from above as if I were in heaven." She paused. "Then, all of a sudden, I saw a huge serpent slithering all across India!"

For a moment, shivers went down my spine. After all this was exactly what had been bothering me and caused so much fear in my life. Satan's power and demonic influence over thousands of years was so real and evident in India. The old lady raised her voice and continued.

"But then, just as suddenly, a huge foot of Jesus appeared out of heaven, stamping on the snake and crushing it to death!" In that moment, the power of the Holy Spirit touched me powerfully.

This was God speaking to me in such a strong way as if He were saying, "You have been hypnotized by that serpent, but you should be looking at My victory in Jesus over Satan and his whole army!" Immediately, I was very convicted and repented on the spot of my lack of faith. God restored me and filled my heart again with peace and strong faith in His everlasting victory. With tears in my eyes, I thanked this old lady for helping me overcome my fear. This was the best message I had heard in a long time.

"The weapons we fight with are not the weapons of the world. On the contrary, they have divine power to demolish strongholds." (2 Cor. 10:4 NKJV)

NINE GIFTS FOR OVERCOMERS

"Now about the gifts of the Spirit, brothers and sisters, I do not want you to be uninformed. You know that when you were pagans, somehow or other you were influenced and led astray to mute idols." (1 Cor. 12:1–2 NKJV)

Within a year after our arrival in India, I was asked by the Indian team leadership to become an elder. This was a great honor and a big responsibility after four years of being a faithful team member. It is always easier just to sit back and be led by others. Taking care of others means an increased awareness of the need to be an example to others. It means helping them to reach their individual potential while taking care of their needs. Most importantly it requires a strong prayer life to find out God's will and direction for the team. The four of us elders led a team of about forty to fifty Indian and foreign male and female team members. My specific responsibility was to start and lead our first all-Indian team sent out to the state of Rajasthan. It was made up of twelve Indian members of both brothers and sisters.

In order to prepare this team I organized a special prayer and fasting day to seek God for our outreach and for God to empower us with His Holy Spirit. Teaching from 1 Corinthians 12 the need for and the function of the nine gifts of the Holy Spirit were explained. The three years of Jesus' ministry on Earth were accompanied by extraordinary miracles of healing, the casting out of demons, signs and wonders wrought by the Holy Spirit who dwelled in Jesus. Before his departure Jesus told his disciples that they would do greater things than these when the Holy Spirit would be poured out upon them. Jesus never did such things to show off or to glorify Himself. The manifestation of the gifts of the Holy Spirit are there to proclaim good news to the poor, to heal the broken hearted, to proclaim freedom for the captives and to set the captives free. Furthermore, to strengthen and bless the believers and help them overcome strongholds of evil and darkness.

"There are different kinds of gifts, but the same Spirit distributes them. There are different kinds of service, but the same Lord. There are different kinds of working, but in all of them and in everyone it is the same God at work. Now to each one the manifestation of the Spirit is given for the common good. To one there is given through the Spirit a message of wisdom, to another a message of knowledge by means of the same Spirit, to another faith by the same Spirit, to another gifts of healing by that one Spirit, to another miraculous powers, to another prophecy, to another distinguishing between spirits, to another speaking in different kinds of tongues, and to still another the interpretation of tongues. All these are the work of one and the same Spirit, and he distributes them to each one, just as he determines."
(1 Cor. 12:4–11 NKJV)

For clarification, these nine gifts were presented in three groups:

1. Gifts of Edification
   A. Speaking in different kinds of tongues (languages)
   B. Interpretation of tongues
   C. Prophecy
2. Gifts of Revelation
   A. Word of wisdom
   B. Word of knowledge
   C. Distinguishing between spirits
3. Gifts of Power
   A. Faith
   B. Healing
   C. Working miracles

Sitting cross-legged on the floor in a big circle, we began praying about this teaching. We invited the Holy Spirit to work in our midst to distribute and bless each person with spiritual gifts as He determined. It was so comforting and amazing to experience how the Holy Spirit gently came upon each one of us. While each of us laid hands upon the person next to him or her, these simple Indian disciples of Jesus started to speak in tongues or share prophecies. Some received words of knowledge or wisdom, others faith for healing and working of miracles. The joy of the Lord filled our hearts as God equipped each one of them with the gifts they needed for their future ministries.

Looking back over the past forty years, this time of outpouring of the Holy Spirit proved to be crucial and very important for their preparation and development. All of them learned to overcome the spiritual battles facing them while using the gifts each one of them received. Based on the five-fold ministry, they eventually became powerful evangelists, visionary apostles, caring pastors, gifted teachers and prophetic ministers to save the lost and bless and equip the church in India. Manifold fruit came forth out of the obedience of these Indian disciples as they lived and taught these spiritual principles. They made countless disciples who in turn did the same.

"Still other seed fell on good soil, where it produced a crop, a hundred, sixty or thirty times what was sown." (Matt. 13:8 NKJV)

17
SIGNS AND MIRACLES

"When Jesus had called the Twelve together, he gave
them power and authority to drive out all demons
and to cure diseases, and he sent them out to
proclaim the kingdom of God and to heal the sick."
(Luke 9:1–2 NKJV)

"So they set out and went from village to
village, proclaiming the good news and healing
people everywhere." (Luke 9:6 NKJV)

DRIVING LICENSE

Before leaving my home country I had not had the time
to complete the lessons to get a Dutch driving license. In India
I first practiced in our long, yellow van which had been driv-
en overland. To step into such a vehicle and start driving from
scratch in the middle of a bustling Indian city is quite an adventure. After some time of practice, I went to the local Region-
al Traffic Office (RTO). Behind a miniature office window, a
sleepy RTO official asked me what I needed.

"I would like to get a driving license," I answered.

"Koi baat nahi!" (No problem), "but first you have to get
a health check," he answered, pointing to somewhere outside
around the corner. Next to a roughly painted cardboard sign
with "Doctor" written on it, a very old man crouched underneath a black umbrella, hiding from the burning sun.

"I need a health check," I said while standing in front of him.

Looking up to me through his thick glass bottomed glasses the following amusing conversation developed:

"Are you healthy?"

"Yes, I feel fine!"

"How is your eyesight?"

"I can see you quite well!"

"Tik hai" (All right), he said shaking his head back and forth affirmatively, and he signed the paper. "You can go for your driving test now."

Walking with me up to a huge old Tata truck parked in the compound, the instructor told me to get into the cabin. Hoisting myself up, I plunged into the worn-out driver's seat, started the engine and tried to yank the drive stick out of neutral into gear. In those days the stick shift was an enormous steel stick bent in various directions. Only by sheer manpower and double clutching could it be moved and forced into doing its job.

"Now drive backwards!" came the instruction. Revving up the engine, I slowly moved the truck backward as far as I could about 165 feet and stopped.

"Well done, you passed the test," came the surprising answer.

After paying IRS 50 (approximately five U.S. dollars in 1981), I received my All India driving license enabling me to drive cars, trucks, coaches and buses all over India! Based on this license I eventually got the international driving license which I needed to drive in Europe and overland to Asia as well. It was a true miracle! In those days getting a driver's license in India was no big deal to overcome at all.

Apart from the yellow van, the team also had an old travel bus from the fifties. Driving that vehicle required some sensitivity. The first time I drove it I decided to try out going a bit faster on the main road outside town. When I reached the 'high speed' of about forty-four miles per hour, all of a sudden the whole vehicle started shaking uncontrollably! Barely able to hold on to the steering wheel, I desperately tried to keep the bus on the road and from hitting another vehicle. Only by drastically reducing speed it started to act normal. I never tried that again.

ALTER EGO

"Picture, picture!!" Some very excited Indian teenagers approached me in broken English as I was walking along a street with two brothers from our team. Street evangelization in India was never boring and foreigners always attracted attention.

"Why are they saying that?" I asked. "I do not have a camera!"

"They think you are a film star," one of them answered.

"What, me? A film star? How can that be?!" I exclaimed.

"You look like an Indian film star they know from the movies!"

Now I was really confused. *How could a tall and skinny white Dutchman ever look like an Indian film star?*

Television was not yet widely available to most Indians at that time. People were crazy about going to local cinemas featuring films with all of their heroes. Located in the city of Bombay, the Indian film industry, nicknamed "Bollywood," is bigger and produces more films than Hollywood in the U.S. Most films were still quite innocent and told a love story or a family drama set in a village area. Two, good-looking, very decently dressed male and female actors, a notorious villain and a mean policeman were standard fare. Spiced with a lot of lively music, singing and dancing, each film usually ended up with the highlights of a long-distance kiss, the villain getting caught and the family peace being restored.

Whoever this Indian film star was that I resembled, it was clear to me, that our faces must be quite similar. I met people everywhere who seemed to know me better than I knew myself.

On one busy train station I was suddenly surrounded by a

bunch of youngsters insisting that I must be the film star. "Tom Alter, you are Tom Alter!" Speaking all at once in Hindi, they even got a bit irritated when I tried to tell them I could not speak Hindi yet. "Tom Alter speaks Hindi, so why don't you?" they argued. They were convinced I was telling a lie. With the help of an Indian brother translating, I was able to calm them down, reveal my true identity and share the reason why I had come to India. They all heard the message of salvation for the first time in their lives.

Over and over this happened to me in many similar situations all over India. Learning to be very thankful for this strange sign from God, I started to look forward to these God-sent opportunities and open doors to tell many about their Savior Jesus Christ. God's sovereign ways are higher than our weak ways! It wasn't until later that I finally found out how Tom Alter truly was my doppelgänger and "alter ego." Two years older than I was, he played roles in many Bollywood films. The son of American missionaries, he was born and raised in India and had learned to speak Hindi fluently. He was the only foreigner acting regularly in the Indian film industry and therefore known by all. My curiosity was raised, and I started to pray for an opportunity to meet him. One day this prayer would be answered in a very special way.

DEAF AND DUMB HEALED

"May I know the name of your god?" I asked this question of a young Indian with a small idol tied around his neck during an evangelistic street meeting in the city of Belgaum (Belagavi) in the state of Karnataka. He eagerly explained all he knew about his god.

"Why is your god so small and why do you carry your god around your neck?" I countered. "Would you like to hear about my God?"

"Yes, why not?" he answered.

"Well, my God is so big and powerful, I could never carry Him around my neck. In fact my God carries me!" I happily explained.

The atmosphere at the dusty grounds of our open-air evening meeting in that same town was filled with great expectation. A multitude of Indians from all walks of life were sitting cross-legged on thin tarpais (rugs), men and women seated separately from each other. Their shiny, dark eyes reflected the bright tube lights set up in long rows to lighten up the meeting grounds. They clearly enjoyed and were touched by our team's testimonies and joyful singing in Hindi and English amplified by loudspeakers from the brightly lit stage in front of them.

Now it was my turn to grab the microphone. This was the first day of this open-air meeting and my first time ever to preach in front of so many people. With all of my heart, I briefly shared the good news about salvation, healing and deliverance available to anyone willing to believe this message. The Holy Spirit was very much present. After my message I exclaimed with a heart full of faith: "Nothing is impossible with our God; if you are sick come up to the stage and we will pray for God to heal you in Jesus Name!"

Immediately people started to line up next to the stage. An old lady accompanied by a much younger man clambered slowly up the stage. In front of the crowd for all to hear and see, I asked her what her problem was.

"My son here cannot speak; he is deaf and dumb."

"Oh no, I thought while starting to panic. Lord, why first a deaf and dumb person? Why not let me begin with a common cold or a headache!?" In a flash I was reminded of what I had told that Hindu young man on street: my God is big and powerful, and He carries me. Now was the time to overcome my unbelief and practice what I had preached and believed to be true.

"Lord, how shall I pray?" I cried out in my heart.

"Just do what I did while I was on Earth!" came the answer.

"Oh, yes, I remember!" So I put my fingers into the man's ears. Then I spat on my hand and touched the man's tongue with one hand and laid my other hand upon his head. Looking up to the Lord with a deep sigh, I prayed out loudly: "Ephphatha, ears be opened in the name of Jesus!" That was it.

Then it was time to check out if he could hear something. After snipping my fingers close to his right ear, he nodded yes. Then his left ear. He nodded again.

"Can you say: J-E-S-U ?" I asked in Hindi.

"JJ . . . EE . . . SS . . . UU . . . !!" he stuttered, moving his hands in exultation.

The crowd, hearing all of this, broke out in spontaneous applause. Jesus had healed him on the spot! He never spoke before, so he had to start from scratch. This man's ears were opened, his tongue was loosened and he began to speak plainly.

"J . . . E . . . S . . . U . . . !, J . . . E . . . S . . . U . . . !": he repeated over and over again. Then at once very clearly: "J-E-S-U!!" beaming like a child. Hallelujah!

"Can you please also pray for my other son?" the old lady asked excitedly.

He was next in line.

"Well of course, what is his problem?"

"He is deaf and dumb from birth as well," she replied.

My heart sank. "Oh, no, not again!" I thought. There was no way out but to repeat the whole process all over again. God was faithful and healed his brother and others suffering from various diseases. Many turned away from idols and gave their hearts to Jesus that evening. All glory to God who makes all things well!

"Then Jesus left the vicinity of Tyre and went through Sidon, down to the Sea of Galilee and into the region of the Decapolis. There some

people brought to him a man who was deaf and dumb, and they begged Jesus to place his hand on him. After he took him aside, away from the crowd, Jesus put his fingers into the man's ears. Then he spit and touched the man's tongue. He looked up to heaven and with a deep sigh said to him, '*Ephphatha!*' (which means 'Be opened!'). At this, the man's ears were opened, his tongue was loosened and he began to speak plainly." (Mark 7:31–35 NKJV, author's emphasis)

CAPTIVES SET FREE

During our evangelistic open-air meetings all over India, God proved over and over again that the time of Acts in the Bible was not over yet. Faithful foreign and Indian team members prayed and fasted regularly for God to pour down His Holy Spirit upon the spiritually hungry people of India. Two sisters in our team received grace to fast for forty days after the Lord told them to do so.

The spiritual darkness that keeps men and women bound and blind can only be overcome by the spiritual weapons of prayer and fasting. No wonder people got delivered from demonic bondages during those meetings. Especially the proclamation of the name of Jesus during times of worship and praise at the beginning of each evangelistic open-air meeting seemed to make demons very nervous. Often, demon-possessed people started to bounce around, scream and fall over in the middle of the meeting. In order not to disturb the rest of the meeting, these people were usually taken to the back of the stage. There, in a separate place, team members would pray in authority for deliverance. Many captives were set free this way.

An infamous ruthless Gunda, a gangster of small stature but greatly feared by all in his district, attended one of our meetings in his area in the state of Gujarat. He was delivered from demonic bondages and was convicted of his sins. His life was changed by asking forgiveness and turning away from his sins and evil deeds. When he appeared on the stage to share what Jesus had done in his life, people in the crowd first were afraid and some even wanted to run away. After listening to him there was a great relief, but it still took a long time before his former victims started to trust him. Eventually he became a pastor shepherding the Lord's sheep in his area.

A LEPER HEALED

Long before our team came to India, an important foundation for the spreading of the good news was laid by many faithful men and women of God. Known as the father of modern missions, William Carey, for more than thirty-five years, fought against the practice of Sati (bride burning). In December 1829 Sati was banned in the entire British Empire, including India.

Carey's greatest gift and focus was translating the Bible into local languages and helping people become literate so they could read God's Word. Carey translated the Bible into Bengali, Oriya, Marathi, Hindi, Assamese, and Sanskrit. He also translated parts of it into twenty-nine other languages and dialects. With great self-sacrifice and suffering, Carey and countless other dedicated indigenous and foreign workers of various ministries after him helped to build the church in India. We should always remember those who went before us as we continue to build on their foundation.

During the years 2016 and 2017, a total of 135,485 new cases of leprosy were detected in India, and it is still a problem today. Leprosy is a slowly progressing bacterial infection that affects the skin, nerves in the hands and feet, and mucous membranes of the nose, throat, and eyes. Destruction of the nerve endings causes the affected areas to lose sensation. Occasionally, because of the loss of feeling, the nose, fingers and toes become mutilated and fall off, causing the deformities that are typically associated with the disease.

In a village area in India, our ladies team stayed with and worked together with a missionary who had left her homeland in the US and worked hard at a home for lepers. While observing the dedicated lifestyle of our sisters, and participating in their evangelistic meetings, she became very convicted about the absence of the assurance of salvation in her own life. She had been working for the Lord in her own strength, which had caused many frustrations. In one of their meetings she gave up her pride, surrendered her heart wholly to Jesus and has been a very happy and spirit-filled worker for the Lord ever since. While traveling through her area on the way to conduct meetings elsewhere, I stopped by at her home for the lepers.

"Why don't you preach to our lepers this evening?" she asked. I consented gladly. Soon I found myself in front of about thirty lepers, men and women seated separately on the ground in a small and dimly lit chapel on their property. Tears filled my eyes as I looked around upon their marred faces, hands and feet. Most of them had become believers in Jesus. Their eyes were filled with hope as they listened eagerly to my message. With compassion rising up in my heart, I prayed fervently.

"Lord, you healed ten lepers, and one returned to say thanks, so please do it again today I pray!" At the end of the meeting, I prayed a general prayer for healing by faith in the powerful name of Jesus. Soon I had to leave that place again. Much later I heard that one of those lepers was completely healed. This miracle was medically attested to by a physician. All glory to God!

A BLIND MAGICIAN SEES

The sweltering evening heat was overwhelming. Exhausted and bathed in sweat, I stood there on the stage as our open-air evangelistic meeting in a remote area of India had come to a close. Many people had been touched and healed by the Word of God that was preached that evening. Most were illiterate and simple farmers or daily wagers. People in India always enjoyed our singing and preaching which was usually accompanied by a lot of "Hallelujahs."

Hallelu, the first part of hallelujah stems from the Hebrew verb *hallel*. More than simply "praise Jah" or "praise God," the word *hallel* in Hebrew means "a joyous praise in song, to boast in God." When people were healed, we would always ask them to tell us publicly who healed them in order to give glory to God. Sometimes they answered: "Hallelujah! Hallelujah healed me!" Having heard that word so often, they concluded that *hallelujah* was a new god among the many other gods in India. Of course, we explained to them it was Jesus, the Son of the One and only Living God who had healed them.

Most people had left the meeting grounds. Only one old man, dressed in a dhoti, remained standing still right in front at the stage. A dhoti is a garment consisting of a length of cloth wrapped around the waist, passed between the legs, and tucked in at the waistline. From underneath his colorful head wrap, he looked up to me as if he wanted to ask a question.

"What can I do for you?" I asked.

"I came to tell you that I was blind and now I can see for the first time in my life!" he answered softly. Praise God, what a wonderful healing that was!

"I want to change my life," he continued. "I was a very bad man, a magician, and I did much harm to others and I want to ask God to forgive me." He gave his heart to Jesus right there. This man had been a powerful sorcerer with the ability even to kill those who opposed him by putting a curse on them. People in that area feared him greatly. Now this blind man could see clearly both physically and spiritually and was set free to become a blessing instead of a curse.

18
DISCIPLESHIP
AND DISCIPLINE

A *disciple* is a dedicated follower of Jesus. A true disciple imitates both the life and teaching of his master, Jesus, to become a living copy of his Lord. *Discipline* is the means by which discipleship is achieved through self-control, learning, hearing, seeing and doing with God's help.

Jesus warned us all clearly that our spirit is willing, but our flesh is weak. Our willing spirit can easily be undone by our weak flesh. The key to overcome this challenge is to watch and pray and to discipline our body and keep it under control. Life in India was very hard on the flesh. Our willing spirits could easily get discouraged by the many challenges we were facing in the flesh. The apostle Paul understood this important principle very well when he wrote these words to the Corinthians.

> **"But I discipline my body and keep it under control, lest after preaching to others I myself should be disqualified." (1 Cor. 9:27 NKJV)**

In Matthew 4:1–11, you can read how Jesus, after he was baptized, was led by the Spirit of God into the wilderness to be tempted by Satan. This may raise some eyebrows. How could God the Father allow Jesus to be tempted by Satan and use the Holy Spirit to lead Him into this situation? Well, God is sovereign, but He will not allow anybody to be tempted beyond their capacity. Trials and temptations are a part of God's training program to teach discipline and His ways to overcome Satan's tricks.

In this case Satan tempted Jesus three times. The way Jesus resisted these temptations is very significant. After each temptation Jesus answered Satan the same way by saying: "It is written!" Jesus did not use his own ideas but simply and very effectively used only the Word of God to counter Satan's proposals and lies. There is no other way to overcome in our battle with the forces of darkness than by using the written Word of God. You may have noticed that this book, *Born to Overcome,* uses this principle. Each challenge poses a need to overcome, which is only done by using the power and authority of God's Word. First knowing and then applying the appropriate Word of God for each challenge will help you to overcome.

> **"Watch and pray so that you will not fall into temptation. The spirit is willing, but the flesh is weak." (Matt. 26:41 NKJV)**

TERRIBLE TRAIN TRIP

"Chai, special chaiiii, time pass, tiiiime pass!" The sleepy and monotonous cadence of train wheels rumbling down the tracks was abruptly disturbed by the raspy voice of a skinny tea seller. Entering our swaying train wagon, he balanced a round tray with tiny earthenware cups and a kettle of tea on his head. He climbed and stumbled over suitcases and countless passengers packed like sardines on three tier berths. They were even spread out all over the dirty floor. Tirelessly, he tried to convince somebody to buy his tea. The train hooted as it went by a railway crossing. Hot wind carried suffocating coal dust and smoke through the open windows. Traveling for days on end in slow passenger trains pulled by steam locomotives and powered by coal was one of our main ways to get from point A to point B in India.

This was my first trip by train, and I had tried to make myself somehow comfortable on a narrow, hard top berth using my few belongings as a mattress and pillow. Normally I would have asked the tea seller to pour me a cup of tea, but I did not feel like it at all this day. Suffering from recurring stomach cramps and a bad case of diarrhea, I was forced to leave my berth every fifteen minutes to relieve myself in one of the two toilets at the back of the wagon. Making it to the toilet in time became a real ordeal. Like the tea seller, I had to scramble over this mass of humanity and travel equipment to reach the toilet, hoping desperately no one else had to empty his tubes. Over and over again, I had to make the round trip back and forth from my berth to the toilet, irritating other passengers on the way. I felt so bad, discouraged and oppressed by negative thoughts.

"Is trying to reach Indians worth all this trouble?" I asked myself while wrangling over my fate. Physically and mentally exhausted and weak, I finally reached the town where our team was based. As soon as I got there I rushed to the toilet once again. Seated on the toilet, it suddenly dawned on me what was happening. Either I was going to continue in misery, or I would have to start resisting this attack on my body and spirit. In that moment a holy anger at what Satan was trying to do to me welled up in me.

"In the Name of Jesus, I command this diarrhea to leave my body right now!" I shouted.

At once the liquids in my intestines dried up. Strength returned to my body. I was instantly healed.

"Thank you, Jesus!" I exclaimed. It was a great lesson to learn true discipleship by overcoming the weakness of my flesh and by strengthening the willingness of my spirit by faith in God's unlimited power to heal.

BONE TWO

India is the most populous country in the world with about 1.4 billion people. This country of many contrasts has enjoyed

growth rates of up to 7% in 2024 and is one of the largest econ-
omies in the world with a gross domestic product (GDP) of 3.89
trillion U.S. dollars in 2024. Only a small percentage of the Indian population has benefited from this impressive economic
boom so far. Two-thirds of people in India still live in abject poverty: 68.8% of the Indian population lives on less than $2 a day.
More than 30% have less than $1.25 per day available—and are
considered extremely poor. This makes the Indian subcontinent
one of the poorest countries in the world. Women and children,
the weakest members of Indian society, suffer most.

The way our team, Indians and foreigners alike, lived in India
was very much in line with the way most people in India lived
and still live. We were poor, and we did not have a big influx
of foreign money to count on—not enough to stay in three-star
hotels. This was not at all convenient for the flesh, but it made
us one with the average Indian. They accepted and loved us and
were willing to share whatever little they had. Almost every area
of life was a big undertaking, and many times a huge battle.

The first ten years of my life in Asia, I never had a place
to call my own. The nature of our ministry required constant
traveling to various places. We slept in churches or—due to the
heat—on top of our bus or on the flat roofs of the homes of
Indian Christians. A sleeping bag or a thin straw mat was rolled
out on the floor to make a bed. Because of the scarcity of water, taking a bath meant filling a bucket of water, which had to
suffice to wash your whole body, hair and all. Some even used
the same amount of water to wash a few clothes in the process.
During the few winter months, a heating coil was used to warm
the water in the same bucket.

Hindus are mostly vegetarians, so meat was hard to find.
Cows are off limits. Even if available, the poor creatures like
chickens or goats had hardly any meat on them. Our diet con-
sisted mainly of white rice and dal (lentils) and sometimes a

chapatti—a round, flat unleavened bread made of whole wheat flour. Never enough to feel satisfied. Sometimes we were invited to Christian homes where we were usually fed better yet very spicy food. Most of us lost a lot of weight. For me personally this was not the biggest problem since the constant heat dampened my appetite. Living basically off peanuts and garam chai—hot Indian tea—salty biscuits and watermelons, I became extremely skinny. Somebody called me "Bone Two" since there was another foreign brother even skinnier than me called "Bone One."

THE FILM DIRECTOR

In those days mobile phones were yet unheard of. Because of my contacts in Europe, one day I had to try and make an international phone call. In order to do this, I had to travel from wherever we were for one or two days by train, crammed in with people and sometimes animals to the huge city of Bombay (Mumbay). After arriving there, a rikshaw (three-wheeler) bounced me through this bustling and overpopulated metropolis to the Main International Calling Station. You had to wait in line to book your call, which could last hours, and then wait patiently for your call to come through. Even when a connection was finally made, the line often was very bad. Through constant crackling sounds, you could barely hear the person on the other side. Calls like this were excruciating and quite expensive as well. Such situations were the ideal environment for the much-needed spiritual fruit of patience to grow.

Taking a seat at one of the tables, I ordered some hot special chai—delicious spiced tea—and waited and waited. People came and went. A well-dressed, middle-aged Sikh, an adherent of Sikhism, pulled back a chair to sit down and threw his bag on my table. His tall stature, colorful dark blue turban and full, black beard made him stand out in the crowd.

The Sikh Religion is a monotheistic religion with about 27 million followers founded by Guru Nanak Dev in the fifteenth century in the Punjab, North India. It emphasizes the unity of the creation and worships a shapeless and genderless creator god. Their teaching rejects superstition and the traditional rites of Hinduism. All Sikhs must follow a code of conduct, which includes the hair and head. Sikhs are expected to keep all hair uncut and the head covered. The rule of dress for every Sikh man is to tie up their hair and wear a turban and carry a Kirpan, a ceremonial dagger.

This very friendly and smiling Sikh immediately started up a lively and lengthy conversation. Offering to pay for my tea, he happily chattered away in English, sharing jokes and telling me about his job as a film director in the south Indian film industry. He appeared to be a jolly good fellow. My intention was to somehow share the gospel with him, but it was quite hard to find an opening. I started to pray in the Spirit.

"Tell him he is happy on the outside, but extremely sad in the inside!" This penetrating voice and urgent impression coming from deep within my spirit startled me.

"Lord how can I say that? What if it is not so? I will embarrass him and myself!"

"Do not argue. You cannot know this by the natural mind. This is a word of knowledge through the Holy Spirit," came the answer. Taking a deep breath, I interrupted the Sikh's narration.

"Sir, I am serving the living God who just gave me an impression that I would like to tell you." This effectively stopped him in his tracks. First, he looked a bit puzzled and awkward. Then he became curious. Indians are an amazingly spiritually minded people and always respectful towards religious matters.

"So, what is it?" he asked with a shy smile.

"You are a very happy person on the outside but deep inside you are extremely sad." This struck him like lightning. In an instant all happiness disappeared. His mood changed completely.

With tear filled eyes he asked me softly:

"How do you know? Who told you this? It is so true!" Grabbing me by my hand, he poured out his heart and told me his tragic story.

After making a lot of money as a successful film director, he decided to take his young wife and child on a trip to the U.S. They enjoyed themselves a lot until disaster struck. While driving a rented car at night, he fell asleep behind the wheel. His car crashed, and his wife and child were instantly killed. He was the only survivor. Now it was my turn to be shocked and sad. My heart was filled with compassion for him.

He paused, breathing deeply before he continued:

"I have been very reluctant to talk to anybody about this, and here I am telling all of this to you a complete stranger! I am so thankful you told me the truth and are willing to listen to me."

"Well, there is a Father in heaven who loves you and wants to heal your hurting heart and comfort you," I answered.

From there on, I had a very attentive listener whose heart was opened to receive the good news. When we parted ways he was a different man. Discipline to overcome doubt and unbelief was needed. I had to obey the prompting of the Holy Spirit and use the Word of Knowledge. This wonderful gift of the Holy Spirit became a great blessing to this very lost Indian soul.

"He who has an ear, let him hear what the Spirit says . . . !" (Rev. 2:29 NKJV)

PRAYER IS STRIKING THE WINNING BLOW

"A lack of prayer in your life! Too much confusion and fear in your life. The Lord wants to use you more and more" (Surat, India, April 1980). This short and very penetrating prophecy was spoken over me by a precious Indian brother during a time of prayer. It helped me to shake off confusion and fear by making the decision to spend much more quality time with God.

> **"During the days of Jesus' life on earth, he offered up prayers and petitions with fervent cries and tears to the one who could save him from death, and he was heard because of his reverent submission. Son though he was, he learned obedience from what he suffered and, once made perfect, he became the source of eternal salvation for all who obey him."**
> **(Heb. 5:7–9 NKJV)**

Although without sin, Jesus lived his life on Earth in a physical body just like us. He was exposed to the same physical challenges such as heat, cold, homelessness, hunger, thirst, loneliness, rejection, hatred, fear, danger, etc. Jesus did not rebel against these circumstances but suffered through them to learn obedience, and he made the biggest sacrifice to become the source of salvation for all mankind.

Jesus prayed for guidance and strength in places of quiet solitude. At regular times he separated himself from his disciples to spend time in fellowship with his heavenly Father. He prayed both in the morning and in the night, in the wilderness, on top of a mountain or in the Garden of Gethsemane.

> **"Very early in the morning, while it was still dark, Jesus got up, left the house and went off to a solitary place, where he prayed." (Mark 1:35 NKJV)**

> "But Jesus often withdrew to lonely places
> and prayed." (Luke 5:16 NKJV)

> "One of those days Jesus went out to a mountainside
> to pray, and spent the night praying to God."
> (Luke 6:12 NKJV)

My personal challenge was to find such a lonely place to pray. Lonely and especially quiet places are hard to find in India. People are moving around any time during the night or day. Loud music from tea stalls and religious chanting from Hindu or Buddhist temples or prayers from mosques can be heard at all times. Nevertheless, I loved waking up early when the temperature was still somewhat enjoyable to spend time praying on top of our bus or the home where we spent the night. Waking up early to pray requires discipline because we have to overcome our weak flesh wanting to slumber and sleep.

In the meantime, I was asked to become one of the elders of our two teams in India. Leadership increases responsibility, not only to lead but to be an example to others as well. In this capacity I always tried to encourage others to take enough time to seek God in prayer. One day I asked an Indian brother why he always woke up so late. Assuming—falsely—that he started the day without prayer, I asked:

"When do you take time to pray?

To my great surprise he answered:

"I always wake up at night around 2 a.m. and pray for two hours."

In the end it is not about what is the best time or place to pray, but about doing it. The more responsibility you receive in the kingdom of God, the more time you need to spend with your heavenly Father. Even Jesus could not do anything of his own accord. Whatever his Father did and told him to do, he did. Nothing more, nothing less. Here lies the secret of how to overcome any situation, obstacle or problem: learn to hear His heavenly voice by spending much time in His presence and then obey His directions! A faithful man of God, S. D. Gordon, once so aptly said: "Prayer is striking the winning blow. Service is gathering up the result." We all have to learn this truth: without ministering to God, there is no power to minister to men.

"So Jesus said to them, 'Truly, truly, I say to you, the Son can do nothing of his own accord, but only what he sees the Father doing. For whatever the Father does, that the Son does likewise.'" (John 5:19 NKJV)

ENLARGING THE VISION FOR ASIA

"He who has an ear, let him hear what the Spirit says to the churches. To *him who overcomes* I will grant to eat of the tree of life, which is in the paradise of God."

(Rev. 2:7 NKJV, author's emphasis)

19
THE LAND OF
SERENDIB

Waking up abruptly from a deep sleep, I faintly heard somebody calling my name from a distance: "Antoine!! Antoine!!" I was lying on a thin mat on the floor next to the door of a house in Colombo, Sri Lanka, and drowning in sweat, trying to catch whatever cooler air might come in. Straining my ears, I heard it again. Was God calling me?! My heart started to pound. Shall I answer like young Samuel? "Speak Lord, for your servant is listening!" The sound came closer and closer until I could finally clearly hear somebody slowly shouting: "Paaa . . . an! Paaa . . . an!" Outside, a small cart appeared being pushed by a man trying to sell bread! In Singhalese, the language of most Buddhists in Sri Lanka, the meaning of *pan* is bread. Somehow in my groggy state *Pan-pan* sounded a lot like *An-toine*.

Just days before, an American brother of our team and I had arrived in Talaimannar in Northern Sri Lanka from Ramaswaram, India, by ferry. From Talaimannar, an old-fashioned steam train slowly transported us through the jungle to the capital of Colombo. While traveling, the Holy Spirit started to burden my heart for this new land. I sensed a great urgency to work very hard *now* because time was running out. How true this impression later proved to be. It was the year of 1980, and we were sent by our leadership to spy out the land. This meant finding out how we could establish a base there to train new workers and to share the good news. We were to contact local Christians to find out how to obtain visas, recruit local workers and, in general, to figure out the best way for our team to be a blessing to Sri Lanka.

As early as AD 361, one name for the island of Sri Lanka or Ceylon was Serendib, which is the classical Persian name for Sri Lanka. The name Serendib, Arabic in origin, is a corruption of the Sanskrit compound Siṃhaladvīpa (Dwelling-Place-of-Lions Island). The word *serendipity* stems from *serendib* and means "an unexpected pleasant surprise." Soon I was to make my own unexpected pleasant surprise in this land of Serendib. Sri Lanka, the land of Serendib is truly a beautiful paradise-like island. Due to regular seasonal rainfall and its location near the equator, the subtropical southern part has abundant flora and fauna, and much wildlife.

Many spices and delicious fruits such as guava, jackfruit, sapodilla (chiku), pomegranate, pineapple, all kinds of bananas, wood apple, papaya—just to name a few—thrive well in this very humid climate. The average humidity is about 80% and the annual temperature varies from 27°C in the coastal lowlands to 16°C at Nuwara Eliya, in the central highlands (1900 meters above sea level) where all the tea estates are located. The east and north of Sri Lanka are much drier. Sri Lanka's maximum length of 432 kilometers (268 miles) and a maximum width of 224 kilometers (139 miles) combined with a climate range from hot sunny beaches to cool lush rain forests makes Sri Lanka an ideal tourist attraction.

DISTRIBUTING LIVING BREAD

The local Christians were very kind, cooperative and willing to help us get started. Already at that time, about 86% of the Sri Lankan population of 15 million was literate, a very high rate in comparison to neighboring countries in Asia. Maybe God did speak to me when I thought He was calling me by my name, when I heard the word *pan*. The Living Bread—or Pan—which comes from above, is what Sri Lanka urgently needed.

We rented a small house near the beach in Colombo. Team members in India or Pakistan whose visas had run out could come to Sri Lanka. Soon, small teams were sent out all over the country to distribute gospel portions and tracts. Local people were friendly and eager to receive and read them. The Bible Society was very helpful and amazed to see these motivated young people swarming out over the country distributing thousands upon thousands of Gospels in the Singhalese and Tamil languages. Bibles were also given to Muslim Imams in mosques all over Sri Lanka. We ordered so many Gospel packets from the Bible Society that they asked us to come in and put our own packets together as they couldn't keep up. We even printed our own gospel tracts.

Sinhalese, Tamil, and Muslim ethnic groups make up 99% of the Sri Lankan population. Both Sinhalese and Tamil trace their immigration to the distant past, with Sinhalese alone accounting for nearly 75% of the people. The Tamils consists of Sri Lankan Tamils and Indian Tamils. The Sri Lankan Tamils are a native minority. In 1981 they numbered about 2 million, or 13% of the population. They make up more than 95% of the population in the Jaffna Peninsula in the north, more than 70% of the population in Batticaloa District in the east, and substantial minorities in other northern and eastern districts. This pattern reflects the historical dominance of Tamil kingdoms in the northern half of the island. The Indian Tamils were brought in by the British to work on tea plantations in the mountains of Sri Lanka. More than 90% of the Sinhalese are Buddhists; Tamils are mostly Hindus. Christianity belongs to 7%, and 3% are Muslims originating from Arab spice traders and Asian Muslim workers brought in by the Dutch. For centuries the island was ruled by many kings divided into numerous kingdoms. From the sixteenth century, some coastal areas of the country were also controlled for commercial reasons by the Portuguese, the Dutch and the British for about a century each. Independence was finally granted in 1948, but the country remained a Dominion of the British Empire until 1972.

SILENCING BIRDS

A local pastor asked our team to participate in open-air meetings he was conducting in various towns in Sri Lanka. This was a welcome extension of our ministry since we had lots of experience with open-air evangelism. Our team was responsible for making the meetings known by hanging posters about the meetings and handing out invitations during the daytime. In the evenings they did the worship and shared their testimonies from the stage. As a result of these meetings we soon became known all over Sri Lanka as the International Gospel Singers (IGS). In each town we came to know young people who either were saved during these meetings or were already born-again Christians before we met them. Some of them requested that we teach them to serve the Lord. Soon a small team of young local male and female believers from both Sinhala and Tamil backgrounds became a part of our ministry.

Living and working closely together made it easier for us to disciple them into dedicated followers of the Lord Jesus Christ. For practical reasons English was chosen as the team language which sometimes caused hilarious situations. Once, walking by the toilet in our team base in Colombo, I heard a Sinhala brother practicing what he had just learned during English lesson. Very confidently he proclaimed: "I am . . . the toilet!" Before our evening meal another brother earnestly prayed, "Dear Lord, bless the prepared hands . . . !"

There was much openness and freedom to share the gospel. Soon IGS was asked to come and do their own open-air meetings in various towns. Open-air meetings in Sri Lanka were not as well attended as the ones we were used to in India where people tend to be more curious. The Buddhist population in Sri Lanka was especially standoffish. Due to a lack of finances our team was ill-equipped to do open-air meetings, but we learned to overcome this problem by making the best of it with the Lord's help.

We were always happy to leave our overcrowded base in Colombo, situated in the low coastal area with extremely high humidity, for ministry in the much cooler mountainous areas. During one of those meetings in Badulla, the capital and largest city of Uva Province, situated about 680 meters (2,230 feet) above sea level in the lower central hills of Sri Lanka, something very special happened. Surrounded by lush green tea plantations, this city is almost encircled by the Badulu Oya River and overshadowed by the Namunukula range of mountains with the highest peak 2,016 meters (6,614 feet) above sea level. A suitable place with a small stage in the middle of town surrounded by huge, shady Bunyan trees was found for our open-air meeting. The men's and women's teams were accommodated separately in the local church building or with local Christians. During the day they went out to invite people to the evening meetings.

The responsibility for this first-ever, Christian open-air meeting in the city of Badulla rested entirely upon my shoulders. In between I had to find enough time to prepare myself to preach in these meetings. There is always a spiritual battle involved in every attempt to bring the light and truth of the Word of God to people living in great darkness. Slowly people started to show up before the start of the meeting. Two bald-headed men dressed only in long, orange robes wrapped around their body and loosely slung over one shoulder suddenly approached the stage: Buddhist priests!

They started to come on stage and walk up to the microphone.

"What can I do for you?" I asked them politely.

"We also want to speak to the people in this public meeting!" they answered.

"Well, this is a meeting organized by us Christians, but it is open for all to attend so please sit down and wait for the meeting to start," I replied.

"If you wish to speak publicly you will have to arrange your own meeting next week, ok?" Finally they left reluctantly but remained standing in the shade of a Bunyan tree to observe what was going to happen.

Two of the American team sisters were supposed to come earlier to the stage to get ready for worship. One played piano, and the other one sang along with me as I played the guitar. They were late so I was getting nervous. When they finally showed up, the pianist could not get the piano in tune with my guitar and vice versa. "Give me a G! No, that's not a G . . . try again!" Time was running out and my frustration mounted. The meeting was supposed to get started.

"Forget about the piano," I snapped impatiently.

"We just do it this evening with no piano!" It was not an ideal way to start the meeting but in my mind this was all resistance from the enemy.

We sang a few songs and someone gave a testimony. Now it was my time to get up and preach. I welcomed the people who attended the meeting. As soon as I started my sermon an enormous swarm of black birds descended upon one of the Bunyan trees opposite of the stage. Immediately an ear-deafening cacophony of extremely loud chattering and shrieking broke loose. The noise was so overpowering I could not continue to be heard. Startled for a moment, I looked up to the tree. Then a holy anger welled up within me. In a flash I was reminded of Jesus who stilled the storm. Pointing my finger up toward the tree, I shouted at the top of my voice:

"You birds in that tree, I command you to be still in the name of Jesus Christ, right now!"

There was instant silence...

A great hush came over the audience. Not even a single bird dared to open its beak after that. No words were needed to emphasize that a miracle happened. It was a sign and a wonder coming straight out of heaven. Everyone present, whether Christian or not, realized that the Living God was there in a very special way to confirm His Word. All glory to Jesus!

The meeting continued peacefully after this breakthrough. The message in English was translated by two Sri Lankan team sisters into both the Sinhala and Tamil languages. Their fiery and rapid way of translation made it feel like having two machine guns at my side spraying bullets of the Truth. Many lost souls got saved, healed and delivered, and quite a few became true disciples of Jesus in that town. Some might say: "One miracle, sign or wonder from God speaks louder than a thousand words." I would rather say: "One miracle, sign or wonder from God confirms the true divinity, authority of the Word and love of God, the Father, for lost humanity."

God sometimes allows certain uncomfortable circumstances to teach us how to do the works He did while on Earth. Our childlike obedience and unwavering faith in His omnipotent power and ability is the key to overcome the unbelief and fear that may try to hinder us from doing greater things than these.

> **"Very truly I tell you, whoever believes in me will do the works I have been doing, and they will do even greater things than these, because I am going to the Father." (John 14:12 NIV)**

ONIONS FOR SRI LANKA

Our old vehicles were bound to break down sooner or later. While driving the yellow van from India to Sri Lanka, where we planned to import it and use it for the team there, it broke down in South India. It was a complete engine failure so there was no way to go on. We had to arrange for the van to be loaded up on the back of a truck. Boards were laid from the ground toward the truck. Such events always attracted crowds. While our driver steered, at least 100 curious onlookers volunteered to push it up onto the truck amid a lot of shouting, arguing and yes, even pushing. Eventually they succeeded with cheerful jubilation.

The yellow van was then dropped off at the ancient port of Tuticorin in Tamil Naidu, South India. The Portuguese, the Dutch and later the British were in or ruled India at different times. The Portuguese sailed into Tuticorin in 1532, and in 1649 the Dutch captured it. My job was not to capture anything but to make sure the van would be transported by ship from Tuticorin to Colombo in Sri Lanka.

While my teammates left town I checked into a cheap guesthouse and lay down for some rest. When I woke up due to the noise of many voices outside, it was evening. Looking down from my window onto the street below I saw a huge and happy crowd of ladies, men and children all moving into one direction. Some carried what seemed to me to be books under their arms.

"What are they doing and where are all these people going?" I asked someone in the guesthouse.

"They are all going to Dinakaran's meeting in town," I was told. Not knowing who Dinakaran was, I became curious and decided to go down and join the crowd. Someone who spoke English explained that a famous Tamil preacher was conducting an evangelistic open-air meeting in the city of Tuticorin. The books they carried were Bibles! I decided to check it out. When we all came to the meeting ground, I was quite surprised to see the size of that meeting. Lit up by thousands of tube lights, a huge crowd of at least fifty thousand people seated on carpets on the ground had gathered in that place!

The atmosphere was loaded with excitement and anticipation. The Tamil preacher spoke that evening. Although I was not able to understand anything, it was a great blessing to see their eagerness and hunger for the Word of God. People were worshipping the Living God with all their heart; many were getting saved, healed and delivered from darkness. What an encouragement and privilege it was to be able to experience this move of God in such an unexpected place.

After waiting two weeks in Tuticorin for the port official to return, it took another week of running around to get all the official paperwork done. Finally the yellow van was hoisted up by crane and let down into a wooden vessel bound to sail to Sri Lanka. When it arrived many days later, I went to pick it up at Colombo seaport. After filling out many documents, a port official took me to the place where the wooden vessel was moored. From the quay I looked down in surprise at the boat below. There was no yellow van to be seen.

"Where is the vehicle?" The only thing to be seen and smelled was a boat filled to the brim with onions!

"It is there, sir, underneath the onions," he answered very matter-of-factly.

"No way, underneath all those onions?!" He went down to the boat and moved a layer of onions revealing the yellow roof of our van.

Somebody in India had seen a great business opportunity. Our team had already paid for the transportation of the vehicle in advance. That person had come up with the grand idea to fill up all that wasted empty place with a few onions to be sold for a good price in Sri Lanka. It took us many months to get rid of the penetrating smell of onions!

AN AWKWARD BUT PLEASANT ENCOUNTER

The sister who played the piano during the meetings in Badulla would not get off my mind. Apart from doing worship together there had not been any other communication between us. I did not know anything about her. Our Asian team totally adjusted to the local culture and contact between the sexes was off limits and kept to a minimum. Yet out of the blue there was this nudging feeling and impression that we somehow belonged together. It made me suspicious of myself.

Trying to overcome it only made it worse. It was like pushing and keeping a ball under water. The deeper you push it down the higher it jumps up when you let it go. Sometime later some of the foreign team members were seated in the living room in our team office house in Colombo. We were dutifully listening to an audio cassette teaching on divorce and remarriage. The message was interesting but the monotonous whirring sound from the rusting fan hanging from the ceiling made us all a bit sleepy. The everlasting high humidity heat in Colombo can be quite overwhelming.

One of the drowsy listeners yawned, stood up stretching his legs and arms, and left, soon followed by somebody else and again others. Suddenly the pianist and I were left alone in that room, listening together to a teaching about marriage. It felt very awkward! We both realized it at the same time and jumped up to quickly leave the room through separate exits. However, there was only one very narrow path between two walls leading out of the compound.

When I came around the corner the pianist also came around her corner of the house. To our great consternation, we were now forced to meet each other again. Without looking each other in the eye or speaking a single word we both tried to escape by squeezing past one another without touching. In that moment it happened again. This soft, but compelling voice: "You BELONG together!" However, I needed more confirmation and wanted to be sure about this truly being God's will for her and my life. I deliberately put off thinking about it as I knew I had to wait upon the Lord.

JEHOVAH JIREH

My four-month permission to stay in Sri Lanka ended. It was the beginning of September 1980 and time for me to return to Germany to prepare our yearly one-month of fundraising meetings in October. My flight schedule was arranged from Colombo, Sri Lanka via Bombay, India to Frankfurt in Germany. One of our team leaders was to fly a month later to join me and preach in the meetings while I translated. So far I had never been on a plane because we had come to Asia driving over land. Our team had printed a whole load of brochures, nicely packed in two heavy boxes, which I had to take along.

Only 20 kilograms of luggage was allowed, and I carried more than 20 kilograms overweight! Since all our money was spent on airfare, I was not given any money to pay for overages. It could cost more than five-hundred U.S. dollars! This was quite a dilemma. I was willing to try it by faith but told my leader I would have to leave the boxes behind in case I was charged money for it.

The first miracle happened when I was about to fly from Colombo. The president of Sri Lanka had to leave his country unexpectedly for an important meeting abroad. My flight was canceled because he needed our plane. All passengers were re-booked on the next flight out. While checking in for the flight I was given a seat in business class without having to pay extra. This also meant my luggage went along without any extra charge!

Upon arriving in Bombay, I stood in a long line to check in for the flight to Frankfurt. Waiting for my turn, I was getting a bit restless. There was no money to pay for the weight of my extra luggage. Finally my turn came. I put the heavy boxes on the scales to be weighed. The pointer of the scale swung to the right. The lady behind the counter looked up at me.

"Your luggage is overweight. You will have to pay extra."

Bewildered, I answered: "Well, then, I will have to leave these boxes behind because I cannot pay." Not knowing what to do next I stood there quite lost for a moment feeling very embarrassed with all the other passengers looking on.

"So then . . ." the male voice of somebody next in line broke the silence. "Please put his extra weight on my name." It took me totally by surprise.

"Why would you want to do that for me?" I asked the young

man behind me.

"Unfortunately, I lost all my luggage on a flight in India, so I can offer to take yours." The lady behind the counter agreed, and off my boxes went down the conveyor belt. After thanking my unexpected helper, we asked to be seated next to each other in the plane.

An amazing miracle of God's provision had just happened. Jehovah Jireh was true! It means "God will provide," as it was with Abraham when he was to sacrifice his son Isaac. About to sacrifice my two boxes with literature, God had provided a perfect solution. Not knowing what to do, I had given up, but God obviously had not. Wow, what a lesson! The refrain of the good old song "Trust and Obey," which was written by John H. Sammis in 1887, came to my mind: "Trust and obey, for there's no other way, to be happy in Jesus, but to trust and obey." Overcoming financial difficulties can only be done when you stay in the center of God's will for your life and continue to trust Him to provide even if it looks impossible.

After the plane had taken off and had settled at cruising speed, I turned to my companion. "Whatever happened to your luggage?" He explained that he was an artist from Czechoslovakia and had traveled throughout India painting at different locations. After his flight to Bombay, on his way home, all his paintings that he had checked in never showed up and were lost, a devastating loss of much hard work. Feeling very bad for him, I tried to cheer him up a bit. We came to know each other, and I shared about my life as a disciple of Christ. Unknowingly and unwillingly, he had been used by God to bless me. I owed it to him to share about God's love. He was open and listened with great interest. Spontaneously he drew a beautiful picture of the "way of life" on the flyleaf of my pocket Bible. An eternal seed of life was sown in his heart.

Soon I was back in Germany. The pastor from Grasellenbach, a tiny health resort in the middle of the legendary Oden-wald forest picked me up at the airport in Frankfurt. Worried about my skinny appearance, his dear wife fed me lots of very delicious German food. After World War II, this elderly couple had fled from Eastern Europe and spent years living under harsh circumstances in the nearby forest with their five children. They knew what it meant to be hungry and homeless. With the help of a loan from the government, they had finally been able to build the tiny house where I stayed with them.

The first two weeks were spent making many phone calls to contact German pastors and church leaders about the possibility of a mission meeting in their fellowship. Most of these contacts were very interested in our ministry in Asia. They were thankful for the many fruitful times our teams from Italy had spent in Germany to be a blessing for their churches. Bless, and you shall be blessed! The schedule quickly filled up with approximately twenty-five meetings in Germany alone—apart from a few that I could arrange in the Netherlands. In between I helped the pastor collect firewood in the forest or ministered in their small fellowship in neighboring Michelstadt.

These fundraising meetings were quite intense as it involved nonstop traveling day and night to cities all over Germany and the Netherlands. In each meeting we showed slides about our ministry in Asia and challenged the churches to get involved in reaching the people in India, Sri Lanka and Pakistan. Translating each sermon, plus every conversation, from English to German and vice versa was very tiring. For that, the result was very rewarding. Not only finances but much prayer support was raised for our ministry. Once again, the truth of Jehovah Jireh, God's provision under sacrificial circumstances was confirmed. In the process we were also helping Germany and its generous Christians to become a blessing for Asia.

20
THE LAND OF
THE PURE

Soon we were on our way overland once again. With the help of our team in Italy, a secondhand van was repaired, prepared and painted. Equipment for the evangelistic open-air meetings and ministry in India was purchased. Off we went on the long and tedious overland journey back to Asia. The situation in Iran was becoming more and more complicated and dangerous. That fall in 1980, neighboring Iraq had just started a very bloody confrontation with Iran. An estimated 1 million persons were killed in a war that lasted eight years and ended up in a stalemate. Iranian children were told to sacrifice their lives for Allah by walking ahead of troops to clear the landmines. Iraq's main reason for the invasion was to cripple Shia-dominated Iran and to prevent Ayatollah Khomeini from exporting the 1979 Iranian Revolution movement to the Shiite majority in Iraq. The replacement of Iran as the dominant state in the Persian Gulf by Iraq was another motive. Iran could threaten the minority Sunni dominated Ba'athist leadership of Saddam Hussein by internally exploiting religious tensions in Iraq.

While traveling through Turkey and Iran, the war made it very hard to find enough diesel for our vehicle. Luckily we had anticipated this problem by bringing some containers and a barrel to stock up on surplus diesel whenever we had a chance. The Iranian Revolution had dramatically changed the atmosphere in Iran. Women who previously dressed in Western attire were now completely covered by burkas. Moving like fluttering black bats, they hurried anxiously down dusty streets in the villages and towns we passed. The religious spiritual darkness was very tangible. Stern-looking Iranian Revolutionary Guards heavily armed with Kalashnikov machine guns were ever present. We made haste to pass through this country as fast as we could.

The way through Afghanistan was shut. The situation there was even worse after the Russian invasion. Some of the last hippies who wanted to travel to India via Afghanistan died trying. We did not try. The only other way was by traveling south more than 300 kilometers from Zahedan, Iran, to Quetta, Pakistan, through the dry and arid desert of the wild Baluch territory. The still largely unreached people group of the Baluch inhabits the Baluchistan region of the southeastern-most edge of the Iranian plateau in Iran, Pakistan and Afghanistan. We were on our way through to the Land of the Pure.

The name *Pakistan* literally means "a land abounding in the pure" in Urdu and Persian. It remained to be seen and experienced how pure Pakistan really was. At the time there was at least no war going on in this Land of the Pure. About 75% of Pakistanis are Sunni Muslims and 20% are Shiite. Five percent of the population are Hindus, Christians, etc. In 1980 the population was 78 million which increased to 220 million by the year 2020. The 3,180-kilometer-long (1,976 miles) Indus River cuts straight through Pakistan, fed by the five major tributaries of the Punjab region. The Indus civilization was the earliest known urban culture of the Indian subcontinent—one of the world's three earliest civilizations, along with Mesopotamia and ancient Egypt. The Karakoram Mountain range in Pakistan is home to eighteen summits more than 7,500 meters (24,600 feet) in height, with four exceeding 8,000 meters (26,000 feet). One interesting proverb among the Pashtun people group in Pakistan and Afghanistan states: "There is no mountain so high that there is no pass to cross over it." Spiritually we were confronted with the towering heights of the religion of Islam, ago-old superstition, widespread corruption and poverty. However, there is no mountain so high that it cannot be overcome and moved in the name of Jesus!

GODLY WOMEN IN A MALE DOMINATED SOCIETY

"Allahu Akbar! . . . Allahu Akbar! . . . God is great!" At sunrise, an ever-increasing crescendo of the first call to prayer broke the relative silence of the night in the city of Lahore in Pakistan. Waves of overlapping prayer calls out of loudspeakers from minarets on mosques heavily blanketed the whole town. My own habit to meet God early in the morning was greatly distracted and challenged by these wailing and eerie sounds descending on my eardrums. This call was repeated five times a day. Traditionally, the calls were made from the mosque's minaret without amplification. Nowadays most modern mosques use loudspeakers so that the faithful can hear the call more clearly. The actual prayer times are dictated by the sun's position. While living in Asia you cannot help but notice the dedication to prayer of Muslims, Hindus and Buddhists. They serve gods or teachings many do not know or understand personally. Yet they faithfully cling to their rituals to please their gods or fulfill their religious duty in the hope of attaining salvation. How much more should Christians who know the Living God spend more and regular times in prayer in the presence of God Almighty?

> "After he had dismissed them, he went up on a mountainside by himself to pray. Later that night, he was there alone." (Matt. 14:23 NKJV)

Our teams were warmly welcomed by the local Christians in Pakistan who showered upon us the traditional hospitality practiced by Christians and non-Christians alike all over Asia. We were simple and mostly single Christian workers living by faith in God's provision without big support bases in our home countries. For Pakistanis, our poverty was not a hindrance but a reason to bless us. Their simple logic was that it was their Christian duty to take care of these servants sent by God from faraway lands to bring Good Tidings. The few men, a couple and the ladies lived separately in the homes of local Christians. For weeks on end our Pakistani hosts in different towns and villages would feed and host us.

After prayer female team members went out during the mornings to distribute literature from house to house in the city of Lahore. There was relative freedom to do so because Pakistani women mostly stayed home while the men were working. Our team prayed, did worship, gave testimonies, preached and ministered in churches and fellowships all over Pakistan. Amazingly in that male-dominated society our international team eventually developed into an indigenous all-women team. This faithful band of women was led by two sisters who voluntarily gave up their right to get married. To this day they are plowing, sowing and raising up godly women of God to bring the good news to the Land of the Pure. Fortunately, the spiritually hard and crusty soil had been broken up and plowed by the prayers of a very special man of God.

THE LEGACY OF PRAYING HYDE

When the Lord sends us to other nations it is very important to find out about and give credit to those who fruitfully ministered there before we came, as we are building on their foundation. John Hyde, an American missionary, was called to the Punjab in Pakistan (at that time still a part of India) in 1892. Because he was partly deaf, he had a hard time learning the language and his ability to communicate was impaired. The first nine years he saw little fruit. Once John decided to start praying and fasting, everything started to change. From 1899, persistent prayer—even praying all night—became his passion. People called him Praying Hyde and also "the man who never sleeps."

Revival came in 1904 in the first Sialkot convention where John started the Punjab Prayer Union. Yearly revival conferences are still held there to this day. The victory of those meetings was not won in the pulpit but in the closet of unceasing prayer. After many years of no one coming to Christ, John saw fifty baptisms in 1907 and 800 in 1909. God gave him increasing faith to ask for one to four souls to repent each day of the year. The glory of the Lord rested upon these conventions in a special way. Praying without ceasing is the key to overcoming the spiritual darkness and setting the captives free.

THE RIGHT HAND OF GOD

I personally experienced the legacy of Praying Hyde when I was asked to speak in a Christian convention in the city of Faisalabad in the Punjab, Pakistan. When I got up on the stage to speak, all of a sudden, the power of the Holy Spirit overwhelmed me. God's presence was so strong I was not able to utter a single word. It felt so small and feeble to be in the presence of such Majesty. *Who was I, a mere saved sinner, to speak in the name of Jesus, the Son of this awesome God?* I humbly asked God to step aside a bit if He still wanted me, his earthly son, to say something. No wonder God moved powerfully in that meeting. Many people were saved and healed that day. A lady testified that she had seen me come and preach in their town in a vision a couple of days before the meeting. One young girl, an orphan adopted by a couple without children, testified that she had seen a vision of Jesus coming back on the clouds! Some Muslim students had also attended and walked up to me after the meeting. One of them had a very special question:

"You preached today about Jesus standing at the right hand of God."

"Yes, that is right," I answered. In my sermon Acts 7:55–56

was mentioned:

> **"But Stephen, full of the Holy Spirit, looked up to heaven and saw the glory of God, and Jesus standing at the right hand of God. 'Look,' he said, 'I see heaven open and the Son of Man standing at the right hand of God.'"**

"But how do you know that God has a right hand?" That was quite a question indeed. I tried to give a simple answer.

"Well, we are all descendants of Adam, who was created in the image of God. So we have faces, hands and legs and are only reflecting the image of God who created us."

I sensed they were not genuinely interested in the answer but more out to challenge me. Not willing to get into an endless and useless religious discussion, I cried out in my heart:

"Lord, show them who you are!"

"Touch his forehead!" an inner voice spoke clearly.

It was not my habit to lay hands on or pray out of the blue over unbelievers. But I obeyed anyway. As soon as my hand touched his forehead he fell backward toward the ground. His friends were just as surprised as I was. We all looked at him lying there quite still. His eyes were closed but a smile was on his face.

"He will be ok," I reassured them. After some time he came to himself and stood up.

"Do you still not believe that Jesus is standing at the right hand of God?" I asked him.

With a broad smile flashing all over his face he answered:

"Yes, I do believe! I just saw Him at the right hand of God!"

There was not much discussion or arguing after that experience. All of them opened up like sunflowers toward the sun. It was the first time I experienced God using a vision to open the eyes of a spiritually blind Muslim. And it would not be the last time.

Worldwide during the last thirty years, God has been revealing Himself through dreams and visions to many Muslims. In answer to prevailing prayer, our sovereign God uses His own sovereign methods to overcome the spiritual blindness of those bound by religious darkness.

21
FAVOR FROM
THE LORD

"He who finds a wife finds what is good and
receives favor from the LORD." (Prov. 18:22 NKJV)

Something was not complete and missing in my life, and the time had come to find it. Asian culture is in many ways so much different from Western culture. Regular contact between unmarried men and women are off limits in the Asian culture. Most marriages are arranged by the parents. The groom and bride to be hardly know each other. Living in Asia as well, I sensed my dear Father in heaven was arranging something very special for me in line with this Asian context.

In the city of Badulla and afterward, through the strange encounter in Colombo, Sri Lanka, the Lord had begun to speak to my heart about His intention for me to marry Chris. She was the American team sister who was supposed to play the piano during the open-air evangelization in Badulla. To be surer about it being God's will, I had deliberately put it off in the first place and decided to wait upon the Lord. There was no way to know whether she liked me. It did not seem like she showed much interest in me. In fact, I had the impression she avoided me.

During the beginning of February 1981, the Lord started to speak strongly to my heart again, constraining me to consider a marriage with Chris. So I asked the Lord to put a true love in my heart for her if He wanted her to be my wife. On February 10, I felt a great urge to propose a marriage to Chris. Asking a woman to become my wife made me quite nervous. The timing, where to do it, how to do it, what to say and how she would react all appeared to be insurmountable obstacles. I needed to somehow overcome by faith.

"How shall I go about this, dear Lord?"

"Just ask her!" came the sobering and scary answer.

"Tell her not to say yes or no but to pray about it for a month and then give you an answer."

"Ok, dear Lord. Great idea; yes, of course, your will shall be done," I hastily uttered.

Majestic, beautiful and shady Banyan trees stretching out their branches indefinitely into all directions surrounded the Christian compound in the city of Anand (which means Joy!). Aerial roots hanging down all over from their branches had taken root in the soil to become new trunks. Our ladies team was accommodated in that compound. Chris oversaw making a huge banner to be used in the upcoming open-air evangelistic meeting. This gave me a good excuse and an opportunity to meet her alone. Outside the house, under the shady Bunyan trees, we met to see the banner and "discuss" some things about the banner. This was the cover-up for my strategy.

Chris immediately started to feel uncomfortable about meeting and talking alone outside to a single brother. There was no time to lose now. Overcome by my own nervousness and insecurity, I completely messed up and forgot what I wanted to say. Coming to the point quite unromantically I said: "Chris, I want to talk to you because the Lord wants me to ask you to become my wife."

Then I added most awkwardly:

"Don't think I am asking you because you are so beautiful; it is only because the Lord told me to!"

While I heard myself saying this, I caught her eyes for a moment. She did not speak a single word, but what I saw completely wiped out my insecurity. Those two beautiful, bright blue eyes lit up with a mixture of happiness, joy and expectation. It meant more to me than a thousand words of explanation. Encouraged, I said,

"You do not need to say yes or no right now! "Just pray about it for a month, and then give me your answer."

We spoke only briefly, but already then she told me that she knew this would come. During the month of waiting, the Lord did confirm my step of faith and obedience by giving me a genuine, strong and pure love for Chris. I just knew that it was different from any other time I had been "in love" in my life. It was a love motivated by an overwhelming peace about this being God's will. At the same time, realizing this new responsibility brought an awareness of sole dependence upon God for every coming step. Since my yes should be yes and my no a no, I had to act accordingly.

On March 6, 1981, during a hectic open-air evangelization in the city of Ahmedabad, I had to find and force a time to talk to Chris. One sweltering evening I parked our overland truck in a dusty and barely lit, narrow alley behind the house of local Christians where the team kitchen was located. Chris was on kitchen duty. Standing near the dim light of a street lantern, I gathered up all of my courage and walked slowly up to the back door. In that very moment the door opened and out came Chris, her hands full with some garbage she wanted to dispose of. We both stood there staring at each other for a moment.

"Aren't we supposed to talk to each other?" she said breaking the silence.

"Oh yes, quick, come with me, we can talk in the truck!" I whispered.

"Oh no, not there, what will happen if somebody sees us?" her voice squeaked in desperation. Grabbing her by the hand, I pulled her behind me toward the vehicle.

"There is no other way and place, let's go!"

We hopped into the cabin of the truck and closed the door

behind us. Without losing much time or words, Chris told me that she agreed to marry me. The Lord had clearly spoken to her even before He had spoken to me about it. Great! So good to finally hear that. We jumped out again. Ahead of me, she quickly walked back to the kitchen. Suddenly the kitchen door swung wide open once again. Out came the wife of our team leader with a big inquisitive look on her face. Seeing Chris and then me in the background, trying to hide in the darkness, her female senses immediately picked up what was going on.

"Oohh! Aahaahh?! So that's where you were! Oh, how nice . . . !"

On our yearly trip to share in churches in Europe with her husband, and on one of our overland trips together, we had become friends and knew each other very well. Threatening her jokingly I said:

"Listen to me: if you tell your husband about this before I can talk to him, I will kill you!" There was no more time to lose now. That same day I met with the elders who agreed that Chris would be the right woman to become my faithful companion.

THAT VERY CLEAR VOICE

Yes, I, Chris, was the American pianist who couldn't manage to get her piano to tune in Badulla! Sitting there in disgrace on the top of the stairs at the back of the stage, I suddenly heard a Voice, very clear: "You will have to learn to understand him when he is like that, because one day you will be his wife." I was shocked. I thought, well, either that is the voice of God or the voice of the devil. Right then I decided I was not going to do anything whatsoever. If this is of God, then this guy will come to me and ask. In the meantime, I made up my mind to push this whole thing as far away as I could. I did not want to get married. I was living a wonderful, fulfilled life, lots of responsibility, leading the girls' team, literature outreaches, preaching. Marriage? What a bother, and then kids! Yikes!

So it was almost nine months later Antoine did come and ask. It was amazing what happened, just like in the movies! From one second to the other, I was totally in love. The sun was shining, I heard bells ringing, birds singing, the whole lot! As soon as I could get away from him, I ran behind the little rooms where the sisters were quartered and sat on top of the sewer slab to obediently pray about it, as I had been told to. Again came this very clear Voice: "Why are you asking? I already told you." For me, this "very clear Voice" business was somehow, mercifully, a very real part of my spiritual life and very helpful in overcoming doubt and unbelief.

Maybe it was because I had very godly parents who were praying for me. I was born south of Chicago where my father was the Mennonite pastor of a black church in the sticks. There is a book about Pembroke, as it was infamous for being one of the poorest communities in Illinois. My daddy certainly was doing his best to help lift that community. My childhood was generally happy and unconcerned. It didn't bother me to be the only white spot in my church, kindergarten, school.

I have a very clear memory of the day after Dr. Martin Luther King Jr. was assassinated. One of my little girl friends came up to me and said,

"You killed Dr. Martin Luther King. I am not going to play with you anymore."

"Yeah right, I killed somebody," I thought sarcastically to myself. But in my little second grade brain, somehow I understood this girl; she was angry. Later I realized that all this was excellent preparation for going into the mission field. I was already used to living in a different culture.

My parents raised me, my two brothers and one sister without fear. My brothers and I were left free to wander all over all those dirt roads, exploring the woods and hanging out at the church to watch the guys play basketball, etc. Several times I was wandering somewhere alone on my way home when a car would drive by and some guy would say, "Hey, my, you are beautiful, wouldn't you like a ride?" Somehow I just shrugged it off. Although there was a little gospel church on every corner, the neighborhood was actually quite dangerous as drugs, alcoholism and prostitution were rampant. But in the midst of it my parents raised us with a genuine appreciation and understanding for folks that were different and definitely to have a heart for the down and out.

The first time I heard this "clear Voice" was when I was seven years old. My mommy had put me to bed, and I was supposed to sleep. But suddenly I heard the voice of God, and I knew that it was time for me to give my life to Him. I was very excited about this and called to my mommy to come so she could pray with me. But alas . . . my mommy had put me to bed and no amount of calling changed that for her. Disappointed, I was lying there when I suddenly realized, *well, if God can talk to me, then I can talk to God. I don't need my mother.* So I prayed to give my life to Jesus all by myself.

Eventually, somehow, I felt that both God and my father kind of left it up to me to figure a lot of things out for myself. After the assassination of Dr. Martin Luther King Jr. and the ensuing race riots and upheavals which I experienced firsthand in our "integrated" high school, more and more loneliness started to govern my life. It was no longer popular to be friends with a white girl. And that very lonely girl started looking for attention in all the wrong places. Finally, one time while I was walking home alone late at night, I heard that Voice again.

"Chris, it is wrong what you are doing!" It was so clear that I answered back out loud,

"But it doesn't *feel* wrong."

Just as clear came the answer:

"It's wrong, because My Word says it's wrong."

Boom. I felt like I had just walked into a wall. Suddenly before my feet I saw a deep gulf open up, leading down into utter darkness. Right then I made an absolute 180-degree turnabout. Spiritually that is. It took me awhile to get everything straightened out, but I climbed right out of that hole. Around this time my parents decided to move from this area and my father took a pastorate in a small, white farming town in northern Illinois. I never asked them if they did that to get me away from the mess in that neighborhood. But it did give me a chance to start anew, also with the Lord.

"My sheep listen to my voice; I know them, and they follow me." (John 10:27 NKJV)

Around this time, the charismatic movement was sweeping through many denominations in the U.S. and also in Mennonite congregations. My mother dragged me to every charismatic happening she could find. She was spontaneously baptized in the Holy Spirit during her private prayer time. My mother was always a praying person. I have a very early memory of answering the door to find a man standing there, asking if my mother was home. I must have been very little as I only came up to his knee. I told him he had to go away because my mama was praying and nobody was supposed to bother her. Indeed, every afternoon after lunch my mom would tell us to be quiet, and she would go into her bedroom and kneel by her bed with her Bible open before her. It was during one of those times that the Holy Spirit just came over her. She described it as "waves of love!" At the time I was just a mixed-up teenager, but I did see the big change that the Holy Spirit made in the lives of my parents. I thought that if old people could change so much, there must be something to it.

One day my mom convinced me to go with her to a Charles

and Francis Hunter meeting held in a huge cinema hall. My mom and I were sitting way up in the back balcony just watching all these "goings-on." It was prayer time and people were lined up in big, long prayer lines backed up to the doors, and folks up front were falling out on the ground left and right. While observing all this suddenly it was announced that they were going to pray for all pastors.

"Yeah, see now you gotta go," I said poking my mom.

"But I'm a pastor's wife," she said.

Just that quick came another announcement over the loudspeaker:

"And if the pastor is not there, the pastor's wife should come!" I laughed at my mom and told her,

"See, now you have to go."

So she did. I sat there watching her slowly move up toward the stage in that long line, and I was thinking, *If my mother falls over like all these folks are doing, then I will know that this is for real.* I knew my mother would never fall over just to please anybody.

Finally she got up on the stage and the first minister prayed for her . . . nothing, so they passed her down the line. The next one . . . still nothing happened. My mother went through the whole line, standing up the whole time. I was really disappointed, *"What a bunch of nonsense; this is all not true."* But suddenly there was that clear Voice,

"No, Chris, this is not the way to judge. If you want to know about My Spirit, then you read in My Word." *Huh*, I thought. *Okay!*

A CLEAR CALL

This clear Voice was also there for my call to the mission field. By time I was attending Eastern Mennonite College in Virginia, majoring in Biology. I—a straight-A student—was on my way to becoming a doctor. But I started to get letters from my best friend. We had gotten filled with the Holy Spirit together and tried to get a Bible club going in our high school. They refused and told us we had to meet off the school premises. She had started her college study at Illinois State, but now she was writing to tell me that she had quit college to join a Jesus People movement called "Christ is the Answer." And boy, was she excited about it.

Her parents, of course, were not at all amused; they even tried to get my pastor daddy to talk her out of it. Before they had avoided all contact with my family, as they had no understanding of their daughter's interest in all this Christianity business. But my Daddy seemed to realize that she had a real calling. In the end he also could not convince her to come home.

Along came spring break, and I had to decide what to do with it. I could stay on campus and study hard like a good straight-A student. I also had been invited by a person I was dating to go home with him to meet his parents. And my friend invited me to come visit her in Tampa, Florida, where the Christ is the Answer (CITA) team had their evangelistic tent set up. I was on my way to the campus post office as I mulled over this decision in my mind.

Hmmm, meet his parents . . . that is kind of an escalation in the relationship . . . *am I ready for that?* Yes, he was a wonderful guy studying theology, planning to go into the ministry . . . *Hmmm* . . . As I walked into the post office, I walked past the clipboard where all the opportunities for rides were posted. As it was spring break, all the students were scattering and everybody was offering rides in just about every direction. Suddenly, right in the middle, my eye was drawn to a tiny piece of paper offering a ride to . . . TAMPA, FLORIDA.

I just knew—the Voice was clear as a bell—I was supposed

to go there.

Even without an address, I found my friend in her long, Jesus People denim skirt—and she was ecstatic. It was not hard to find such a huge tent and there were posters all over the city. Besides, there was a big controversy going on and bad publicity about this group being a sect. There were camera men and news people all over all trying to get a good story. The whole place was buzzing. Somewhere close to the end of my visit, my friend took me out for a cup of coffee at the Walgreens. A rare treat for those poor Jesus People, I must say.

As we were sitting there, there it was again, this clear Voice:

"Chris, I want you here. They have something you need, and you have something they need." So, I suddenly said to my dear friend,

"Well, I have decided to join."

My goodness, she started jumping up and down and was shouting for joy all over the Walgreens store! Later I found out that she and another team member had both prayed and fasted for forty days that I would come and join the team. Guess there was no other choice! Yes, they had beseeched the Lord of the Harvest to force out this laborer. Our Lord of the Harvest truly has His own ways to overcome the lack of workers in His kingdom. In Greek, the word for "to send out," which Jesus used in the Scripture below is *ekballo*, which literally means "to force out."

"Then he said to his disciples, 'The harvest is plentiful but the workers are few. Ask the Lord of harvest, therefore, to *send* out workers into his harvest field.'" (Matt. 9:37–38 NKJV, author's emphasis)

Once back at the tent, I went to the leader and told him that I wanted to join. But first I would go back up to college and settle my things. And I needed to go and tell my parents; and then I would come back. Looking at me through his long Jesus

People hair he said,

"Oh, you don't need to worry about your parents. We will swing back up to Illinois by the summer and then you can go tell your parents."

I exclaimed in dismay,

"You are crazy; if I just disappear, my parents will have the police out looking for me. Of course I have to go back and talk to them."

He smiled; what could he say? He was sure he would never see me again. But, as I was traveling back to college and praying about all this, I put three signs before the Lord: "If this is You, then I want the blessing of my big brother Michael, the dean of my college and of my father."

First was my brother. He was a senior at the same college, and we had a good relationship. I trusted him as he was a very vibrant Christian. When I told him my intentions, he looked at me and said, "Man, I wish I could do something like that!" One down! Two to go!

I had to quit college, and that entailed talking to the dean of the college who was responsible for the spiritual development of the students. He also led the charismatic Bible study that I attended on campus. As he listened to me, he suddenly said: "Well, this could be a good experience for you; would you like me to call your father for you?" Now that reaction did surprise me. After all, it was his job to keep students *in* the college! My father was a different story. When I called to tell him, he told me to get on the next plane and come home. So, I borrowed money from my grandma (just about all my father's family were involved in this college) and flew from Harrisonburg, Virginia, back home to Chicago.

When I walked into my house, who was sitting in the living room but an ex-CITA team member. My father had dug him up from somewhere and had him there to question him about the team—and to talk to me. Wonderfully, he was able to answer all the theological questions that my father had. I had no idea what they actually taught about anything. They were about preaching the gospel—that's all I knew! At the end, this person assured my daddy that CITA was not a sect; they were genuinely preaching a clear gospel, maybe a bit strong on discipleship, but a good ministry. So, what could my father say? Actually quite a lot.

Every afternoon we spent in his pastor's study, and he asked me all kinds of questions and was doing his level best to convince me that this was not the way. I could go be a Mennonite missionary; why this team? The "living by faith" part was hard for him. He tried to get me with the Scripture where Paul wrote to Timothy that anyone who does not provide for their own household has denied the faith and is worse than an unbeliever. With all my eighteen-year-old confidence, I didn't get it. Folks paid him a salary to preach; likewise, people also give the Jesus People donations to preach. I didn't see any difference and told him so. The last day came, and as we were sitting around the breakfast table I said, "So, Daddy, what is it now? Do I have your permission or not?"

There was a long silence. Very long. Then, "Weeeell . . . yes."

That was it! I was gone. To the amazement of the team leader, I showed up again. Later I found out that my mother had fasted and prayed about the situation, and the Lord had also given her a "yes!"

In order to get me to India, the Lord had to simply overrule me. After some time in the team, they decided to send out new missionaries—some to strengthen the CITA team in Italy, and others were to be sent on to India where a new work had been started. We were all to pray and ask God if we were to be sent out. My friend and I were both sure that we were to go. As I had never been anywhere out of the U.S., I thought Italy was far enough. So

I signed up for Italy and she—ever the 100% person—signed up for India. All took part in the same training to get us ready to go and we all flew over together (after praying in our ticket money!)

We landed in Paris where two buses were waiting to take us to our respective teams. The Indian team was to go first to Sweden for a time of fundraising and preparation before driving overland to India. The leader, who was also the bus driver, had a list and he was calling out names and directing us to the right bus. I heard my name called to get on the bus that was going to Sweden, eventually India. I thought,

Hey, I never said I would go to India! But, just as quick, came that very clear Voice:

"Chris, this is My doing." Well, that was that.

I did go and talk to the leader, telling him that I needed to call my parents. I thought I should tell them if I was to be in India and not Italy as that is quite a difference! He graciously granted my request. I never found out what happened. I suspect they mixed up my name and the name of my friend as she ended up in Italy. She eventually married one of the team mechanics. They have a beautiful family and are still serving in the Italian CITA team. There are times when it is not about overcoming; it's about letting yourself be overcome!

MALARIA AND A MIRACLE

Graciously, an arrangement was made by our leadership for Chris and I to go to our team in Sri Lanka for a while. The kind of life we lived in an Asian culture where the sexes were mostly separated did not give us much time to come to know each other. The culture in Buddhist Sri Lanka was similar, but people there were more used to foreigners who frequently visited this beautiful tropical island. The steady sound of mighty Indian Ocean waves rolling in and crashing down surrounded us as we strolled around the beach near our team's office. I reached out and held her soft, warm hand for the first time. This was the beginning of a life of walking together in Jesus' footsteps.

We were engaged, and my wife-to-be was and still is not a woman of many words. The few words we exchanged were soon interrupted. A heavy tropical rain suddenly forced us to run and hide behind a hut made of straw. She stood there completely drenched and soaked, water dripping slowly down her beautiful, long blond wet hair on her lovely face. It made me love her all the more. This precious time was short, and soon I was on my way back to go oversee our all-Indian team.

They were ministering in Rajasthan, a very hot and dry state in India with various ancient Hindu holy places. Nomadic camel herders roamed the countryside in search of food and water. Hindus there were very devout and ready to defend their religion with violent means. It was a quite a challenge for our team made up of young disciples. We had been sent out entirely by faith. There was no promise of financial support coming in regularly. We entirely depended upon the sure promises in God's word.

> "Look at the birds of the air; they do not sow or reap or store away in barns, and yet your heavenly Father feeds them. Are you not much more valuable than they?" (Matt. 6:26 NKJV)

Young people are usually quite hungry, especially the male team members. At times it was hard to see them suffering when there was not much to eat. Nonetheless they hardly ever complained and were willing to overcome these trials by faith in Jehovah Jireh. There was always great rejoicing when our faithful God provided us with the things needed for life. The few Christians and small churches scattered in various places were more than willing to help and accommodate us whenever we came. A glass of cool water from their "refrigerating" clay water jars was always offered first. No matter how poor these hospitable people were, we were offered a simple meal or at least tea and biscuits.

Once after a particularly hot and dry afternoon of ministry outside we stumbled into the main hall of a small Bible school in Jaipur where we were accommodated. It was like entering heaven. An amazing drop in temperature occurred as soon as we entered. At the end of the room I discovered a big box stuck in the window. It was covered on all sides by straw matting through which a small pump slowly dripped water. A big ventilator sucked the hot and dry outside air into the box and it was blown out of the other side, cooling the room down effectively as well as adding much-needed humidity. This was my first encounter with an amazing Asian invention: the water cooler. We all dropped down on the floor basking and falling asleep in this unexpected, revitalizing, wonderful climate caused by this simple technology. The God who created us has given mankind creative abilities to also overcome practical problems.

Time went by fast, and I was looking forward to meeting my fiancé, Chris, again. She was going to join the sisters in our team located in the city of Jodhpur near the desert of Rajasthan. This gave me a chance to meet her once in a while and discuss our wedding plans for the end of the year. Soon we would have to leave the country together as our visas would expire. All of a sudden I started to feel quite weak and very sick.

I was bitten by just a very small mosquito. Normally we used mosquito nets in humid areas swamped with mosquitoes. But in this dry desert climate, with few mosquitoes, we slept without them. Malaria is a major health problem in western Rajasthan. This was unknown to us at the time but would not have stopped us from going there. However, it is a serious and sometimes fatal disease. Usually, people get malaria by being bitten by an infected female. Only such female mosquitoes can transmit malaria after taking blood containing microscopic malaria parasites from a previously infected person. The World Health Organization estimates that in 2020, globally 241 million Anopheles mosquito cases of malaria occurred. Roughly 627,000 people died of Malaria, mostly children in Africa.

About a week after getting infected I was very sick with high fevers, shaking chills and flulike illness. In spite of this, Chris and I had to pack up our few belongings to start travel to South India. By the time a bus ride had taken us from Jodhpur to the city of Ajmer in Rajasthan, my condition had worsened. The malaria parasites in my body caused me to have short spells of feeling very cold. My battered body needed blankets although the outside temperature exceeded 35 °C (95° F). Soon afterward my body temperature shot up very high, and I had to throw the blankets off again. These extreme changes are very hard on the body, and especially on the heart, when it continues for too long.

For the night we were staying with an evangelical reverend in Ajmer. While lying on a hard rope bed covered by a thin mattress, this dear brother gently rubbed cool ice all over my body to keep the high temperature down as much as possible. I will always remember his kindness because it was very helpful. A nurse from their church gave me some quinine medicine. This helped to get up the next day for the long trip to Madras (Chennai) in South India. Barely able to carry my small briefcase, I was very glad to have Chris by my side to help me. After an exhausting 2,000-kilometer train ride lasting thirty-seven hours, we finally arrived in Madras where we were accommodated in a Bible school. The next day was a Thursday. After our engagement, Chris had decided to always fast the same day I fasted weekly, which was Thursday. To be honest I did not feel like fasting. Exhausted, skinny and weak, I was not very motivated to suffer even more. We discussed it but finally decided to fast anyway. Why break a good and helpful tradition just because I was feeling unwell? So, we brought a sacrifice of praise unto the Lord.

**"Give thanks *in* all circumstances; for this
is God's will for you in Christ Jesus."
(1 Thess. 5:18 NKJV, author's emphasis)**

This doesn't mean that we are to give thanks *for* everything but give thanks *in* everything.

Seated on a thin mattress with our backs to the wall on the roof of the Bible school, we started to praise and thank the Lord in this situation and pray for the things upon our hearts. After spending some time in prayer, it suddenly felt like a warm hand was slowly laid on my chest. Opening up my eyes, immediately I saw—that except for Chris—nobody was there. The heat increased, and for ten minutes a powerful sensation flowed through my body. It felt like a constant current of high-voltage electricity flowing through but not harming my chest. It was so strong that I did not dare to touch Chris fearing she would get shocked. Awestruck, I waited. When it was over I just knew I was healed! My physical strength miraculously returned. We both just sat there for a long time, overwhelmed by what our awesome God had done to overcome this huge physical challenge.

A 12,000-KILOMETER (6,214-MILE) DRIVE TO OUR WEDDING

"Oh, Antoine, this time only your spirit has come!" Our dear German pastor and mission coworker was a bit shocked when he picked me up at the airport in Frankfurt, Germany.

"Du bist nur noch ein Strich in der Landschaft!" (You are just a line in the landscape!), he added in dismay. He was right. My physical appearance had diminished a lot after a year in Asia and my battle with malaria. I told him what had happened and how God healed me. His precious wife was even more concerned about my pathetic condition. Immediately she started to make up for all the weight loss by fattening me up with her specialty: French fries and fried chicken. Not too healthy but it helped a lot.

Time went by fast with translating and recording the German text for the *Super 8* film we had made about our ministry in Asia. We showed it in many churches in Germany, motivating many believers to pray for and support our work. It was an intense time of traveling and meeting people, but it was worth the hard work. As the years went by, the body of Christ in Germany became a true blessing for the emerging church in Asia.

During a short stay in the Netherlands, we had a nice surprise. A nice, young Dutch couple whom I knew from my time with the Jesus People decided to join our ministry. The wife was German but spoke Dutch fluently. They were an answer to prayer because I needed an extra driver to help me drive a vehicle overland to India after the meetings were over. My dear parents were delighted to hear I was planning to get married upon my arrival back in India. They apologized for not being able to come due to their age. Instead they decided to buy and pay for our wedding rings, which was another answer to prayer.

In Munich, Germany, we bought a secondhand van with the funds we had raised in Germany, as well as equipment needed for the ministry in Asia. Getting a Carnet de Passage (a sort of passport for the vehicle in my name to cross through all the countries on the way to India) was a lot of paperwork. While getting it done we stayed with an elderly Christian lady in her beautiful home shaded by trees near the Inn river. She was a real blessing. We could always count on her accommodating and feeding any of our team at any time, even when we came unannounced. In her desire to show hospitality to the servants of her Lord Jesus Christ, she never complained about anything. She gladly did what the apostle Paul told the church in Rome to do.

**"Share with the Lord's people who are in need.
Practice hospitality." (Rom. 12:13 NKJV)**

As soon as I arrived from Germany, our team's skilled mechanics in Italy started a complete overhaul of the vehicle. All vital parts and the chassis were checked and, if necessary, renewed or welded. The complete body of the van was repaired and newly painted. Extra headlights and spotlights were added to the front of the vehicle to cope with the challenges of driving in Asia. It was a delivery van with a large, open cargo space in the back. This was going to be my third time driving the long, difficult trip overland. The previous experiences had given me a good idea of how to make best use of such cargo space.

By dismantling the side covering, the inner steel-chassis was laid bare, providing a strong support base for a long row of sturdy, wooden horizontal beams from the back to the front. On top of these beams, two thick, foam mattresses were laid to provide for a relatively comfortable place for two persons to sleep. This made the vehicle look a bit like a holiday camper. Below the beams there remained about two-thirds of the cargo space to store lots of equipment and supplies needed for the teams in Asia. From the outside it was hard to estimate how much stuff was stored beneath the beams. This was important because at each border crossing, nosy customs officers could possibly check the inside of the vehicle and give us a lot of trouble about the items we were transporting.

While all this was being done I visited some Italian churches to share about our ministry in Asia and to raise more funds for the trip. This was not very hard to do in compassionate Italy. Brought to tears by the stories of physically and spiritually starving parents and their bambini in Asia, the Italian believers, themselves quite poor, would gladly bring their sacrificial offerings. This touched me and taught me a lot. When by God's grace we learn to overcome our need for self-preservation, we are ready to give liberally with joyful and thankful hearts.

Our wedding date was set for December 14, 1981, in the city of Ahmedabad in the state of Gujarat, India. My parents had already engraved this wedding date on the inside of the wedding rings, which I carried on me. A large, evangelistic open-air meeting was planned there by our team. During one of the evening meetings our wedding was to take place. It would take about three weeks to drive to India. Time was ticking by, so I was eager to get going with my two Dutch companions.

Finally, after five years of communicating mainly in English or German, it was a special treat to be on the way with my own people and speaking my own language for a while. In the truck, the space underneath the bed was stuffed with equipment for the team and supplies for the long overland trip through Greece, Turkey, Iran and Pakistan to India. Very well-meaning Italian believers, convinced that we might starve to death in Asia, also brought big bags of Italian pasta to help us survive. Rather grudgingly, I squeezed them in. Large barrels were filled with extra diesel to keep us driving where no diesel would be available.

This was very necessary. The bloody war between Iran and Iraq was in its second year. In September 1981, a stalemate between the warring parties came to an end. Since then the Iranians had launched a series of successful offensives driving the Iraqi army back. Diesel, normally dirt-cheap in Iran, was heavily rationed because of the war and often not available. This made driving overland even more of a challenge. Just driving through Iran meant covering an uncomfortable and unsafe distance of about 2,400 kilometers (1,500 miles) in a country at war.

Passing borders was particularly nerve-wracking. We prayed a lot for the eyes of border guards to be blinded so they would not check us too much. All borders in Greece, Turkey, Iran and Pakistan were crossed without much questioning. At one border, the guards asked us to open the back of the truck. We tried hard but could only open a crack in the door. Something was stuck. Peeping through the crack, we noticed a big bag of pasta prevented the door from opening. The border guard soon lost interest and waved us on. I was suddenly very grateful for all that pasta!

A big problem awaited us at the last and famous Wagah-Attari border. After a long, hot dusty drive and brief visit to our team in Lahore, Pakistan, we said goodbye and proceeded to the nearby border between Pakistan and India. The Pakistani side of the border is named after the village of Wagah. Attari is the name of the village on the Indian side. At this border, the lowering of the flags ceremony takes place each evening before sunset. It is a daily show-like practice that the Border Security Forces of India and the Pakistan Rangers have jointly kept up since 1959.

The marching soldiers perform elaborate and rapid, dance-like maneuvers, raising their legs as high as possible. It is a symbol of the two countries' rivalry. At the same time also a vague display of brotherhood and an attempt to show cooperation between the two nations. At one point, a single soldier from each country high-step strides right up to the border—like two proud roosters. Shaking hands, they turn around briskly to take off in the opposite direction. All of this is cheered on loudly by thousands of Indians, Pakistanis and the handful of foreign tourists who daily attend this event on public stands at both sides of the border.

Passing this border by day, this time we unfortunately missed this spectacle. The Pakistani side was crossed uneventfully. We had almost made it through. Just one more border left before entering into India. The Indian border guards did not bother us, but the Indian customs officers had their own kind of spectacle in store for us. We were told to drive the van under some trees, shading us from the burning sun.

"Open up the back of the truck!" ordered one of the customs officers dressed in a khaki uniform with his well-fed belly bulging over his broad brown belt. My heart sank. One by one we slowly started to take out some of our baggage. They insisted on checking out more.

"What is behind that stuff there?"

Now I was getting nervous. Halfway hidden was all the equipment we needed for our open-air public meetings in India. Of course, I could not tell them that. They discovered different boxes and packages.

"Take out these boxes and lay them on the ground outside the vehicle!"

"What do you need this for and where are you taking all of this?" one of them wanted to know while taking much time opening each box to examine its contents. It required a quick and good excuse to answer this question without getting into trouble.

"We are traveling through India on the way to Sri Lanka," I quickly answered. This was not a lie. After reaching the team in India and unloading the vehicle, I would get married. My Indian tourist visa was valid for six months. Afterward, I would have to take the vehicle to Sri Lanka. This was the original plan.

"In that case, we have to wrap all these boxes in burlap bags and seal them with our official custom seals," the man in khaki explained very businesslike.

"What . . . ?" I exclaimed in desperation. Unimpressed he continued.

"After presenting them to the customs officers on the other side of India, before leaving for Sri Lanka, you are free to take them with you from there." The whole process of packing and sealing would "just take a couple of days," I was told. My frustration was mounting, but I tried to conceal it knowing that getting upset at them would make matters worse. I tried out another trump card.

"Sir," I pleaded, "I am on my way to get married in India on December 14. Due to this delay, I might miss my own wedding.

Would it be possible to shorten the process a bit?" Indian weddings are celebrated extravagantly and at great length. For the bridegroom not to show up in time was a no-go. Wagging his head slowly from left to right and back the way Indians do, he tried to encourage me:

"Definitely. Don't worry, sir . . . we will try our best to get you out of here in time."

This did not quite comfort me. Previous experiences had taught me "don't worry" usually meant it was time to start worrying. As the saying goes: foreigners have watches but Asians have time. Why worry if you have time? It proved true this time as well. Under the watchful eyes of khaki-clad officials comfortably seated on chairs, some skinny, poor daily laborers were put to work. While squatted, with elaborate movements of their hands, they slowly sewed burlap bags on each of our boxes. When finished, each box was sealed with an official red wax, custom seal. All of this took three long days. It seemed like three weeks to me. My level of patience was utterly tested, and I was only able to overcome by remembering what the Word of God says about trials.

> "Consider it pure joy, my brothers and sisters,
> whenever you face trials of many kinds, because
> you know that the testing of your faith produces
> perseverance. Let perseverance finish its work
> so that you may be mature and complete,
> not lacking anything." (James 1:2–4 NKJV)

As soon as this ordeal was finally over, we jumped in our van to continue our way as fast as we could down the Grand Trunk Road (GTR). The GTR road is an important 2500-year-old trade route stretching 2,400 kilometers (1,500 miles) between Pakistan, India and Bangladesh, still used today. Our first stop was New Delhi, the sprawling overcrowded capital of India. In a high-rise apartment we met and stayed with a precious Indian sister, a widow. She always accommodated whoever passed by from our team.

"I received a telegraph message for you," she immediately told me while offering us refreshing, cool glasses of water. These were still the slow days of telegraph messages, a method of sending and receiving messages by electric signals and printed out on paper. In the hope of it being a message from my fiancé, Chris, I nervously opened the envelope. It read:

"Wedding Ahmedabad canceled . . . Stop . . . Team moved to Kurnool, Karnataka . . . Stop . . . Come soon . . . Stop . . . Chris . . . Stop."

"Oh no!" I groaned and just could not believe it. My fiancé, Chris, had worked so hard to organize the wedding to take place during an open-air meeting in the city of Ahmedabad in the state of Gujarat, India. Her lovingly designed wedding cards proclaiming Ahmedabad as the venue were now obsolete. Much later I found out that deadly communal riots between Hindus and Muslims had forced the team to find another location. However, the distance between Delhi to Kurnool by road is another 1,794 kilometers (1,115 miles), and we had already driven more than 9,656 kilometers (6,000 miles) to get this far. Facing another trial of faith, I had a hard time "considering it all joy."

There was no other option but to "let perseverance finish its work in order to become mature and complete, not lacking anything" as the Scripture above says. Patience, a much-needed fruit of the Holy Spirit, in general, and especially while working in Asia, is sometimes the only way to overcome frustration.

Without much delay we hit the road again. My Dutch friends were very helpful driving the vehicle and standing with me in these trials. In Pakistan and India, vehicles drive on the left side of the road. Our left-hand drive vehicle made driving on the two-way highways very intense. The constant heat causes a driver to feel very drowsy. Our vehicle did not have the luxury of air conditioning. On the crowded roads, elaborately painted trucks, the occasional private car or taxi, rikshaws, motorbikes all bellowed out choking exhaust fumes. In addition, ox cars, bicycles, people of all walks of life, camels, water buffalos, goats and a few elephants were all competing for space and attention.

Luckily 24/7 tea stalls located underneath shady trees could be found all along those roads. Sturdy, wooden, woven beds cushioned with cotton mattresses invited the weary traveler to take some well-deserved rest. Invigorating, strong special chai was served in small clay cups. Delicious vegetable samosas and other Indian finger food were available night and day.

For driving at night, we were well equipped. As darkness fell, which happens early and quickly in Asia, the usual light flashing competition started. Trucks and buses in India are road bullies. During the day their loud horns and sheer weight help push everything else aside. At night while speeding in the middle of the road they flash their main lights off and on continually to blind, intimidate and chase opposite traffic off the road. Our strategy was simple. In Italy our mechanics had installed a second set of very strong flood lights on the top of our van. When an opposite truck flashed its lights, we first flashed our normal main lights in return. When that did not help and they came closer, we drowned them with our overwhelming flood lights! This caused the on-coming truck driver to see absolutely nothing. At once they had to slow down and move to the side. It was a very effective secret weapon—and lots of fun to use it and see the reaction.

My excitement increased as we finally approached the city of Kurnool. After all this travel I would finally see my beautiful bride-to-be! In order to find out where the team was, we just had to ask for the location of the Christian colony in that city. The team members met us with great joy.

"Where is my fiancé, Chris?" was my first question.

"She is gone; she went to Bombay to pick up her parents who are coming to attend the wedding," came the unexpected answer. Once again my heart sank. Bombay is located more than 800 kilometers (497 miles) from Kurnool.

"When will she be back?" I asked impatiently while trying to hide my discouragement.

"We don't know, exactly. She was supposed to be here already." That was not very helpful.

One of the older sisters knew Chris had planned to arrive by train in the city of Hyderabad about 200 kilometers (124 miles) away from Kurnool. Although very tired, I was not going to be stopped from driving there at once. Love never gives up, never loses faith, is always hopeful, and endures through every circumstance. True love overcomes any distance!

"Love is patient and kind. Love is not jealous or boastful or proud or rude. It does not demand its own way. It is not irritable, and it keeps no record of being wronged. It does not rejoice about injustice but rejoices whenever the truth wins out. Love never gives up, never loses faith, is always hopeful, and endures through every circumstance." (1 Cor. 13:4–7 NLT)

Accompanied by that sister, I took off into another long night of driving. In between, we only stopped briefly for much-needed tea breaks to help keep us awake. Early in the morning we arrived in Hyderabad and drove straight to the main train station. Leaving the sister behind to watch the parked van, I started walking up toward the entrance. All of a sudden I heard a female voice shout: "Stop!" A nearby rikshaw came to a screeching halt. A wildly gesticulating white woman dressed up in a shalwar kameez jumped out of the rikshaw and ran up to me. It was my fiancé, Chris! Leaving her poor father, surrounded by clamoring coolies, to watch over the luggage alone at the train station, she and her mother had taken off to arrange a bus ticket to Kurnool.

Immediately a huge load of worries and anxiety fell off both our shoulders. Hugging my beloved wife-to-be, I knew everything was all right now. Finally we were together again!

Chris had her own story to tell. Deciding not even to try to explain to her parents that the wedding was changed from one side of India to the other, she simply telegrammed them: "Don't fly on to Gujarat. I'll pick you up in Bombay." On the way from the U.S. to India, her parents had stopped by missionary relatives stationed in Africa. From there they were scheduled to fly on to India. The plane landed in Bombay, the passengers got out, but no parents! They were not on the flight. Chris had absolutely no way to contact them or to find out what happened. As it turned out, they had missed their flight on that side. So the only thing to do was to find out when the next flight from Addis Ababa would arrive. A time was given. So the next day at that time she came roaring up to the airport in a rickshaw.

Already outside the airport, she suddenly spied a crowd on the sidewalk. To her dismay, in the middle were her forlorn and desperate parents surrounded by a swarm of coolies. They had been standing with their luggage on the sidewalk waiting there for hours! Her parents were courageous Mennonite ministers and very humble and pleasant folks to be around. For the first time I finally met them and they were also eager to get to know their new son-in-law. Soon we were all on the way back to Kurnool. Although we had not slept at all there was no more time to lose as the wedding was to take place the next day.

AN EXTRAORDINARY INDIAN WEDDING

My desire had been to marry in a place where people would hear the gospel and get saved. The best place and time for that to happen was in one of our open-air meetings which our team had organized in the city of Kurnool. On the fifteenth of December

1981, amazingly only a day later than planned, our wedding finally took place. A crowd of about six thousand people gathered on the meeting grounds for the evening meeting. The bride and groom, Chris' parents, my sister and her husband, who had joined the team in Sri Lanka, were all there. Together with the best men and women, some Indian and foreign team members, we all arrived at the back of the meeting in the team bus.

Dusk had set in as my beautiful bride, Chris, adorned in a snow-white Indian sari and accompanied by her father, walked down the long aisle being watched by thousands of curious Indian eyes. While accompanying her mother, dressed in a sari as well, I noticed she was quite nervous. A sari commonly worn by married Indian women is a very long strip of cloth that women wrap around their body. With more than five thousand years of existence, the Indian sari is considered to be among the oldest form of garment in the world still in existence. Later on I found out that Chris´ mother was very concerned about her sari. Wearing such a thing for the first time, she was terribly afraid it would suddenly unravel and drop down to the ground while she walked through that crowd. Fortunately, this did not happen.

The team band led the worship, a team leader preached a short message on marriage, we exchanged wedding vows and put on our wedding rings. Afterward, we cut a simple cake and enjoyed some finger food with our team. Indian weddings can last a whole week and are very expensive because the whole village must be fed as well. To avoid going bankrupt, we had informed the crowd that this was a foreign wedding where this was not the case. To be honest I was suffering from quite a bad headache on my wedding day. The stress from all the weeks past took its toll.

Nonetheless my heart was jubilant, and I was eager to start this new chapter in my life. Chris had tried to figure out how to get legally married in India. The local district police chief, who as special guests attended the wedding with his wife, had assured Chris,

"Why, don't worry, of course you can get married here."

Afterward, we were handed some document, but we had a funny feeling about all this assurance. In India people get married according to their religious affiliation. The Hindu priest, the Muslim Iman or the Christian reverend, pastor or priest must perform wedding rituals and sign the marriage certificate. Two foreigners getting married in India was obviously an unprecedented case, at least in Kurnool. This officer had promised us that these papers from a public notary would be enough. The same police chief was so kind to offer us the use of the local government guest house to spend our wedding night which we gladly accepted. Normally such accommodation is only reserved for visiting high government officials. Our heavenly Father made us feel honored and special. After all, Jesus is the King of Kings, and we are His royal family members. We spent two days alone in that nicely furnished government guesthouse. The second day we decided to take a walk along a small canal near the guesthouse. Far away we saw something floating in the water. A man was standing nearby looking down at it. Coming a bit closer, we found out it was the bloated body of somebody who had drowned there some time ago. Some things one never gets used to in India!

We were quite poor and apart from each other, our passports, our Bibles, a few clothes and our wedding rings, we owned absolutely nothing. A nice apartment or furnished home filled with modern appliances and comforts to call our own were not waiting for us to start our married life. The van was our home for now. It had a thick mattress in the back, so at least we had had a place to sleep. Chris' parents had brought us a wedding gift of one-thousand U.S. dollars. Because I was responsible for the Indian team, we decided to use this amount to buy new tires for their bus. The old tires were completely worn out, and it was dangerous for the team to keep on using them.

Since we had to take Chris' parents back to Bombay for their flight home, we planned to buy the bus tires there and transport them back to the team afterwards. We took our time to get there, showing our beloved India to our parents. At night Chris and I slept outside on the rack on top of our "mobile home" and her parents slept on the mattress inside. In Bombay we also had to visit the American embassy to find out about the validity of the marriage document. Unfortunately, the lady shook her head,

"Sorry but we can't accept these papers!"

Fact was we were not yet legally married. We got our bus tires, but as far as marriage, we were back to zero. So what now? For the first time simple faith to overcome an urgent practical problem was required from the two of us as a couple.

" . . . for everyone born of God overcomes the world! This is the victory that has overcome the world, even our faith." (1 John 5:4 NKJV)

The van was registered in my name, and we had to take it to the team in Sri Lanka. This meant we both had to go there because now we were married though not yet legally. Until the day we got married, we had not spent much time together, so we were looking forward to coming to know each other better on this trip. We drove to the coastal town of Rameshwaram, which at that time was only a small, sand-blown sleepy town. It had two main towering temples and was situated on the Pamban Island in the Tamil Nadu state of India. According to Hinduism, Lord Rama built a bridge starting from Rameshwaram right up to Sri Lanka to wage a war against Ravana, the king of Lanka. This king had abducted Rama's consort Sita, mother goddess of beauty and devotion.

When we arrived there we could not find any such bridge to cross over to Sri Lanka. Instead there was a ferry which crossed over to Sri Lanka, only at certain times. But, due to stormy weather, all ferry crossings had been canceled so we were forced to wait for better weather. This frustrated us at first but then we realized God had a wonderful plan for us. As dedicated and long-suffering disciples, the idea of taking time for a honeymoon had not even crossed our minds. The ways of God and the mind of God were obviously higher than our ways.

After finishing our evening meal in the restaurant of a small guesthouse near the beach, the kind owner allowed us to park our "mobile home" on his property. We could stay there as long as needed provided we would take our meals there. This way we ended up celebrating a wondrous two-week, God-given honeymoon. The days flew by sleeping, eating and walking along endless, mostly deserted beaches. Time for praying, talking, reading God's Word, resting, laughing, enjoying each other's presence and God's creation. God is so good!

Hoisting our "mobile home" on top of the deck of the ferry was another adventure. Once it was safely done, we sailed to Mannar Island on the northern tip of Sri Lanka where the vehicle was hoisted down on the quay without any damage. Entry formalities were done at Talaimannar and off we were for a six-hour slow drive through arid areas and lush tropical forests. We had to cover the 325 kilometers (200 miles) to Colombo, the capital of Sri Lanka, where our team base was located.

Sometime soon after, while walking through crowded downtown Colombo, we suddenly noticed a rickety old red sign with the golden letters: "Register of Marriages" in the midst of a row of shops.

"Do you see what I see?!"

"Let's go in and check it out," Chris answered.

The wooden door underneath the sign opened to a very narrow kind of shop. Half-blinded by the bright sunlight outside, we peered into the darkness inside. All the way at the end of the shop stood a small, wooden table. A man half-asleep on a chair behind the table seemed to notice us now.

"Come on in!" He was happy to have something to do. We ventured inside, and walking up to the table, we came to the point immediately.

"We want to get married. Can we do that here?"

"Yes, why not? I am the registrar of marriages." Opening a drawer, he pulled out some very long forms.

"We have to fill out these forms, but first I have to marry you," he said lighting up a cigarette. We looked at each other in disbelief . . .

"Do you want to marry this woman or not?" he asked impatiently.

"Yes," I answered. He nodded approvingly.

"We need two witnesses," he said.

Walking up to a side door, he went in and pulled out a woman.

"Now we have two witnesses, me and this woman."

That problem was quickly overcome! He looked up to me with his cigarette dangling from his mouth and asked:

"Do you want to take this woman as your wife?"

"Of course, why not? I love her!" I answered jokingly. Impressed by my answer, he exhaled a huge cloud of smoke. Turning to Chris he asked:

"Do you want to take this man as your husband?"

"Yes!" she said softly but firmly.

"Now you both are married, and we can fill out these forms with triple carbon copies."

That was it. We signed the documents, paid twenty-five U.S. dollars and thanked the registrar of marriages for his kind and hopefully helpful cooperation. Stumbling over each other trying to get out of the narrow building, we spilled out onto the busy street. Looking at the three marriage certificates in our hands, one Sinhala, one Tamil and one English copy, big question marks hovered over our heads.

Could this be too good to be true?

"We gotta go straight to the American embassy with this," Chris declared. To our great surprise and delight, the next day at the American embassy our marriage certificate was accepted! The next step was to do the same thing at the Dutch embassy where it was accepted as well. Now it was official. By faith in God and trust in His divine guidance, we had overcome this challenge and were finally legally married on January 18, 1982!

DIVINE APPOINTMENTS AND OPPOSITION

"No, in all these things we are *more than conquerors* through him who loved us."

(Rom. 8:37 NKJV, author's emphasis)

22
DIVINE
APPOINTMENTS

It was one of those hot, dry days in the city of Jaipur in the desert state of Rajasthan, India, where Chris and I were ministering with our all-Indian team. As a couple we were accommodated at the home of a local pastor where a sister from Australia happened to visit as well. She walked into the living room where we were relaxing and said:

"I have a word from the Lord for you. Do you mind if I tell you what He is saying to you?"

"Yes, of course. Go ahead!" we answered, taken a bit by surprise.

"The Lord gave me a vision and its explanation about how God is going to use you. In that vision, I saw a two-pronged winnowing fork in the hand of God. Like this winnowing fork, you both are going to be used to throw up the wheat in the air so the chaff will be separated from the wheat," she shared briefly.

Before we could respond she walked out again. Looking at each other, we wondered how this vision and these words would be worked out and come to pass in our lives. John the Baptist, the waymaker for the Lord Jesus Christ, prophesied the following words about the One who would come after him:

> **"His winnowing fork is in his hand, and he will clear his threshing floor, gathering his wheat into the barn and burning up the chaff with unquenchable fire." (Matt. 3:12 NKJV)**

The best way to make sure whether a vision or prophecy is true is to find out whether it is in line with the Bible and to wait until it is fulfilled. God is interested in wheat, not chaff. It was clear the Lord was speaking to us about His Harvest and the need to separate the wheat from the chaff. But how was He going to use us as His winnowing fork? And what about this burning up of the chaff? Soon we would find out how and why.

MEETING MY LOOKALIKE

Bombay, which is now called Mumbai, was the metropolitan city where I had to go once in a while to cash the support check for our all-Indian team. Traveling there and back on long, second-class train rides was a part of the procedure. Upon leaving the bank, I stuffed a large heap of rupee bank notes into an ordinary plastic bag. A briefcase would have drawn undesired attention from potential pickpockets. Chris accompanied me this time as we checked into a well-known Christian guesthouse. We were very tired and in need of a washing up after all the dusty and sweaty traveling.

Refreshed, we walked into the cozy, communal dining room afterward. A small company of foreigners was already seated around the dining table, chatting away before the meal was served. We sat down and listened to the conversations. A young man on the far-right side of the long table drew my attention. He was busy talking to somebody opposite the table. He looked very much like me. I poked Chris' arm and nodded in his direction to find out if she noticed what I saw.

"We were shooting a movie on the beach in Japan." I overheard him saying. No doubt now.

"It can only be Tom Alter, the foreigner acting in Hindi movies who looks so much like me that people all over India mistake me for him," I whispered near Chris' ear. She nodded in agreement.

It is very strange and awkward to meet somebody who looks

just like yourself. It's like looking into a mirror and seeing your image become flesh and alive right in front of you. My heart started to beat faster. All this time I had been praying to meet him one day to tell him what God had spoken to me about him. Now this day had come, but it made me a bit nervous.

"Excuse me. You must be Tom Alter, right?" I asked him after most other guests had left the room. He stopped his conversation and turned to me in surprise.

"Yes, why and how do you know about me?"

"You cause me a lot of trouble. Everywhere I travel in India people mistake me for Tom Alter, and they refuse to believe me when I insist I am not!" Noticing our similarity, his eyes lit up and he seemed pleased and proud to hear it. We struck up a lively conversation about the funny situations I experienced as his lookalike.

"Every encounter ended up in a wonderful opportunity for me to share the good news about the Lord Jesus Christ, for which I am very grateful," I shared. Tom's parents were Presbyterian missionaries in India where he was raised in the Indian culture and had learned to speak fluent Hindi.

"Dear, Tom, I have a word from the Lord for you," I finally said. "Are you willing to receive it?"

"Sure!" he answered not knowing what to expect.

"Ever since I came to know about you and your popularity as a foreign actor in Hindi movies, I started to wonder why God had called me to India. I was not born in India, not used to the heat, a stranger to the local culture and unable to speak Hindi. You were raised in a Christian missionary family in India, are used to the culture and climate and speak Hindi fluently. So why are you who looks like me not sharing the gospel in this country instead of me? God told me to ask you this question whenever I would meet you."

A shadow passed over his face as he pondered this question

for a while. "Guess you are right," he admitted sadly. He went on and shared how he was going through quite a difficult time in his life. His father had just died and his career in the movie business was going downhill. I tried to console and encourage him to make the right choice in his life. I never met him again and left the result up to God.

> "What do you think? There was a man who had two sons. He went to the first and said, 'Son, go and work today in the vineyard.' 'I will not,' he answered, but later he changed his mind and went. Then the father went to the other son and said the same thing. He answered, 'I will, sir,' but he did not go. 'Which of the two did what his father wanted?' 'The first,' they answered. Jesus said to them, 'Truly I tell you, the tax collectors and the prostitutes are entering the kingdom of God ahead of you.'"
> (Matt. 21:28-31 NKJV)

A Divine Appointment is an unexpected leading by the Holy Spirit in order to accomplish God's purpose in a person's life or situation. It involves a meeting with another individual that God has specifically and unmistakably arranged. The Holy Spirit sets up such encounters because someone needs what He can offer them through you. It takes quite a bit of faith and discipline to overcome doubt and obey and act upon such urging of God's Spirit.

FLIGHT DELAY WITH A PURPOSE

My flight from India was delayed. Once a year I would fly back to Europe to conduct our annual fundraising meetings in Germany and the Netherlands. Long distance flying can be a tedious and tiring business. Because of the different time zones, most flights take place at very odd times. In the eighties we were at least spared the ordeal of the extensive security checks of today. Flight delays have always been common and bothersome but sometimes they serve a special purpose. Having to wait out an especially long delay, I had to stay overnight. Food and drinks were offered at one of the restaurants at the airport. An almost empty table in a far corner looked like a good place to have my meal in peace. Only one man was seated on the opposite site of the table. Immediately he started chatting away about the delay and a whole bunch of other matters. After some time, I started to pray in the Spirit for an opening to share the gospel with this person.

"Unclean spirit!" All of a sudden the Holy Spirit spoke these penetrating words into my spirit about him. "Lord, I do not know this man, how am I supposed to say this to him?" I pleaded with God. Desperately I looked around. Secretly I hoped somebody else would join us at the table so I would have an excuse not to bring up this embarrassing subject. Nobody showed up. The urging of the Holy Spirit increased. There was no way out now. My companion was still jabbering away so I had to interrupt him.

"Sorry, God just spoke to me and gave me an impression about your life. Are you willing to hear what He is saying?" He paused abruptly. Looking at me with great surprise, he said.

"Yes, what is it?"

"God told me you have a problem with immorality, and He wants to set you free!"

It struck him like a hammer.

"H . . . h . . . how do you know this?" he stammered when he had halfway gathered himself.

"I am a servant of the living God and He knows everything."

He rose behind the table.

"Come with me to my room. I want to tell you something!"

This idea did not quite appeal to me. Wild thoughts like falling into the fangs of a serial killer, mass murderer or sex offender crossed my mind. Who knows what he had done and could do to me once I would be alone with him in his room?

"Get up and go with him!" the Holy Spirit urged me.

Reluctantly I followed him into his room. Ready to run, I made sure the door was right behind me and not locked.

"You are right," he sat down on his bed and started pouring out his heart to me, a complete stranger.

"Yes, I have a big problem with immorality, and it is destroying my life." He seemed very eager to finally being able to talk to somebody about this dark side of his life.

"I am an Indian citizen, but I live abroad now. It all started out like this . . ." He then told me as a young man he had molested and raped a young girl in a rice field. Nobody found out so he was able to hide his terrible secret. However, he was haunted from that day on by unclean thoughts and immoral deeds, which only got worse when he moved abroad. He cheated on his wife and much more than that. He had wanted to change his life, but he was not able to do it. All of these things and more he confessed.

"Freedom and forgiveness starts with confession and repentance, so turn away from these things; do not sin anymore and God will set you free," I shared. He was very relieved and thankful God sent me into his life. Thanks to God who had given me the grace to overcome my fear and obey the prompting of the Holy Spirit to help save a life. Jesus came to seek and to save what is lost.

"When they kept on questioning him, he straightened up and said to them, 'Let any one of you who is without sin be the first to throw a stone at her.'" (John 8:7 NKJV)

TICKET COUNTER ENCOUNTER

We were all standing in line at the ticket counter at Delhi airport on the way home from a blessed time of ministry in India. A young Dutch couple had accompanied me there. Both were former drug addicts whose lives had been transformed by the power of the gospel. All foreigners waited neatly and patiently for their turn at the counter. Local passengers, however, did not seem to notice any waiting line. As usual they started to push forward toward the ticket counter from all directions. Turning toward a surprised, young foreign lady traveler standing behind me I said:

"Do you know why they do that?"

"No, why?" she asked.

"They believe all ways lead to God as well as the ticket counter," I answered jokingly.

She laughed heartily and at once we entered into a lively conversation about spiritual and cultural matters in Asia. After finally finishing our business at the ticket counter, we all sat down waiting for our flight to London. She was a practicing Buddhist for ten years and had just come back from one of many trips to Buddhist temples and holy places in Tibet. She had to make countless exhausting prostrations, clockwise around Buddhist monuments, keeping the temples to her right. This was meant to bring her great religious merit. But now she was very tired of all of this. All three of us shared with her about our experiences with the Lord Jesus Christ.

For about an hour she listened eagerly to our stories and was very touched by what she had heard from us. When we entered the plane for a night flight, I suggested we could meet at the end of the flight. Next morning, I found her all the way in the back of the plane seated in the last row. The seat next to her was empty so I asked her if I could join her there.

"Did you think about what we told you yesterday?" I asked.

"Think about it! I did not sleep the whole night thinking about it!" While bursting into tears she admitted, sadly, "I looked for truth everywhere except for Jesus. I have never given Him a chance in my life."

"Well that can change today!" I encouraged her to start following Jesus. She left the plane a much happier person.

"Jesus answered, 'I am the way and the truth and the life. No one comes to the Father except through me.'" (John 14:6 NKJV)

REACHING THE UNREACHED

As I happened to look out of the window in a small church in one of the 664,369 villages in India, I noticed a group of Adiwasis. Adiwasis are local tribal people who are traditionally organized in small communities. Some distance from the church, they were all squatted in the heat around a rectangular box covered with a cloth. Their colorful tribal clothes were faded and worn out. The uncombed hair of their women hung loosely over their shoulders. Turning to the pastor of the church, I asked him who these people were. He only knew they were Adiwasis.

"Did you ever try to tell them about Jesus?" I asked him. The answer was negative. "Why not?" He shrugged his shoulders.

"Then I will go and meet them!"

When I stepped out of the church my eyes were blinded by the bright sunlight and the heat enveloped me like a cloak. Slowly I walked up to them. All of a sudden an older man hastily stood up and rushed away from the scene toward the bushes. He must be frightened seeing a white man for the first time in his life, I thought. A younger man also stood up but acted friendly when I greeted him with *namaste*—the Indian salutation of respect and reverence. A traditional Indian greeting, it literally means "I bow to you."

After a short conversation he accepted my invitation to have a talk in the much cooler church building. The pastor kindly translated when I started to ask him about his belief system.

They were from a bird-hunting tribe, and the god they worshipped was hidden within the box they carried around. The old man who ran away was his father and also the tribal shaman.

"Where do you come from and what do you believe?" the young tribal man wanted to know.

While sharing the message of salvation in a very simple way, I could see his eyes light up. He was very curious and asked lots of good questions about the reason why Jesus had come to this earth. After about an hour of answering his questions, I asked him whether he would like to meet Jesus personally. He was very surprised and delighted about this offer. By then he had realized he was a sinner in need of forgiveness and salvation.

"We can ask the Lord Jesus to come into your heart when you repent of your sins," I told him. He was immediately ready to do that, bowed his head and prayed the sinner's prayer with us. When he opened his eyes, his faced beamed with a newfound heavenly joy. Then he started a conversation I will never forget.

"How long do the people in your country know about this wonderful way of salvation?"

"Since a long time; about thirteen hundred years ago," I answered.

"Around the year 690 after Jesus was born, an English monk named Wilibrord, along with twelve companions, crossed the North Sea to bring the gospel for the first time to my country, the Netherlands." Looking at me with sadness in his bright, brown eyes, he asked:

"Then why did it take so long for me and my people to hear about this good news?"

These words penetrated my heart like a sharp sword. I bowed my head in shame and sadness. I felt so bad that nobody had come earlier.

Jesus told his disciples to go and make disciples of all nations more than two thousand years ago. How much more our King and Savior Jesus Christ must be grieving over all this delay! This divine encounter strongly motivated me to help overcome this huge challenge of reaching the unreached. From then on I committed myself to motivate others to go until all have heard. India is home to more than one-third of the unreached people groups in the world. There are over 1 billion people in India who don't know Jesus and 2,445 people groups in India that have never heard the good news.

> "How, then, can they call on the one they have not believed in? And how can they believe in the one of whom they have not heard? And how can they hear without someone preaching to them? And how can anyone preach unless they are sent? As it is written: 'How beautiful are the feet of those who bring good news!'"
> (Rom. 10:14–15 NKJV)

SAVING A LOST SHEEP

A Brahman preacher of the goddess Kalima wanted to commit suicide because as he said his god was not delivering him. He laid down on the railway tracks, but some people saw him and dragged him away before the train could kill him. They tried to take him to the temple, but he did not want to go there and was just sitting by the roadside. Our Indian team sisters passed by and tried to give him a tract, but he was angry and refused to take it. A bit later the sisters were on their way to a village meeting when their way was blocked because of too much rain. They took another route, which led them straight to the place where the Brahman was still sitting. The sisters asked their team leader to talk to him. Since they were on their way to the meeting, he told him to wait until they returned. They went on, but again the road was blocked forcing them to return. Then the Lord clearly spoke to the heart of the team leader:

"I want to save this lost sheep!!"

It shook his heart, but when he went to him, the Brahman would not listen. Finally the team leader convinced him to come to their house. While ministering to him, the Holy Spirit strongly fell upon the Brahman. He started to cry when he heard about the love of God for lost sinners and wanted to receive Jesus right then into his heart. Very convicted of his sins, he put away his holy book, tore off his holy thread and all kinds of rings. The peace of God filled his heart. That night he stayed, and the team continued to minister to him. The next day he got up and decided to go home to start his new ministry.

"As I did many things for false gods, now I want to do more than that for Jesus Christ," he said.

23
TROUBLE IN PARADISE

In the fall of 1982, on my fourth trip driving overland from Germany via Italy, Greece, Turkey, through the desert in parts of Iran and Pakistan to India, we broke our own record. Accompanied by a Swedish brother, we completed this tedious and exhausting trip within eleven days! We managed this feat by taking turns driving for two-hour stints continuously, only stopping to sleep from midnight until 4 a.m. During the two-hour stints, one of us would keep on driving. The other would try to "sleep" or rest on a thick mattress in the back of the van, swaying and shaking nonstop on bumpy roads. While driving through Iran, once more we experienced the oppressive atmosphere of fear in that country. Passing through towns and villages, we got a grim glimpse of the repression and arbitrariness of the Iranian regime. Covered by black, hooded cloaks, men stood on wooden platforms. Their hands were tied on their back and their heads bent down while undergoing public denunciations and awaiting execution. We were not eager to stay much longer than necessary in Iran.

A BASIJI IN IRAN

On the way from Tabriz in northwestern Iran, a small but sturdy man dressed in a shabby semi-military outfit waved us down. Most revolutionary guards, called Basiji, were dressed that way. Our vehicle screeched to a halt. Opening up the window, we asked what he wanted.

"Tehran!" he answered, a bit surprised to find out we were foreigners. Without waiting for an answer, he climbed up into our van. Plopping down into the passenger seat, he started scratching his unkept black beard. Nobody in Iran would oppose or contradict a Basiji. They were ruthless, volunteer paramilitary forces fighting alongside the national army during the Iran-Iraq war going on at that time. Iranian boys as young as twelve were recruited to join the Basiji. They used human-wave assaults, in which young boys at the cost of their lives walked across mine-ridden battlefields to clear them for the advancing army. Basiji also enforced the Sharia laws upon an unwilling nation. Now we were stuck with one of those Basiji for the 600-kilometer (373 mile) drive to the capital of Iran.

After some small talk in broken English, the Basiji realized his golden opportunity to win me, a foreign infidel or kafir for Islam. He did his best to promote all the qualities of his religion while I listened without interrupting him.

"Would you like to convert to Islam?" he finally asked me.

"Yes, I would like to convert to Islam . . . ," I said and paused for a moment to let it sink in. A victorious smile swept over his face.

" . . . but only if you can answer a question that I have for you." Fully convinced he would know the answer, he sat up straight in his seat.

"At the moment your country Iran is at war with your neighboring country Iraq."

"Yes, and Iran will win this war!" he exclaimed interrupting me.

"Now, in this holy war fought for Allah, Iranian Muslim soldiers and Iraqi Muslim soldiers on both sides are dying and thus become martyrs expecting to go to heaven." Before he could say anything, I continued.

"My question to you is: Who will go to heaven? The Iranian Muslim soldiers or the Iraqi ones?"

A great silence followed. Obviously my question had caught him totally off guard. "I cannot answer this question," he finally admitted, reluctantly.

Now it was my time to turn the tables on him.

"Would you like to know what the difference between Islam and Christianity is?" He agreed.

"Our Lord Jesus Christ did not require his followers to defend their faith by killing those who oppose Christianity. God is strong enough to defend himself. Jesus Christ, the son of God gave up his sinless life and died as a sacrifice for sinful mankind. Then he rose from the dead to save us from sin and give us eternal life." To my great surprise, he did not react negatively at all. He seemed to be puzzled and stayed pensive all the way to Tehran. A small seed of Truth was sowed into this religious Basiji mind.

SIR ATTENBOROUGH

After we finally arrived in New Delhi, the capital of India, we stopped at a five-star hotel just to have a quick cup of coffee and enjoy the air conditioning after all this stress. While relaxing, we were suddenly approached by a waiter who handed us a folded, white piece of paper.

We opened it and read a short message:

"Sir Attenborough wants to see you!" I looked up to the waiter, handed him the paper back and said:

"Tell Sir Attenborough we do not have time." Off he went. My Swedish companion who had been reading the local English newspaper was not amused.

"Don`t you know who Sir Attenborough is? He is a famous film producer; I just read he is currently shooting the film *Gandhi* in India!"

"Well, I am sorry, but who knows what he wants from us? Maybe he wants to use our vehicle or use us to act in his film. Our vehicle is loaded with supplies for the team, and they are waiting for us. You and I do not want to become actors, right?"

The English film director Richard Attenborough worked about twenty years on his film *Gandhi* about the life and death of Mahatma Gandhi. He was the leader of an Indian independence movement against the British Empire during the twentieth century. Gandhi was known for his stand on nonviolence and religious all-inclusiveness. The production of this film involved much effort and a budget of 22 million U.S. dollars. In 1982, this historically accurate film that won eight Oscars was shown in cinemas worldwide, earning about 128 million U.S. dollars. Maybe others would not have wanted to miss the chance to take part in such a high-profile undertaking. We, however, were not willing to get sidetracked. Focused on overcoming the challenges before us, we pressed forward toward the mark for the prize of our high calling of God in Christ Jesus.

> **"Brothers and sisters, I do not consider myself yet to have taken hold of it. But one thing I do: Forgetting what is behind and straining toward what is ahead, I press on toward the goal to win the prize for which God has called me heavenward in Christ Jesus."**
> **(Phil. 3:13–14 NKJV)**

WHEN YOU PASS
THROUGH THE WATERS

In the meantime our team was struggling financially. It was decided to sell a vehicle we had brought overland. The place to do that was Nepal. It was registered in my name, so I was asked to take the van there and meet up with one of our mechanics in Kathmandu, the capital of Nepal. That was easier said than done. First of all, to save money, I was asked to leave my sweetheart behind in Lahore, Pakistan, where we were located at the time. That proved to be a big mistake. I vividly remember looking at her through the back mirror. She was standing there by the roadside looking so sad and lonely. While driving away slowly, her figure became smaller and smaller. Finally she faded away from my view. We were true disciples and used to hardship and giving up our personal comfort or desires. However I was now newly married and still had to learn what being one with your wife really meant—and to say "no" if needed.

Secondly, I had to drive there all alone without a buddy, which we would normally not do. On the way to Nepal through the Ganges valley area in India, it started to rain lightly at night. The motor for the front window wipers was not working. Every drop on the window reflected the headlights of oncoming vehicles in a confusing explosion of warped light. On those unlit and narrow, two-lane country roads, this was a very dangerous situation. It became practically impossible to drive on. Somehow I made it through only to find myself the next morning at a wide river before crossing into Nepal. People told me there was no bridge, but another way to cross it was by ferry. Not the kind of ferry you may expect elsewhere. Basically, a very primitive raft made of thick tree trunks laid out in a rectangular square, tied together with ropes. It was not much wider or longer than my vehicle. Two boards were laid down from the riverbank unto the raft.

Wildly gesticulating Indians shouted instructions on how to get the vehicle onto the raft. There was a real chance the vehicle could fall off the boards if I drove over them too slowly. After praying a short prayer, I revved up the engine and took off. Luckily the vehicle made it over the boards onto the raft. Breaking out into cold sweat, I hit the brake to stop the vehicle just in time from going over the deep end. Scrambling quickly out of the cab, I made sure to stay behind the van in case the top-heavy raft would topple over while crossing the river. Indian muscle-power pushed the raft off the riverbank. Two oarsmen standing beside the vehicle started to row with all their might in the opposite direction against the current. Their aim was to get the raft to the middle of the fast-flowing river. Helped by the man at the rudder, they finally managed to get there. It was a crazy situation, and I feared the worst. From there on they let the swaying raft flow with the stream while steering and laboriously rowing it sideways toward the landing place on the opposite bank of the river. When we finally arrived there safely, the same procedure for unloading the truck was done there successfully. A heavy stone was lifted from my heart. Remembering the promises of the Word of God can be very helpful and encouraging to overcome practical obstacles on the way.

"When you pass through the waters, I will be with you; and when you pass through the rivers, they will not sweep over you. When you walk through the fire, you will not be burned; the flames will not set you ablaze." (Isa. 43:2 NKJV)

Driving through dense jungles and up the mountains, I reached Kathmandu, the capital of Nepal where our mechanic had been waiting for me. A very kind missionary family hosted us there. After I found out that the only way to sell the vehicle in Nepal was illegal, I refused to sell it. Of course this would mean the whole trip was done in vain. By phone the main team office in Sri Lanka had to be informed about this decision, which did not make them very happy. By now I was one of the main leaders of our team, so they had to accept it grudgingly. The decision was then made to drive the vehicle through India all the way to Sri Lanka where it could be used for the team. Our hosts had four very cute puppies and one of them was given to me for my two nieces in Sri Lanka. In the meantime, my sister and her husband had joined our team there. I was looking forward to seeing them and, of course, my wife, Chris. She had to travel all alone by train through the whole of India from Pakistan to Sri Lanka so that we could be together again.

GURKHA

Leaving the mountains in Nepal, we drove down winding roads into the deep Indian plains. It was the end of the dry season. The dry season normally lasts from December to June and the months of March until June are the hottest. The parched land, and all languishing nature and man were eagerly awaiting the showers from heaven. In the far distance dark, billowing rain clouds came slowly rolling our direction over the flat Indian countryside. An amazing and awesome sight. We parked the van by the roadside and waited for this huge curtain of rain to reach us. The sky darkened and everything around us held its breath. Coming down like bullets from the sky, the first drops hit the dry ground in explosions of dust. Torrential rain poured down on us, followed by a refreshing drop in temperature. We felt very dirty and dusty. There was no one to be seen, so we undressed to our underwear and jumped outside to enjoy a refreshing, natural shower outside next to our truck.

One evening we had stopped to take some rest and to let our little puppy out for a walk. Afterward, we tied him by a rope to the truck. All of a sudden our tiny puppy barked ferociously at something in the dark while tearing nonstop at his rope. There was nothing to be seen so we tried to calm him down. To make sure, I went behind the truck to check out the situation. Popping out of the darkness, a frightened guru, an Indian holy man, appeared. He was walking down the opposite side of the road, and our puppy had noticed him way in advance and wanted to protect us. Thereafter I named him Gurkha in honor of the courageous Nepali soldiers who fought fiercely on the side of the allied forces during World War I and World War II. After we arrived in Sri Lanka, Gurkha grew up to be a surprisingly big, hairy dog. Very protective to those he belonged to but quite aggressive to outsiders.

When I met a Dutch lady tourist on the beach near our team base in Sri Lanka, I found out his real identity. She saw me struggling with rebellious teenager Gurkha.

"Do you know what kind of dog this is?" she asked excitedly.

"No idea. He was given to me in Nepal," I answered.

"It is a Mastiff, one of the most aggressive dogs there is. In the Netherlands you are only allowed to let him out when he wears a mouth basket!"

The Tibet-Mastiff originates from Tibet where they call this ancient breed of shepherd dog *Do-Khyi*. It means as much as "a dog who needs to be chained up." The famous Greek poet Aristotle described the Tibet-Mastiff as follows ". . . Colossal bones, muscular, heavy with a huge head and wide snout . . ." A very accurate description of our Gurkha. Very kind to all he knew, especially team kids—but unpredictable to outsiders. At our team base in Mount Lavinia, a suburb of Colombo, capital of Sri Lanka, Gurkha's presence was a very effective deterrent to overcome the problem of petty thieves sneaking around homes most nights.

BLACK JULY 1983

Long before it all happened, an old lady shared an awful vision she had received from the Lord. She was a member in a small Pentecostal church in Jaffna, the main town in the North District of Sri Lanka inhabited by a mainly Tamil-speaking population. In that vision she saw their normally peaceful town full of blood—blood everywhere. Nobody believed that what she saw would actually come to pass. But decades of tension between the Sinhalese majority and the Tamil minority eventually culminated in hatred and boiled over in extreme violence.

After one of their leaders was killed by the Sri Lankan army, the Liberation Tigers of Tamil Eelam (LTTE) ambushed an army convoy on July 23, 1983, killing thirteen. News of fallen Sinhalese soldiers set off an anti-Tamil rampage in Colombo and elsewhere. Small mysterious markings started to appear on the homes of Hindu Tamils living among the Buddhist Sinhalese in Sri Lanka in July 1983. Then all hell broke loose.

From the evening of July 24, Sinhala mobs, armed with electoral rolls, targeted marked Tamil homes and businesses, looting, ransacking and burning property as well as the Tamil people inside. They were chased down the street with knives and burned alive in the streets, in vehicles and in their homes. Hundreds of women were raped. Tamil political prisoners locked up in a jail were also targeted as prison guards allowed Sinhala inmates to slaughter them. The army and elected officials did very little to stop it. Only a few Sinhalese Buddhists, Muslims and Christians managed to overcome evil by protecting some of their Tamil countrymen at the risk of their own lives.

"Do not be overcome by evil, but overcome evil with good." (Rom. 12:21 NKJV)

Our team members in Colombo and elsewhere in Sri Lanka—some of them Tamils themselves—became eyewitnesses to this pogrom-like attack which took place between July 24 to 29 in 1983. The team's landlord, a staunch Hindu Tamil, and his family were able to save their lives by fleeing into our office located on his property. More than five thousand Tamils were killed, about eighteen thousand homes and businesses destroyed. Altogether 150,000 Tamils lost their homes. It was a series of deliberate acts, executed in accordance with a concerted plan, conceived and organized well in advance. In the ensuing ethnic crisis, half a million Tamils left the country to seek refuge in India and countries worldwide. Other young surviving Tamils joined the LTTE to take revenge. As a result, beautiful tear-shaped Sri Lanka went through twenty-five years of bloody civil war. The urgency God gave me when I first visited Sri Lanka, and the awful vision of that old lady in Jaffna, had come to pass. Flames of hatred cannot easily be extinguished.

Needless to say, our ministry in Sri Lanka was deeply affected by all of this. We had used the time of freedom given to us. Our team there had worked hard during the past two-and-a-half years. Many young people were discipled, and the good news had been proclaimed in cities, towns and villages all over Sri Lanka. Team members had built geodesic domes structures for an orphanage and even a church.

In 1970, R. Buckminster Fuller received a gold medal for his development of the geodesic dome. The American Institute of Architects called it "the strongest, lightest and most efficient means of enclosing space yet known to man." Fuller discovered that a sphere created with triangles could have unparalleled strength. Geodesic domes are even said to have withstood fires and earthquakes better than rectangle-based structures. Originally invented in Germany in 1922, geodesic domes did not have widespread use until the mid-1970s. Prefabricated kits enticed a generation of do-it-yourselfers. This alternative way of constructing a building was embraced by the "hippie movement." Some of our team members, formerly hippies themselves, had learned to build geodesic domes. However, our project proposals to get visas to stay in Sri Lanka through this geodesic dome-building program fell through because of the instability during the aftermath of the ethnic violence in Sri Lanka.

24
LAND OF THE
WARRIOR RACE

All this hard work was not in vain. A new door was opening for us in Asia. A team member had visited Afghan refugees at the border between Pakistan and Afghanistan. The 1979 Russian invasion of Afghanistan was resisted by Afghan freedom fighters, the Mujaheddin. This bloody war had caused 3 million Afghan refugees to flee to Iran and another 2 million to Pakistan. These Afghan refugees were living under harsh circumstances in crowded refugee camps in Pakistan. Our hearts were burdened by their plight and our leadership discussed how to take on this challenge. It was decided that one of our leaders would work on establishing a Non- Governmental Organization (NGO) with the Pakistani government. Through such an NGO we would be able to get visas and permission to bring aid and have official access to Afghan refugees. Working from our base in Lahore, Pakistan, it took this brother a year and lot of patience to get our NGO finally recognized by the Pakistani government.

The experience of building geodesic domes in Sri Lanka proved to be very helpful in starting the work among Afghans. Using only the top side of the geodesic dome as a roof, our technicians came up with the idea to fit concrete pillars underneath in order to come up with a small building. In between the pillars, sturdy walls were built and a door. This construction could be used as a storage facility. When clustered together and leaving some walls open, they could be used as simple clinics or housing. A positive side effect was that they very much resembled the dome-shaped roofs used in some parts of Afghanistan. Ultimately, through this construction program our NGO was approved and our project proposal was given the go-ahead by the Pakistani

Government. The next step was to get the funding and equipment for this project.

MEETING A HOLOCAUST SURVIVOR

A fundraising trip was planned to take place in the fall of 1983 in Germany. Sadly, I had to leave my dear wife, Chris, back with the team in Pakistan. This was a big sacrifice, but we could be sure she would give us much prayer cover. My job was to arrange more than thirty meetings with churches and groups of believers all over Germany. Furthermore, I had to translate the PR film into German for a German version, and to interpret the speaker in all these meetings. This was all quite intense.

After the meetings were over, we headed for Munich to purchase the vehicles and equipment we needed to start the work among the Afghan refugees in Pakistan. The responsibility to get all the paperwork for the vehicles done and to make the trip overland also fell on my shoulders. In order to drive the two trucks we needed four drivers, two for each vehicle so we could take turns driving to shorten the trip. One decision I disliked very much was that the trip back to Asia this time was not made in the fall but in the winter. Driving in the winter in Turkey and parts of Iran can be very dangerous because of heavy snowfall on very slippery roads. Once again I had to overcome myself and my apprehension of what could go wrong or happen to us on such a long and hazardous trip. Yes, I had to be self-controlled and trust in the Lord to help us through whatever lay before us.

> "Better a patient person than a warrior, one
> with self-control than one who takes a city."
> (Prov. 16:32 NKJV)

Before we left I wanted to buy myself a warm winter coat.

Near the busy train station in Munich I found a clothing shop. While the shopkeeper handed me a priced-down, red winter coat, I noticed that he had a long number tattooed upon his left forearm. This raised my curiosity. Introducing myself with some small talk, I finally asked:

"May I ask you why and how you received this number on your arm?"

Looking at me with a pair of very sad, brown eyes he only spoke this very shocking word: "Sonderkommando."

Having read a lot about the atrocities during World War II, I got chills down my spine when I heard his answer. The SS men kept the people unaware that they were fated to die. They were told that they were being sent to the camp, but that they first had to undergo disinfection and bathe. After the victims undressed, they were taken into the gas chamber, locked in, and killed with Zyklon B gas. When the Nazi guards at the extermination camps killed people in their gas chambers, they forced the Sonderkommando (Special Command Unit) to do inhuman, horrible jobs.

The Sonderkommando was made up of mostly Jewish prisoners who did not kill anyone. They would be killed when they refused to obey. The job of the Sonderkommando was to calm down their fellow Jewish prisoners, men, women and children who went nakedly into the gas chambers. The women's hair was shaved off and all personal belongings of prisoners—especially money and jewelry—and even eyeglasses were removed. After the Nazis had killed their victims, the Sonderkommandos dragged the dead bodies out of the gas chambers. They had to remove golden teeth or tooth fillings and wedding rings that the Nazis wanted from the dead bodies. Finally, they had to burn the bodies and clean the gas chambers to get them ready for the next group of people the Nazis wanted to kill.

This methodical and industrialized way of killing and exterminating all Jews is called the *Shoah* (destruction) or *Holocaust* (sacrifice by burning). It is estimated that approx. 1.1 million people perished in the Auschwitz extermination camp alone in just under five years of its existence. The majority, almost 1 million people, were Jews. The number of prisoners forced to work in the Sonderkommando varied. In May 1944, when more than 350,000 mostly Hungarian Jews were murdered, 874 prisoners were part of it. By the end of October 1944, "only" 100 prisoners worked in the Sonderkommando. Totally, around 2,200 persons were forcibly recruited. Sometimes a whole shift of Sonderkommandos was murdered and replaced by new prisoners to cover up the Nazi crimes. Only about 110 survived until the end of the war.

The Jewish shopkeeper I met in Munich was one of them. He did not have to tell me what he had gone through in Auschwitz. Having found someone willing to listen to him, he started telling me his very sad life story.

"When I came out of Auschwitz I discovered all my relatives had been murdered. I alone was left. Like many other Jewish Holocaust survivors, I decided to move to Israel which became a nation again in 1948. However, I never really felt at home there and decided to leave and go back to Europe. In France I became successful in business, met my wife, started a family and built a nice home. One fateful day the house burned down. So I lost my family and everything once again."

By this time tears welled up in my eyes. How much more suffering could a mortal man take?

"After this tragedy I decided to come back to Germany. All my family had lived there for centuries until World War II wiped them out. Where else could I go?" he continued.

"How can you still live in Germany after all the Nazis did to you?" I anxiously wanted to know. "Were you able to forget all the horrors and forgive Germans?"

His unexpected and confident answer touched me to the core of my heart.

"Of course; I have to forgive them. I would not be able to live here if I could not forgive."

It took my breath away. Here was a Jew who had many good reasons to hate but nonetheless had decided to forgive. Many Christians I knew believed in the forgiveness of their sins through the Lord Jesus Christ but were unable to forgive and continued to hold grudges. Only when we forgive those who trespassed against us are we able to receive forgiveness ourselves and overcome the pain of the past.

"You are very close to the kingdom of God!" I told him as I shared what Jesus did for him. After paying for my red winter coat, I thanked him, said goodbye and never met him again.

"But if you do not forgive others their sins, your Father will not forgive your sins." (Matt. 6:15 NKJV)

A STUBBORN CUSTOMS OFFICIAL

In order to drive overland a Carnet de Passage—a sort of passport for the vehicle—had to be obtained in Munich for each of the two trucks we had bought. This document would give us legal passage through the many international borders we had to cross on the way to Pakistan. Getting these documents was a lot of work at various offices. Some of the permissions we needed to make such trips overland were hard to get. Over the years, a certain agent we had come to know was always very helpful. Dashing into his office I would announce to him:

"Sir, I need another miracle!" He was a handsome, tall, blue-eyed blond man. Very much like the type of person favored in Hitler's SS. He also was a man of very few words. An aura of mystery always seemed to surround him. Looking up at me from behind his desk, he flashed a brief, naughty smile while he told me to take a seat. Over and over again, he worked miracle after miracle for us.

This time, however, we faced exceptional obstacles and a miracle seemed to evade us. It had started snowing, which made me nervous about what was to come. Slowly, our small convoy of vehicles left Munich and drove 330 kilometers (205 miles), reaching the Austrian border in four hours. The German border guards were no problem, but for some reason the Austrian side of the border gave us a hard time. They took a long time to study our papers and finally told me to return to Munich to get another paper, which in their opinion was still missing. Very discouraging!

Leaving one of the trucks behind, I had to go all the way back to Munich to get this document. This happened twice! A lot of time, money and energy was lost driving up and down in all that snow. On the way back to the Austrian border the third time, it started to dawn on me that this was not a battle against border guards, not against flesh and blood. Somebody else was doing his evil utmost to hinder us from becoming a blessing to Afghan refugees. More prayer was needed. At the customs counter I presented the latest papers. The customs official examined the documents and started to find some fault again. By now I was getting desperate. Suddenly I did something which I normally would not do. I spoke loudly in tongues right in front of him! An amazing thing happened. The man behind the counter calmly looked up to me from his desk. As if nothing had happened, he signed the documents and our vehicles passed the border. In a split second an Invisible Force changed his mind and helped us overcome this obstacle.

"In the same way, the Spirit helps us in our weakness.
We do not know what we ought to pray for, but
the Spirit himself intercedes for us through wordless
groans. And he who searches our hearts knows the

mind of the Spirit, because the Spirit intercedes for God's people in accordance with the will of God." (Rom. 8:26–27 NKJV)

TRAILED BY HIPPIES

The way was free now to drive on to Italy where our local team prepared the vehicles for the long drive to Pakistan. While waiting, we shared about our upcoming trip and ministry in Asia in small Italian churches. Once again these precious believers shared the little they had to help finance our overland trip. They worried about us and even tried to make us take a huge balloon bottle along that was filled with wine. I guess it was to quench our thirst on the way through the desert. It took some time to convince them and my German travel companions this was not a great idea while traveling through Muslim countries such as Turkey, Iran and Pakistan.

Winter was well under way when our two trucks boarded the ferry from Brindisi, Italy, to Patras, Greece. The eighteen-hour ferry ride saved us the trouble of driving through an unpredictable communist Yugoslavia. Via the bridge, which spans the Bosphorus Strait, we left Europe and entered Asia. Soon we were confronted with very extremely dense, foggy weather with near-zero visibility. Under time pressure we decided to continue driving very slowly for hours, which was risky and very tiring. Worse weather awaited us in east Turkey. Heavy snowfall had hit the area and snow was piled up meters high along the narrow roads. On slippery mountain roads many trucks had crashed deep down into steep valleys.

"Inshallah, which means "If Allah wills," is the credo of many Turkish truck drivers. They drive recklessly because they believe their lives are in Allah's hands. The logic behind this is simple: it does not really matter how careful or careless you drive—it is

all up to Allah. If Allah wills you don't die, then you just do not die. If Allah wills you die, then you die anyway. So it is not up to your way of driving; it all depends on Allah's will. This is a recipe for pretty dangerous situations, not only for them but for us who were trying to survive on these roads. We thanked the living God for helping us over those mountains unscathed. It was very cold, so we never stopped the engines. After taking a break to sleep we had to build a fire underneath the truck to defrost the fuel filters so we could continue our journey.

On the other hand, Turkish drivers could also be very helpful and generous. Due to the ongoing war between Iran and Iraq, diesel was hard to get. Long queues of trucks lined up in front of gas stations awaiting their turn. One of the German brothers on our team had planned to get married in Germany right after helping us drive the trucks. This put a lot of pressure on me to make the trip in the shortest time possible. Not wanting to wait in line and lose precious time, I decided to drive right up to the front of the line. When I told them we were on our way to help their Muslim brothers in Afghanistan, they let us go first. Thanks to this generosity we could fill up our gas tanks and some of the extra barrels we had brought along to make the long trip through Iran. On another occasion, a Turkish truck driver generously allowed us to fill up our tank from his own supplies. Hospitality toward strangers is one of those very positive traditions in Asia which blessed us and helped us to overcome in many situations.

"'I was a stranger and you did not invite me in, I needed clothes and you did not clothe me, I was sick and in prison and you did not look after me. They also will answer, 'Lord, when did we see you hungry or thirsty or a stranger or needing clothes or sick or in prison, and did not help you?' 'He will reply, 'Truly I tell you, whatever you did not do for one of the least of these, you did not do for me.'" (Matt. 25:43-45 NKJV)

After finally crossing the border into Iran, we found out that a new rule had been implemented for those wishing to transit Iran. We were told an Iranian customs representative had to accompany us all the way through the whole country. Furthermore, we were required to pay a transit fee of one thousand U.S. dollars for our company with two trucks. This was bad news for our very low travel budget.

While discussing this among ourselves, we were interrupted by some German and Italian hippies asking where we were going. They were traveling with their German VW van and told to pay the same fee. Low on funds as well, they suggested we travel as a group with our three vehicles to save money. This meant each party would only have to pay five hundred dollars. It appeared to be a lucrative proposal, and I eagerly agreed. In hindsight it proved to be a big mistake because I had not really prayed about this decision. Unfortunately, my Dutch tendency to save money overruled my usual prayerful cautiousness and common sense. Piously I argued that we could share the message of salvation with them on the way.

Ultimately these new companions proved to be a pain in the neck, especially when it came to paying us for their share of the trip. My fateful decision had yoked us together with some very deceitful and selfish characters. Christian ministry involves fighting a spiritual battle. To overcome, we must base our cooperation with others on righteousness and light and not on wickedness and darkness. Soon we had to deal with the consequences.

**"Do not be yoked together with unbelievers.
For what do righteousness and wickedness
have in common? Or what fellowship can light
have with darkness?" (2 Cor. 6:14 NKJV)**

"Can we smoke weed (hashish) while we travel through Iran?" It was the first question one of them asked after leaving the border.

"Yes, you can, but be sure the Iranian revolutionary guards will hang you from the next bridge!" This unexpected answer suddenly cooled his desire to get high on drugs. I made sure it stayed that way. After sharing some harrowing stories of punishments and executions we had seen on previous trips through Iran, they got scared enough to stay away from drugs. The custom official who was ordered to accompany us while traveling through Iran wanted to stay in hotels overnight. We told him we knew only one very cheap hotel: the inside of our truck. Unwilling to waste any time, we aimed to leave Iran as soon as possible.

In Germany we had bought extra recap spare tires for our vehicles to save money. The bad road conditions in Turkey and Iran caused one after the other to fall apart or blow up, resulting in a lot of frustrating delays. Traveling from the city of Tabriz in the west of Iran, we reached Tehran, the capital. Eastward we passed the holy city of Qom, the largest center for Shi'a Muslim scholarship in the world. Around 20 million Shi'a pilgrims visit that city every year. Driving 2,000 kilometers (1,243 miles) through Iran, we finally reached the city of Zahedan on the border with Pakistan. Our "hippie friends" smelled their freedom knowing that hashish was plentiful and easily available in Pakistan. After crossing the border, they drove off at once without paying us their share of five hundred dollars. They did not get very far.

Before us laid a stretch of 300 kilometers (186 miles) uncharted and unpredictable desert, plus 400 kilometers (248 miles) of bumpy roads through wild Baluchistan within Pakistan. Most of the 5.6 million Baluch live in the Pakistan province of Baluchistan. About 1 million Baluch live in the east of Iran, and about one-hundred thousand in southwest Afghanistan. Islamized from the seventh century, they remain strong and proud Muslims practically unreached with the gospel, even today. The Baluch have an interesting and much-honored, almost Christian tradition called Med o Maraka. In order to resolve a dispute, they accept the guilt expressed by the accused who then goes to the home of the person wronged and asks for forgiveness. We also had to forgive our hippie companions. They had left us empty-handed without saying goodbye.

The Baluch drive their trucks and buses much the same way they used to drive their horse chariots. In the desert there is no recognizable road, so we first tried to follow some vague tire tracks. A Baluch bus passed us, so we decided to follow it in a cloud of sand dust. Suddenly the bus stopped and turned around. When we asked the bearded, turbaned bus driver what happened, he told us that he had lost his way. This was quite unnerving. If he could not find the way, how would we be able to find it? Our slow trucks could not keep up with the bus. There was no other way but to go by the position of the sun. It rises in the east, and that was the direction we were going.

Huge yellow clouds towered up in front of us. A howling sandstorm was coming our way fast. Soon we were surrounded by billowing dust and our visibility was next to zero. The fine sand penetrated the windows. We put handkerchiefs over our mouth. What to do in such a situation? A Baluch truck driver had turned his truck around, probably so only the backside would face the sandstorm. Because of the time pressure to get our brother back to Germany for his wedding, I decided not to stop but to drive on slowly. I figured the storm would pass by and we could be out of it sooner that way. This turned out to be right, but in the end I was wrong anyway. The engine needs air. The air filter sucked in sand, which ultimately slowly damaged the engine. We only found that out at the end of our trip when our mechanics in Peshawar, Pakistan, checked it out. They were not amused.

After hours of driving we approached some sandy hills. When we reached the top and were able to look down into the valley, we saw a remarkable sight. Before us in a sandy pit lay the VW bus with a broken front axle, unable to move. Next to it, our former hippie companions were relaxing and lying around high on hashish. Those who use hashish experience a pleasant-to-intense euphoria, a sense of relaxation, an elevated mood and altered perception of time. All of this resulted in their crash. In their carelessness they had driven their VW bus way too hard and too fast. The condition of the road did the rest. When we drove closer, one of them jumped up waving at us to stop. Bent on teaching them a lesson, I pretended to drive on waving back at him. Wildly gesticulating, he came running behind our truck. Finally we stopped.

"What do you want?"

I asked quite aware we could not leave them there alone in the desert.

"We need your help!" came his timid answer.

He knew well why we were not so excited about that.

"What about paying us back our money?!"

"Oh yes, sure. We will do that, but please help us."

"You left us without doing that, so how can I trust you?"

"We will do everything you tell us to do!"

They were now totally dependent upon our mercy—and mercy they received—but at our conditions. The first big city named Quetta was still hundreds of kilometers away. We decided to hook up the front side of their broken VW bus with most of their hippie passengers behind our crane truck. They could only move quite slow and would meet us in Quetta later on. Our condition was that their leader would come along alone with me, and the brother who was planning to get married. We three would drive ahead of them in our smaller truck. He was supposed to pay us back in Quetta. Driving as fast as we could through dangerous tribal territory, we finally got there. While staying in a small hotel for the night our hippie-turned-prisoner tried to find more excuses not to pay. He seemed to be more interested in fleshly pleasures.

"Is it possible to mess with the local girls in Pakistan?" he asked casually.

"You could," I answered, "but you will end up with a bullet in your head the very next day. Pakistani men can be quite jealous, you know." We had met plenty of men armed with Kalashnikovs, so it was not hard to convince him that this was one of his bad ideas. By threatening to call the police on him, he finally turned up with the money.

Time was running out for my German co-driver on the way to his wedding. Luckily our brother made it all the way to our team in Lahore, Pakistan. From there, my dear wife, Chris, performed the miracle of getting him a ticket plus a flight back to Germany. He arrived the day before his wedding. His dear wife-to-be, truly a woman of faith, had resisted all pressure to postpone the event! An important lesson was learned, and a hard-won victory earned, in spite of a wrong decision. All glory to God who in his mercy helped us to overcome in this awkward situation.

"Search me, God, and know my heart; test me and know my anxious thoughts. See if there is any offensive way in me, and lead me in the way everlasting." (Ps. 139:23–24 NKJV)

THE WARRIOR RACE

Kalashnikov-toting Mujaheddin swarmed all over the bustling city of Peshawar where our team was based. They made the city into a hotbed for the acquisition of weapons, funds, drugs and shady alliances with foreign powers. Some just came to lick their wounds or to take a break from fighting the Russians. After the delivery of our trucks in Peshawar, Pakistan, on the border with Afghanistan, our relief work among the Afghan refugees increased and became quite effective. Millions of displaced, traumatized and poverty-stricken Afghans had poured into Pakistan. With nowhere to go they simply camped out in the desert.

Our NGO provided visas for our foreign workers and our project proposals were accepted by donor organizations. Many small homes for widows, invalids and orphans as well as warehouses and clinics, based on our dome building system, were constructed. A milk distribution program was started using excess milk powder donated by the EU. Milk powder was mixed with clean water in large, mobile, stainless-steel containers called "Milk Cows." Daily our teams distributed 12,000 liters of milk in two refugee camps to many thousands of Afghan kids. These projects created jobs for two hundred Afghans who implemented these programs supervised by our foreign staff. Soon international NGOs were stumbling over each other to help alleviate the needs of 3 million refugees.

"A man's gun is his jewelry" is a popular proverb among Pashtuns, the dominant ethnic community in Afghanistan. They comprise 47% of the population. About 18% of 49 million Pashtuns live in Pakistan. Practicing Buddhism before the arrival of Sunni Islam from the seventh to the tenth century during Arab conquests, Pashtuns today are very strong and orthodox Muslims. The Pashtuns have a distinct tribal code called Pashtunwali or the "way of the Pashtun," which makes them different from other Afghan ethnic groups. It is an unwritten set of values, customs and cultural codes that governs daily life. Pashtuns must defend their motherland, grant asylum to fugitives irrespective of their creed or caste, offer protection even to his deadly enemy and wipe out insult with insult.

Pashtunwali is the responsibility to uphold individual and tribal *nang* (honor). It revolves around *zan* (woman), *zar* (gold/wealth) and *zameen* (land). The responsibility of upholding individual and tribal honor rests with the males carrying weapons, as a visible expression of the code of honor. Like most Asians, the way of the Pashtuns also includes *melmastia* (hospitality) by welcoming and protecting guests. Hospitality increases the power and prestige of a Pashtun among the tribesmen. The wider a Pashtun spreads his *dastarkhan* (tablecloth), the more respected he is. Even a stranger seeking refuge can count on such hospitality. Honor requires a Pashtun to show mercy to his enemy when he shows up at his doorstep. By forgiving his enemy, he shows generosity and grace, which enlarges his power and prestige. Little did I know that later my young family would spend three-and-a-half years of our lives living and working among them. This land of the warrior race was to face more than forty years of continuous war, displacement, suffering, hunger, death, internal political and religious strife.

ENDURANCE PRODUCES CHARACTER

"I have told you these things, so that
in me you may have peace.

In this world you will have trouble.

But take heart! *I have overcome the world.*"

(John 16:33 NKJV, author's emphasis)

25

A SHARP
DISAGREEMENT

"Some time later Paul said to Barnabas, 'Let us go
back and visit the believers in all the towns where
we preached the word of the Lord and see how
they are doing.' Barnabas wanted to take John,
also called Mark, with them, but Paul did not think it
wise to take him, because he had deserted them in
Pamphylia and had not continued with them in the
work. They had such a sharp disagreement that they
parted company. Barnabas took Mark and sailed for
Cyprus, but Paul chose Silas and left, commended
by the believers to the grace of the Lord."
(Acts 15:36-40 NKJV)

The ministry in India, Pakistan and Sri Lanka, as well as the
work among the Afghan refugees, was increasing day by day.
Our funding base in Germany was solidified and strengthened
when we decided to start a German charitable trust in 1984.
Previously we had just collected donations in Germany through
the yearly fundraising meetings each fall. During the year, a simple newsletter was sent out to inform our contacts about the
ministry. We did, however, not give any account to the German
government about these funds. Moreover, before we started the
trust we could not issue any tax deductible receipts to our do-
nors. With the help of faithful German believers and supporters
of our ministry, the trust was registered in Germany as a Christian nonprofit organization.

This was an important step toward building accountability,
trust and acceptance in Germany. During a meeting we attended in the city of Nuremberg, a preacher while praying for us

received the following foreboding prophecy: "The Lord shows you are like a trumpet before him, announcing good tidings in distant lands. You are like Gideon, leading a small band of men to undertake great things for God. The Lord also shows dark clouds gathering in the sky. Many times you will say 'What have I done to deserve all of this?' But the Lord will lead you through and strengthen you."

It all started completely unexpected. A sharp disagreement between the leadership of our teams in Asia and those in the U.S. and Italy arose and boiled over. Unfortunately, it ended up with our ministry in Asia having to part company with the U.S. and Italy side. Sadly, not only Afghans but also many Christians at some time in their lives or ministries end up in strife about some more-or-less important matter. In our case, the official disagreement was over a difference in the method of ministry. In the U.S. and Europe our evangelistic teams had always been on the move from one city to the next with a big tent. Like Christian gypsies, they were living in tents not in houses. In Asia the situation was very different. Practically speaking there were not big enough tents to hold our meetings. The teams were accommodated in church buildings, schools or with local believers. Outwardly this unimportant difference became a point of contention. Inwardly, other matters may have played a role. The financial success of our ministry among refugees on the border with Afghanistan may have caused envy or distrust about our leadership in Asia.

Whatever the reasons, the effect of this sharp disagreement was disastrous. In the beginning, each side was trying to prove or defend themselves by writing letters back and forth. It caused hurt, hardness of heart and even more suspicion. As one of the elders in Asia, I decided for myself to stop this. It was obviously the way of the flesh and thus futile and fruitless and not useful to overcome the problem. Satan loves to sow division and set up Christians against each other. The reasoning behind this is quite clear. When Christians fight each other, they will be defeated because they should be fighting Satan and overcoming his darkness instead. To me it became clear that if God was for us, we would not have to defend ourselves but that He would prove us right or wrong. If God was not there to defend us, the ministry would fall apart anyway.

> "The Lord is my strength and my defense; he has become my salvation. He is my God, and I will praise him, my father's God, and I will exalt him. The Lord is a warrior; Lord is his name."
> (Ex. 15:2–3 NKJV)

Things were getting worse and became a severe test of my faith in God. In Sri Lanka, during this extremely emotionally stressful time, Chris found out she was pregnant with our first child. At the height of all this infighting, she started bleeding profusely, which added to our despair. After checking it out, we found out she was still pregnant but had to lie very still in bed. Our finances had dwindled because of bad reports and mistrust sowed about our ministry. The teams in Asia all suffered but continued ministry as well as they could. To make things worse, we heard that team leaders from the U.S. and Italy were on their way to India to take over that part of the ministry. Leaving my wife alone with the Sri Lankan team, I left immediately for India to be with the Indian team when they came.

What happened next was unreal, more like a bad dream. When I arrived in the Indian state of Andrah Pradesh in South India, the team was conducting an open-air evangelistic meeting. Before I met with the Indian leaders I had asked the Lord for wisdom what to do in this situation. The strategy I received was not to fight in the flesh or defend myself. Instead, I decided to fast and pray for three days. I told them about the sharp disagreement that had rocked and divided our ministry. They were very surprised to hear the foreign leaders were coming to take over the ministry. My advice to them was to listen to what they had to say and then make their own decision about which side to choose.

At that time an Indian brother and sister in the team were about to get engaged. To give them the possibility to meet together, I took them with me in the team bus and drove a short distance out of town. All of a sudden an old Indian taxi screeched to a halt near our bus. The doors swung open and out jumped two of our international leaders. They clambered into the bus, claiming it to be their own. Now I was glad to be fasting because I did not have much energy to react or get angry. Staying quiet, calm and composed was the best thing to do in this case. It disarmed their invasive mood and hostile takeover plans at once. I did not have any reason to despise them because I felt a peace that passes all understanding. Now it was all up to God to decide what was going to happen.

Without much communication, they took over command, started up the bus and drove us all back to where the team was. From there I left and went to stay and pray in my room. My presence would have influenced their meeting with the foreign leaders. Deep in my heart I secretly hoped—to my shame—that the Indian team would choose their side. Such a decision would release me from my responsibility for them and set me free to pursue new ministry opportunities elsewhere. It was not to be so.

After two days the Indian team members visited me to tell me that the foreign leaders were gone. "What happened, and what is your decision?" I asked. The foreign leaders had tried to convince them to join their side. During the evenings the evangelistic open-air meetings were still taking place. Non-Christians were getting saved, healed and delivered. But then suddenly, in the middle of a meeting, those leaders came up on stage and told the Indian team members to stop the meeting at once. That was the straw that broke the camel's back. How could they be trustworthy leaders when they stopped a meeting in which people were getting blessed? The Indian team members were very upset and told those leaders to leave at once.

"We want you to stay our leader, and will continue to work with you." was their verdict.

"My sheep listen to my voice; I know them, and they follow me. I give them eternal life, and they shall never perish; no one will snatch them out of my hand. My Father, who has given them to me, is greater than all; no one can snatch them out of my Father's hand. I and the Father are one."
(John 10:27-30 NKJV)

Alea jacta est. The die was cast and there was now no turning back. With a heavy heart I accepted their challenge knowing well that the way before us would be very hard and tedious. First of all, I decided to forgive those who came to take over the ministry. After all, they—especially the leader in Italy—had always been a blessing for our ministry in India. They had done so much to help us fix our vehicles, enabling us to drive overland to Asia. It hurt and made my heart very sad. Those who had turned against us had been close friends with whom we enjoyed sweet fellowship. Accepting this broken relationship was very hard.

"Even my close friend, someone I trusted, who shared my bread, has turned against me."
(Ps. 41:9 NKJV)

It comforted me to know that our Savior Jesus Christ had gone through much worse loss of friendship. Just before his ordeal of suffering and dying to atone for the sins of mankind, his close coworker, Judas, betrayed him because of his love of money. After sharing his bread with them during the last supper, all his disciples, those whom he had trusted, left him when he was arrested.

His main coworker, Peter, even denied three times that he had known Jesus.

Jesus' last words on the cross: **"Father forgive them for they do not know what they are doing!"** and

"Father, into thy hands I commit my spirit," took on a whole new meaning for me **(Luke 23:34, 46).**

In the midst of this, our first child was born in Sri Lanka. Looking down at our baby boy sleeping safely and snuggly in my arms, the Lord spoke to me: "See how this newborn child is totally unconcerned about tomorrow? He does not worry about a thing. He is loved, taken care of, being cuddled, clothed and fed. You are my child, a son of the Living God. How much more will I take care of you and the problems you are facing?"

This reassuring example and simple truth helped me overcome my worries and anxiety over the challenges our ministry was going through. We decided to call our baby boy and first child Jonathan (Gift of God) Elshaddai (God Almighty). The Jonathan of the Bible was a very special person. During his lifetime he was faced with the choice to honor his father or to stay faithful to his friend David. The fact that he managed to do both impressed me very much. To the end Jonathan stayed faithful to his evil and unpredictable father and even died with him in battle. Jonathan was the official heir to the throne but gave up this position because he realized David was chosen by God to be the next king. All of this took a lot of humility and the ability to empty himself of his own aspirations. Jonathan is very much a type of Christ. Jesus left all the comforts of heaven to bear the sins of mankind by emptying and giving himself up so we might live forever. The end of any disagreement it is not so much about who was right or wrong. The ones who overcome in the end are those who stay most Christlike despite everything.

THE TWO HORSES

Faced with very hard choices, we opted for the way King Saul's son Jonathan behaved when he was stuck in between two opposing sides. Of course, this was not the path of least resistance. It took a lot of humility and dying to self. We were in dire financial straits. The birth of our first child had been a caesarean section. To pay for the hospital and team bills we sold whatever team assets we could. Soon after that our little family had to leave Sri Lanka because our temporary visas had expired. From very humid and tropical Sri Lanka we moved with our one-month-old baby back to Germany where winter had set in early. While we were traveling around for fundraising meetings, baby Jonathan caught a severe cold. It was very hard to see and hear him suffer through this ordeal. After prayer and advice from a doctor we exposed him to warm, humid air in a shower cabin and fresh, outside air wrapped up like a little Eskimo. This helped and soon he was cooing happily again. And our dear German pastor friend and his wife did their best to fatten us up again with their huge, delicious meals of fried chicken and French fries.

During one of our mission prayer times, this prophetically gifted pastor received a vision about the leader of our Asian teams. In that vision he saw the leader riding on a big, strong horse. All of a sudden that horse reared up and the leader fell off. He scrambled to his feet and jumped up again. From a distance, a smaller, black horse appeared. The leader mounted that horse but after some time he fell off that horse as well. This vision was not very encouraging because it was a foreboding and warning of more upheaval and stress to come. This vision was fulfilled quite soon.

The main leader of our ministry in Asia had decided to move his office to another, more wealthy country in Asia after our visas for Sri Lanka were canceled in 1983. Ultimately this proved to be a wrong decision and a drain on the ministry finances. The mission account in Germany was way overdrawn. The German mission board could not accept this. Making debts, and especially not being able to repay them, was against our mission conviction. Hudson Tailor, founder of China Inland Mission, faced with a lack of finances, once aptly said:

"To me it seemed that the teaching of God's Word was unmistakably clear: 'Owe no man anything.' To borrow money implied to my mind a contradiction of Scripture—a confession that God had withheld some good thing and determination to get for ourselves what He had not given."

The German mission board decided to bounce any further checks written out on the mission account which was deeply in the red. Until it would be in the black and all debts were paid, there would be no further transactions. Because of this decision, our former leader could not afford to stay in Asia. We advised him to go back to the U.S. and take a rest. He did leave and resigned soon after. This meant that the responsibility for the work in Asia was now on my shoulders, along with two more elders. We had to change the name of our mission and ended up with Vision for Asia.

This situation confirmed the prophecy we had received in India about us being used as a winnowing fork. The wheat was thrown up in the air, and the chaff was separated from the wheat. It did not feel nice to be used as a winnowing fork, but in the end God uses whom He chooses. In hindsight, all of this upheaval was God's way of putting our ministry on a much better foundation.

26
CHALLENGING
A GIANT

The pressure of dealing with all the loss, as well as trying to keep the teams together and provided for, was immense. This burden weighed very heavy on me. One evening when I was staying at the home of our German pastor and mission coworker it all came to a head. The pastor had left for a prayer meeting that night by car. I had decided to stay home to sort out my thoughts and pray. In his childhood, this dear brother was affected by polio which caused him to limp and walk slowly. Getting older and heavier, he always needed a walking stick to support himself. But whenever he would step into his car he was a changed man. To compensate for his physical slowness, he loved to drive very fast. Roads in that wooded part of Germany, called the Odenwald, were narrow and winding up and down various hills. It was late at night, but the pastor did not show up.

My worried thoughts started making up things. The enemy of my soul added a bit as well. I was sure that our brother, speeding home on his way back, had lost control over his car. He must have smashed against a tree in one of those curves. *What would I do if that were true and he is dead?* My troubles were growing over my head already. And now this?! My heart started pounding heavily. It felt like a heart attack.

"Why don't you start to give thanks to Me in this situation?" a soft but sure voice spoke to my spirit in all this confusion.

"What, me? Give thanks under these bad circumstances? No way. Why, there is nothing to be thankful for anyway!"

"Why don't you try at least?" God did not give up on me. Reluctantly I finally decided to give it a try. Amazingly, as soon as I started to thank God consciously with all my heart for all these troubles, something changed. The dark clouds lifted slowly, and the light of the sun broke through the mist of my anxiety. It was one of those lessons that changed my life and can only be learned by experience. Giving thanks to God in *all* circumstances is the best way to overcome any life crisis.

"Give thanks in *all* circumstances; for this is God's will for you in Christ Jesus." (1 Thess. 5:18 NKJV, author's emphasis)

Next Sunday, we were on our way to church. To avoid getting killed, I suggested driving the car that day. On the way I was still trying to cope with some of the challenges before me. Arriving at the church building, we parked the car. Upon entering the church, I was warmly embraced by a dear brother. Before he became a Christian he had been addicted to alcohol. He was a simple but huge man with hands like coal shovels. During his wild years he had been the terror of the town. Under the influence of alcohol, he had once demolished a bar but now he was as meek as a lamb.

"Where are the others?" he asked me.

"What do you mean by 'others'?" I asked. "Only the pastor and I came by car today."

"No, no. I looked through the curtains when you arrived. Two more persons were on the back seat!" He was quite adamant about what he had seen. Now I started to get curious.

"Are you sure? What did they look like?"

"They both had black hair and were dressed in white!" he answered.

When he said that, I felt shivers go all down my spine.

"You have seen angels, dear brother, for sure!" I exclaimed.

He looked at me in distress and doubtful about what he might have seen.

"No, that cannot be. I am sure they were people!"

It took some time for it to dawn on us what had actually happened. While driving, I was worrying away about my circumstances totally unaware that two of God's angelic servants were seated on the backseat behind me. It was as if the Lord was saying: "See, my child, I sent angels to serve, encourage and to minister to you in this special way."

This experience had a profound and lasting impact on my life. Why worry when God and the presence of His angels are so real? Later on we would joke about the reason why our dear brother had angels sitting on the back seat of his car. They could have been flying along. But because of the pastor's fast driving they had to sit inside in order to keep up.

"Are not all angels ministering spirits sent to serve those who will inherit salvation?"
(Heb. 1:14 NKJV)

RESCUE THOSE BEING LED AWAY TO DEATH

Furlough for missionaries is the time to take a much-deserved rest and break from the mission field. Visiting relatives and personal supporters and speaking engagements in home churches are part of it as well. Our furlough, which would take place once in four years, always started with Chris' parents in Pembroke, Illinois. They pioneered and pastored a Mennonite church in a very poor all-Black neighborhood. Their aim was to improve the livelihood of local residents in practical and spiritual ways. Doing a faithful job under very difficult circumstances, they managed to expose and fight prostitution and crime in that area.

Once, while her mother was standing in the bathroom, she moved to get something. In that very moment a bullet shot from a passing vehicle penetrated the wooden wall, narrowly missing her. The first time we stayed with them in Pembroke after our marriage, we had our own experience. In the middle of the night I woke up with a feeling of imminent danger. Not being able to sleep, I felt a strong urge to pray. The next morning we found out a drunken person had set fires which gutted several houses and mobile homes in the neighborhood, killing at least one woman. Our house had been spared. In spite of these dangers, Chris' father had not raised his family to be fearful. The doors of their home were never locked but always open to whoever was in need of encouragement and help.

"Come! Come quickly; the pastor is hurt!" a frightened church member exclaimed while we were staying with Chris' parents. Her father had been doing some maintenance work in the church building that day. Somebody was supposed to hold the ladder while he was exchanging a lightbulb high up on the church ceiling. The ladder slipped, and he crashed down on the hard floor. Dashing half a mile down the road, I rushed into the church. There he lay next to the long ladder, his arms stretched out. He looked very pale and lifeless. A holy anger rose up within me. "No, not him; not my dear father-in-law. He shall not die but live!"

I bowed down over him and kept praying over him until the ambulance took him away. He survived, but both his arms and wrists were broken, knocking him out of commission for a long time. Through this incident and the following Scripture, God spoke clearly to me:

"You tried to rescue your beloved father-in-law being led away to death, and rightly so. How much more you should be concerned about the multitudes of lost souls in Asia staggering toward slaughter! No matter how bad the circumstances are in your life, you are called to overcome for the sake of rescuing those being led away to death and are staggering toward slaughter!"

"Rescue those being led away to death; hold
back those staggering toward slaughter. If you
say, 'But we knew nothing about this,' does not
he who weighs the heart perceive it? Does not he
who guards your life know it? Will he not repay
everyone according to what they have done?"
(Prov. 24:11–12 NKJV)

SURPRISE FAMILY PLANNING

In a daze we wandered through the maternity ward of the hospital. During our furlough in the U.S., Chris had found out she was pregnant again. The nurse doing the ultrasound was at first very friendly. Suddenly she stopped talking and got really intense. Finally, after a long time prodding around with the ultrasound, she took off in a hurry. We were both left wondering what in the world was happening. *Did the nurse find something wrong with the baby? What could possibly be wrong?* All kinds of wild imaginations were flying around in our heads. The nurse finally came back with the doctor.

"Congratulations! You are expecting twins," he said.

"Twins?" my poor wife exclaimed.

The doctor just smiled. It took us totally by surprise. Twins?! Where did that come from?

Nobody on the Dutch side of my family ever had twins. Later on, we found out that Great Grandpa Solomon on Chris' side had three sets of twins—all girls! Plus, there was a great aunt and uncle twin pair, Amandus and Amanda. Dazed by this unexpected diagnosis, we walked straight into the emergency ward trying to find the exit. One thing was certain. Twins were going to change our family and future plans. So far, with our two-year-old toddler, Jonathan, we had been able to continue our extensive traveling schedule. By this time we had traveled between countries in Asia and Europe for ten years without a place to call our own. With this upcoming change we would have to settle our family down in one place. The big question was . . . *where?*

We left the U.S. for Germany, and the first task was to move our VFA mission office from the small village of Grasellenbach in the Odenwald in the state of Hessen, to Nuremberg, the second biggest city in the state of Bavaria. The decision about where to settle our family in Asia had to be soon. In the meantime, Chris had another checkup. The twins within her womb were doing fine. There was only one problem. The doctor told her she would not be allowed to have a natural birth in Germany. Our first child had been delivered by c-section. His heartbeat had been steadily sinking and, as it turned out, the umbilical cord was wrapped around his neck. If we decided to stay in Germany, the twins would have to be delivered the same way for safety reasons.

This was bad news for Chris, who was greatly looking forward to a natural birth. Staying in Germany to give birth was out of the question. "Let's go *now* to Pakistan, they will let me do what I want there!" was her solution. That meant the only option was to join our team in Pakistan working among Afghan refugees. We would be able to get visas through this relief organization which was a registered NGO with the Pakistani government. We were sure Pakistani doctors would allow Chris to give birth without a c-section. After contacting the local team leader, he was happy to help us get a visa and accommodate us. Yes! A future in Pakistan planned by our twins!

Personally, I was not too excited about having to settle in Pakistan and work with our NGO. Gifted with organizational skills, I was definitely useful for that project. However, I dreaded the drudgery of sitting in an office all day and having to deal with labor-intensive project proposals and administration. So far our ministry had been mainly among Hindus and Buddhists who always had been quite open to the message of salvation through

Christ Jesus. In my opinion, Muslims were not very open to that message and seemed to downright reject it according to their belief system. My opinion was confirmed by our experience among the religious Muslims of Afghanistan. They were friendly and hospitable and willing to talk about their faith, but very few were open to the Truth.

Walls would be the best way to describe our new living situation. Walls were everywhere. In India it seemed like half the population lived right out under the stars in the wide open. On the contrary, the Pashtun culture in Pakistan and Afghanistan was very different. High walls surrounded each house compound on all four sides, no matter how big or small. They are called "Purda Walls" after the Muslim practice of secluding their women. The dome homes manufactured through our project were also made with Purda walls and thus well-received by the refugees. Walls around the homes and around the hearts of the people. They seemed to be impenetrable until we considered, well, there are also *doors*! And doors—more often than not—open up if they are knocked upon in prayer.

It took us some time to realize what challenging the giant of Islam really meant. While reading the Bible one day, the following words of Jesus leaped out of the page:

"The Spirit of the Lord is on me, because he has anointed me to proclaim good news to the poor. He has sent me to proclaim freedom for the prisoners and recovery of sight for the blind, to set the oppressed free."
(Luke 4:18 NKJV)

Especially the part, "The Spirit of the Lord is on me . . . to proclaim freedom for the prisoners . . ." pierced my heart. This shed a whole new light on my unbelief and preconceived attitude that Muslims in general were not open to the gospel. Prisoners are in a prison and can only be set free through someone who has the key to the door of the prison. It dawned on me that the people we were dealing with were stuck in a huge religious prison. Every prisoner longs to be free and to get rid of the chains that bind him. Worldwide, 1.8 billion people are stuck in the prison of Islam. King Jesus has the key of the house of David to open and to close. He has given this key, or authority, to open and close to His Body, the church. It became clear to me that through unceasing prayer in the name of Jesus and proclamation of the name of Jesus, this religious prison would eventually have to open up. Prayer and fasting was the key to overcoming this giant.

"I will place on his shoulder the key to the house of David; what he opens no one can shut, and what he shuts no one can open." (Isa, 22:22 NKJV)

First of all, we had to cope with the birth of our twins in a mission hospital set in the hill station of Qalandarabad, Pakistan. Because of ultrasounds, we had been told to expect identical twins, so we dutifully selected two sets of male and female names. The birth went well, of course, without a c-section. To our great joy, out came first a girl named Shekinah, which means "Glory" or "Presence of the Lord." Eight minutes later, to everyone's astonishment and joy—a boy! We named him Mark Hendrik after both his grandpas. All the medical staff couldn't figure it out. There seemed to be only one placenta, which meant they had to be identical. But Mark was definitely a boy and very hungry. Yes, they brought much joy but were also a lot of work.

We were very blessed to finally have our own small but personal place to live in Peshawar. We lived on ground level with a big garden surrounded by Purda walls. Upstairs lived some of the single guys in the team. Even though we lived in a relatively safe part of town, danger was all around. During the years we lived there, a bomb placed at the local airport killed more than one hundred people. Twice, foreigners were kidnapped. This could happen for financial, political or religious reasons. One captive, a Christian professor, showed up alive miraculously after his kidnappers had a dream from God telling them to let their captive go. They set him out on a dirt road and told him to walk, "You have become a bee in our ears!" But a father of several kids was also kidnapped. He never came back and was eventually declared dead. Never will I forget the last picture I have of him in my mind. During worship in our local international fellowship, he was standing with his bushy, curly hairdo while holding his toddler up on his shoulder. He, his wife and family paid the ultimate price for obeying God's will for their lives.

WHEN MANGOES BURST

The seventeenth of August 1988 was a very special day! A happy day with a sad ending. In the morning we celebrated our son Jonathan's third birthday. All his friends had been invited to a big feast in our garden. There were balloons, cakes, presents, games, etc.—an amazing party. There were folks there we didn't even know! After the party was over, we cleaned up the house. The phone rang as we were about to take a nap. One of our team members announced that the American consulate had just passed on a message. The plane of Zia-ul-Haq, the president and military dictator of Pakistan, had crashed that same afternoon in the southwest of Pakistan. As far as was known there were no survivors! That was a real shock. A moment later, another phone call. Indeed, no survivors. Zia was dead. The American ambassador, a number of Pakistani generals, a brigadier and many others were all killed when the plane crashed shortly after takeoff. The cause? Most likely, sabotage. By whom? It all was shrouded in mystery. Something had put an abrupt stop to the solo career of Pakistan's lone ruler. There was an instant political vacuum. When he came to power, Zia had the previous president of Pakistan, Zufikar Ali Bhutto, hanged. Now Zia himself was dead and Bhutto's daughter, Benazir Bhutto, was elected the first female president of Pakistan. The story goes that Benazir Bhutto had gone to a famous Islamic Pir or holy man in Bangladesh to receive a blessing. The Pir prophesied the following over her: "When mangoes burst, your problem will be solved." It was speculated that the bomb that took down Zia's plane was hidden in two crates of mangoes.

The American consulate advised every expatriate to stay at home. My family had planned to go on a one-week holiday to the mountains the next day. I had already promised Chris this holiday when I came back from India and again upon my return from Australia. You know how that goes. Men promise a lot but do little because each time something "important" comes between. This time I was really determined to keep my promise, and now this happened. Chris was crying in the kitchen. This was our last chance before I was to go on a seven-week fund raising trip to Europe. I tried to comfort my wife.

"We will go no matter what! Nothing and nobody can stop us from having our holiday! We have been through a lot more than this." In moments like that you say such things, but the thought of traveling with tiny twins and a toddler in a wild country where crowds can suddenly turn violent did not really encourage me. We prayed together. After consultation with others, we sensed the peace of God. The next morning we left for the mountains. The situation stayed calm and finally our little family enjoyed a well-deserved rest. Fear is a bad adviser. Faith in God's protecting power was able to overcome the fear of the circumstances.

"He got up, rebuked the wind and said to the waves, 'Quiet! Be still!' Then the wind died down and it was completely calm. He said to his disciples, 'Why are you so afraid? Do you still have no faith?'" (Mark 4:39-40 NKJV)

ROBBING THE DYING

Expatriate workers in Peshawar, Pakistan, were always in need of renewal or extension of their residence permits. A special Pakistani official who took care of this business was a good friend of ours. We already had many good opportunities to talk to him about the Lord. One day we came to know that he was not anymore in his office because he had been badly wounded in a traffic accident. At once we tried to find out where he was being treated. We finally found him in a large hospital in Peshawar. He had been there already three weeks, and still looked very bad. Daily he passed blood through his urine, and he was obviously suffering. His whole left arm was in a cast. With much pain, he told us what had happened:

On the way back from the capital Islamabad to Peshawar, he was traveling in a so-called "Flying Coach." These buses transport passengers at such high and uninterrupted speeds that one easily expects to take off any moment. The bus driver tried to overtake a much bigger but slower bus. The worst thing that can happen to any bus driver in Pakistan! Of course, the slower bus driver did not allow him to do that. The Flying Coach driver tried to pass by on the wrong side. After a hair-raising dash, he succeeded in doing so. By that time he was furiously angry and suddenly slammed on his brakes in the middle of the road. The big bus behind him crashed into the backside of his vehicle. Three passengers in the backseat were instantly killed. Because of the speed, the Flying Coach made a complete spin and ended up on the wrong side of the road where it got hit on the front side. Another four passengers died on the spot. The slower bus drove on and left the wreckage of the Flying Coach behind. Our friend was lying between two dead bodies. He was still alive but could not move or feel his left arm. People were moaning and crying. Others were dying. Suddenly a car stopped. In the darkness, some people approached the badly damaged bus.

"Help me, please help me," somebody cried.

Without uttering one word, these people started to take away the personal belongings of the wounded and dead passengers. Our friend's shoes were torn off his feet. Watches, money wallets, jewelry, briefcases—everything was robbed. There was no mercy. The victims were left over to themselves. Only much later, someone else stopped who transported the survivors to a nearby hospital. Upon arrival they were not even able to pay the entrance fee of five rupees (approximately thirty-five U.S. cents). We were utterly disgusted by this awful story.

"What a scandal! Somebody should report it to the newspaper!" we exclaimed.

"That won't help," our friend said sadly, "because such things happen here almost daily!"

We continued to minister to him for quite some time and promised to come back. The following day I brought him some fruit. Our friend's situation had not improved much. So I proposed to pray for him for healing in the name of Jesus Christ. He said yes immediately. It seemed as if he had been waiting for it. It was a wonderful moment. His two brothers, one of them a doctor, all of them Muslims, were also present. Afterward he wept and embraced me for a long time. When I visited him again the next day, he felt much better and the bleeding had stopped.

"Your prayer in the name of Jesus Christ has healed me!" he testified.

AND THE WALL CAME TUMBLING DOWN

The fall of the year 1989 came with two unexpected blessings. The first one was the birth of our fourth child and second daughter, Pauline, named after her grandmother and Shammah which means "the Lord is present." Her presence brought much joy to our growing family, but her second name was also very prophetic. Soon we would need to cling to the presence of God in the midst of very adverse circumstances in Pakistan. The second blessing, and quite unexpected answer to prayer, came when I went back to Germany to organize and conduct the annual VFA fundraising meetings. A German brother from our team in Pakistan accompanied me during these important meetings.

At that time, East and West Germany were still divided by a border wall measuring 1,381 kilometers (858 miles) long and up to four meters (13 feet) high. This was to keep the citizens of communist East Germany from fleeing oppression and poverty. It was a continuous line of high metal fences, walls, barbed wire, alarms, anti-vehicle ditches, watchtowers, booby traps, self-shooting devices and minefields. Around fifty thousand East German border guards were employed to keep watch over this border to keep their citizens in. During its forty-five-year existence, about one thousand East German citizens died trying to cross this border in search of freedom in West Germany. The better-known Berlin Wall was a separate, much shorter border around West Berlin.

In the 1980s, a special seven-year-long global prayer campaign was initiated by a Dutch international mission organization. Believers around the world committed to pray and fast for the persecuted Christians in Communist Eastern Europe. My own Dutch father had experienced WWII, and the subsequent fear of a nuclear war and possible takeover by communist Russia. At our dinner table every day he prayed the following short prayer: "Lord, destroy the power of communism, in Jesus Name we pray!"

On November 9, 1989, we were conducting a meeting in the city of Braunschweig in the north of Germany. Suddenly, the exciting news came that people from East Germany were freely crossing into West Germany en masse. At once we decided to go to the most nearby section of the wall. When we came to that particular border crossing, many Trabis—small East German-made cars— jam-packed with joyfully waving East Germans were crossing the border unhindered. Scores of excited West German citizens waved back, welcoming and embracing them with flowers and various kinds of fruits not available in East Germany.

Watching history unfold right before me, my own eyes filled with tears of joy and jubilation as I stood there awestruck. The fall of the wall and the subsequent disintegration of the Soviet Union without bloodshed was an amazing answer to worldwide prayer. This moving event inspired us to have faith for the downfall of the religious walls in Pakistan and Afghanistan as well. In every German church where we shared about our ministry in Asia, we ended the message with the whole church standing up to proclaim this to happen.

A proclamation is a publication by an authority. In England, proclamations were an openly published declaration of the king's will. As a branch of the king's prerogative, they were binding on the subject. How much more binding is the will of the King of Kings revealed to His Body, the worldwide church, and proclaimed by that church in the authority of the name of Jesus. The church has been given the authority to overcome spiritual darkness. Not to sit by idly and allow darkness to overcome the church.

WARNING THROUGH
AN EVIL DREAM

The visa through our NGO provided stability for our growing family. Our coworkers and other NGO workers shared their resources to start a kindergarten for the many preschool kids. As time went by, an elementary school was added as well. Well, actually a "study center" for kids, because if we started a school we would have to teach Islam. There were plenty of possibilities for fellowship in our team and also with like-minded believers from other organizations. In the beginning, interdenominational church services were held each Sunday with worship and various leaders taking turns to share the Word.

Living in a Muslim country meant Friday was the day of visiting the mosque and taking rest for practicing Muslims. Sunday was a normal working day for our Muslim Afghan and Pakistani personnel. To adjust to this awkward situation, it was decided to move our Sunday worship service to Friday. Our objective was to adjust as much as possible to the local culture to win the hearts of the local population. For the same reason, our men and women dressed up with the all-present Shalwarkameez—very comfy, baggy cotton trousers with a long shirt in various colors. The trouser is wide at the waist and narrow at the bottom and is held up with a drawstring or an elastic belt. The long shirt covers the waist down to the knees. Our team women wore the local covering called a chadar—a large sheetlike shawl that swaddled not only the head but the whole body. Actually, for keeping the sun off and the dust out, it was quite practical. Our men used the Tupi, an Afghan hat made of thick wool.

Once I had a disturbing dream in the middle of the night. Chris and our three kids were all sleeping peacefully around me. In the dream I was lying on my bed next to my wife. On the left side of where I slept, there was a window. In the dream the window curtains were open. Out of the darkness, suddenly the shape of a most evil and witchlike woman appeared. Her piercing eyes were filled with pure evil. Her presence radiated absolute wickedness, vileness and fear. In shock I immediately closed the curtains to avoid having to look at her. I rushed to the front door, which was half open. There stood one of the other leaders of our team. "Shut that door!" I shouted. "There is a very evil woman standing outside!"

He did not seem to worry and walked off. With a loud bang, I slammed the door shut myself. End of the dream. Obviously, the Lord was warning me that we were facing a real spiritual battle, not against flesh and blood but against a spiritual host of wickedness in the heavenly places.

Later I realized that this dream was a prophetic warning about a real problem arising in our team.

"Then the angel who was speaking to me came forward and said to me, 'Look up and see what is appearing.' I asked, 'What is it?' He replied, 'It is a basket.' And he added, 'This is the iniquity of the people throughout the land.' Then the cover of lead was raised, and there in the basket sat a woman! He said, 'This is wickedness,' and he pushed her back into the basket and pushed its lead cover down on it."
(Zech. 5:5–8 NKJV)

While living and ministering on the border with Afghanistan, there were many other well-known NGOs giving aid to Afghan refugees. Most of the workers in such organizations were not Christians. Their motivation was mostly idealism, adventure or simply money. Such NGO workers could earn twice the amount of doing a similar job in their home country. They received a high Danger Pay—a special allowance established for internationally and locally recruited staff required to work in very dangerous locations. In their free time these workers lived out their usual lifestyle as much as was possible in an Islamic society. The American Club in Peshawar was located in a relatively safe area in town. Journalists, aid workers, would-be spies and political operatives would meet there regularly to talk and have a drink at the bar.

Unfortunately, when God had blessed our ministry and it was well-financed and provided for, the spiritual condition of some of our leadership and team members started to erode slowly. Some of them became regular visitors to the American Club for the wrong reasons. Instead of staying on the narrow way and stepping up prayer to overcome the spiritual challenges, a lack of prayer and the temptations of the broad way increased their tendency to become lukewarm. When the door to darkness is left open, just a bit of wickedness will surely creep in.

Our NGO was quite successful and expanded in various ways. More work meant to me the need for more prayer to balance things out. My suggestion was for my fellow leaders and coworkers to start the office day with at least one hour of prayer and worship in the morning before the work started. Originally our motivation was not just to do a lot of relief work and be a blessing in material ways. We were there to proclaim good news to the poor, to proclaim freedom for the prisoners, recovery of sight for the blind and to set the oppressed free as well. Until that point, we had seen very little spiritual fruit. This was totally unsatisfactory and unacceptable to me. The same administrative work I was doing in Peshawar could earn me much more money when done in my home country. I warned them we were up to a spiritual battle. This subject of increasing our prayer base was brought up by me several times. Sadly, my proposal fell on deaf ears. The door was left half open . . .

STRUCK DOWN BUT NOT DESTROYED

Not willing to give up on the need for more prayer, my wife and I decided to start praying together for an hour in the middle of the day. We also encouraged other coworkers to start praying with a partner for an hour at any time suitable for them. Soon housewives and others were all taking part in such prayer times. It was very encouraging to see prayer on all levels and at various times all through the day starting to take place. And when God's people pray, things start to change—or better said—start to be shaken. It was not the kind of change we had expected, especially the way it happened. In short, it was the removal of things that could be shaken so that things that could not be shaken would remain.

> "The words 'once more' indicate the removing of what can be shaken—that is, created things—so that what cannot be shaken may remain." (Heb. 12:27 NKJV)

On May 17, 1990, my family and I had just come back from an outreach to India where we had seen a real move of the Holy Spirit among non-Christians. When we arrived at our team in Lahore on our way back to Peshawar, we received bad news. Our widows counseling center, our factory for the construction of housing and our vehicle workshop all located near a refugee camp outside Peshawar had been completely destroyed. A mullah had falsely claimed that our widows counseling center had been used for "immoral" purposes because bars of soap were distributed to widows.

On April 26, 1990, at the end of Ramadan, the Islamic month of fasting, a mob of eight thousand enraged Muslims ransacked and looted our factory property. In a couple of days, everything our ministry had built up during the past seven years was gone. They looted absolutely everything, even cutting down the trees. Financially it was a loss of at least 1 million U.S. dollars. For those of us who had poured out our lives into building up that ministry, there was no way one could put a price tag on it. Thank God, none of our Afghan workers were harmed in all this although several had to flee or go into hiding for a time.

For a week after we arrived in Peshawar, we tried to assimilate what had actually happened. Then the news came that our factory within Afghanistan had also been looted and destroyed. Tensions remained high as several other relief organizations, even within the relatively safe part of the city of Peshawar, were looted and or robbed within the following week. While all this was going on, we had to switch houses as a family. This was not necessarily a negative thing, but in the midst of everything else it was kind of crazy.

In the aftermath, our local leadership decided upon three goals. Short term goal: We would give it two months. If within that time no drastic financial breakthrough occurred, we would stop the work as we could not go into debt. Mid-term goal: Given a financial breakthrough, we would take it as a sign to continue the work but scale it down. Long term goal: All long-term workers to be given time off to go back to their home countries to find churches to back them up with full personal support. The development of ministry base offices in Germany, the U.S. and Australia was also decided. Amazingly enough, two weeks later on June 13 the desired financial breakdown came through. In a very highly publicized ceremony on the site of our destroyed factory, the Pakistani government gave us a compensation of 5 million Pakistani rupees (at that time, worth 250,000 U.S. dollars). The chief minister personally handed over the check in the presence of many dignitaries. Miraculously, our middle-term goal had been achieved.

Perhaps this event was a bit too highly publicized. Three days later I received a phone call from one of the team members. "Somebody has pulled a gun on our team leader!" he announced without any further details. From what I understood and feared, he had been killed. At once I jumped into my jeep and drove the dusty roads up to the gate of his home. When I opened the sturdy gate I saw the backside of his Pajero jeep. It was riddled with a dozen bullet holes! All my fears were confirmed. With a heavy heart I walked up to the door of his home. The door opened and out stepped my fellow leader, blood stains still all over the side of his head!

"Brother, you are still alive!" I exclaimed joyfully, very much relieved.

He told me the story. He had taken his five-year-old son along by jeep to go shopping in the tribal area outside the city of Peshawar. Upon returning home he saw four men with Kalashnikov machine guns step out on the road. He slowed down slightly, but sensing they meant no good he accelerated past them. The gunmen opened fire, spraying the speeding Pajaro jeep with bullets. It was an absolute miracle that he and his son survived. Bullets entering through the backside of the jeep whizzed by on both sides of his head and exited through the front window. He suffered only surface wounds from broken glass. One bullet went through the back seats and got lodged in the steel reinforcement bar inside the front seat exactly where his son was seated. Both escaped unharmed, but the family was very badly shaken by this terrifying experience. For their own safety they decided to leave the country eight days later and not to come back. Considering the fact that this attack happened in tribal territory, it could have been a "normal" attempted vehicle robbery. But given his leadership position and the highly publicized reimbursement, it could also have been planned out of revenge or envy. At that time various militant religious groups worked actively against the presence of Christian workers.

"We are hard pressed on every side, but not crushed; perplexed, but not in despair; persecuted, but not abandoned; struck down, *but not destroyed*." (2 Cor. 4:8–9 NKJV, author's emphasis)

On my birthday June 25, 1990, our relief organization gave a press release stating that all operations were frozen indefinitely. This was necessary because the danger had not subsided. We would soon find notes between the window wipers of our vehicles, threatening us with death unless we left the city. Since the ministry had stopped there was little to do, so most team members started to leave the country. Some out of fear, which was quite understandable. Others wanted to use the opportunity to return to their home countries to raise their personal support. Another team leader and his wife and family decided to leave as well. Before they left we did some debriefing. Both admitted that they had become lukewarm in their faith and, in fact, felt backslidden. We prayed with them, encouraging them to take a rest and seek the Lord and sent them off. Out of three leaders at our NGO, now two were gone, and I was the only one left. The mantel of responsibility to hold down the fort fell mostly upon my and one other brother's shoulders. In the end only a small team of eight was left. At least the achievement of our midterm goal concerning finances kept the basic things going for a while.

Under normal circumstances, my wife and I were due to go on furlough after three years of ministry. We were hard-pressed on every side and really needed a break from all this tension. We were perplexed. Should we now despair and just give up? What would happen if we decided to leave as well, we asked ourselves. It was sure to us that this would mean the end of our NGO and ministry to Afghan refugees. When we prayed about it, the Lord reminded us not to just see the natural, but also the spiritual aspect of what was happening. We realized that through the increased prayer level the Lord had started to shake up our ministry. We sensed that God was using us as his winnowing forks to separate the wheat from the chaff. Once again the prophecy given to us years ago in India was confirmed. Obviously this was the outcome, and now we had to wait and see how God would work this out.

It was a question of overcoming or giving in to defeat. To choose either to belong to those who shrink back and are destroyed, or to those who have faith and are saved. I decided for myself I was willing to stay and take up this challenge even if it would cost me my life. This was easier said than done. I was not alone, but with my dear wife and four sweet little kids. While daily traveling up and down to the office, I could easily be killed. Kalashnikov machine guns were widely available and evident all over the city's streets. Two would-be killers on a motorbike could easily strafe my vehicle with bullets and kill me while passing by. A new habit was already firmly established to watch for suspicious individuals spying on me. Before or after I would drive or arrive by car or go anywhere I had to check my surroundings. Driving the same way twice to the office was a no go. My wife had to make her own decision. If she would say no, we would go; if yes, we would stay.

"But we do not belong to those who shrink back and are destroyed, but to those who have faith and are saved." (Heb. 10:39 NKJV)

THE PEACE WHICH PASSES
ALL UNDERSTANDING

At home we sat down on our bed to discuss the situation and to make the final decision. Taking my precious wife by her soft, warm hand, we prayed. Both of us decided to stay no matter what the cost would be. We will never forget that moment. Suddenly, an overwhelming sense of peace came over us. It was supernatural—and, in a way, unnatural. After that decision, while driving the car around the city, all fear of getting killed had completely vanished. Strangely enough, deep in my heart I was almost looking forward to the first bullet coming my way. There was a sense of expectation and excitement to be able to finally meet my dear Lord in person.

In our personal newsletter on June 29, 1990, Chris wrote the following to our family and supporters:

"How are we doing? Well, it amazes me also the peace and grace that God can give in such circumstances. The leadership now wants to take the next couple of months to really wait on the Lord and see how He leads and not just 'how things develop!' The Lord reminded me of something he spoke to me several years ago in another one of those times. The devil seemed bound and determined to finish us off once and for all. I will never forget it; it was almost as if I could literally see the devil leering at me . . . 'Ha, ha. Now you are finished!' But the Lord spoke so clearly in my heart. 'When you pray, that is one thing; it's like kicking the devil. But when in the midst of such circumstances you can rise up and bless me, that's like slapping the devil smack across the face.'

Well, I can tell you, I rose up then and started to praise God! Literally jumping up and down on my bed for joy, I experienced a great victory. He has his plans and purposes for us and for this place. I am totally unimpressed with the devil's plan and purposes for us and this area. In our small prayer groups, we have taken up the challenge of spiritual warfare for this place. I should hate to have to back off now. So I really do ask you to *pray*! Not only for us and for our ministry here in particular but against the spiritual principalities and powers of darkness in this place: the religious principalities, the powers of lawlessness, corruption, fear, violence and murder. Wonderful things are happening, but we can't write about it here." The letter ended with this Bible verse:

> "Surely the righteous will never be shaken;
> they will be remembered forever.
> They will have no fear of bad news; their
> hearts are steadfast, trusting in the Lord.
> Their hearts are secure, they will have no fear; in
> the end they will look in triumph on their foes.
> They have freely scattered their gifts to the
> poor, their righteousness endures forever;
> their horn will be lifted high in honor. The
> wicked will see and be vexed, they will gnash
> their teeth and waste away; the longings
> of the wicked will come to nothing."
> (Ps. 112:6–10 NKJV)

I AM DOING A NEW THING

Because we could not go on furlough, we decided to have a short holiday and break away from the city of Peshawar. Feeling thinned and stretched out, we took off for Kalaam which is as far as you can go in the beautiful Swat Valley. In hindsight, driving the four-wheel-drive jeep with four small kids, up and down unpaved steep mountain paths, was quite risky though. Surrounded by snow-covered mountain tops, lush valleys, waterfalls and rivers with crystal clear water, we found healing for our heavily laden souls and spirits through this breathtaking landscape. We had a great time of just resting, relaxing, fooling around with the kids, reading, fishing for and feasting on trout with local tribesmen—or just doing nothing.

Refreshed, we came bouncing back to Peshawar ready to face "whatever." This time "whatever" was a death threat to one of our new team leaders and threats to some of our Afghan workers. Within a week, we were off for a special team retreat we had planned to have for debriefing and to take time to evaluate and make decisions about the future. There was a flurry of last-minute packing, arrangements and picking up guests from in and outside the country. And the Lord did meet us as He always does! A wonderful minister and friend from Germany had come especially for that retreat. He was really used by the Lord as he led us through the basics of forgiving the Afghans, making sure there was no resentment or bitterness left, and praying for our enemies. The secret to overcome such fleshly tendencies lies in overcoming evil with good.

**"Do not be overcome by evil, but overcome
evil with good." (Rom. 12:21 NKJV)**

The theme of all his messages was about "Hearing God" and taking time together to practice that. One of the things that came through clearly was "I am doing a NEW thing" in Isaiah 43:18, 19b:

**"Forget the former things; do not dwell on the past.
See, I am doing a new thing! I am making a way
in the wilderness and streams in the wasteland."**

There was a lot of affirmation and encouragement like "I love you and I am with you." Soon it became clear that the Lord was not yet finished with us and the greatest work indeed lay ahead. The word for the overall mission often seemed to be about expansion, like "new countries and new doors opening."

The word for our local relief work in Pakistan was more about "death and a subsequent resurrection," or "dying and then new life springing up" as when a seed falls into the ground, or "failure or breakdown but then a new beginning." During our very last meeting together at this debriefing and time of seeking the Lord, this pastor asked us to respond to all God had so clearly spoken to us. Right then Chris had an experience with the Lord, something I heard about much later.

Here she tells it in her own words:

"The pastor had just challenged us all to stand to signal our "yes" to God; indeed to be willing to go on expecting something NEW. Suddenly I heard in my head that unmistakable Clear Voice:

"Would you be willing to go to Germany?" I was shocked, incensed even.

No, I am not going to Germany. I had been there with Antoine during fundraising meetings; it was a cold, gray place and I could not imagine living there. After all, I was in love with Asia! I was sitting at the piano, and I thought,

"I am not going to stand. No one will notice I am not standing, because I am sitting here at the piano. Oh, my. One could just imagine our wonderful Father God gently smiling up above.

"It's okay, Chris, I'll give you a little more time!"

The Lord had clearly spoken to us about His strategy for the local ministry through the following Bible verse:

"Go, my people, enter your rooms and shut the doors behind you; hide yourselves for a little while until his wrath has passed by." (Isa. 26:20 NKJV)

We decided to do exactly that. The practical work was reduced to a minimum, and we laid low for about a year. As a team we opened our doors for intercession and shut the doors of business behind us. While hiding for a little while, until wrath had passed by, the Lord blessed us and kept us safe. The seed of the local ministry had to die and fall into the earth. Eventually new life started to sprout forth again as we overcame by faith in the resurrection power of the Lord Jesus Christ

EARTHQUAKE THWARTED
BY PRAYER

"The words of Amos, one of the shepherds of Tekoa—
the vision he saw concerning Israel *two years* before
the earthquake, when Uzziah was king of Judah
and Jeroboam son of Jehoash was king of Israel."
(Amos 1:18 NKJV, author's emphasis)

Strengthened by the encouragement and helpful instructions we had received from the Lord during the retreat, we returned to Peshawar. The situation there remained unpredictable and dangerous. On top of that it was very hard emotionally for those left behind to see so many good friends departing one by one. Each goodbye party or rather "sad-bye party" left the remnant of those holding the fort more vulnerable and lonely. If it were not for what the Lord had spoken to us, and the uplifting times of increased team intercession, we probably would have given up.

One morning, during one of my private times of Bible reading and prayer, I read the above Scripture. When I came to ". . . the vision he saw concerning Israel *two years* before the earthquake . . ." the Holy Spirit suddenly came strongly over me. In my spirit I clearly heard the following urgent and quite disturbing words:

"My son, after *two years* there will be an earthquake in the area where you now live, but it can be thwarted when God's people intercede in prayer!" Those words startled and shook me up. We already had enough challenges in the area we lived, and now this bad news—an upcoming earthquake. What was I supposed to do? Pray, of course! A bit further in Amos 3:7, I read:

> **"Surely the Sovereign LORD does nothing without revealing his plan to his servants the prophets."**

At first I understood that the Lord revealed this to me personally so that I would start to pray urgently for it not to happen. The name Amos means "borne by God; bearer of a burden." The Lord had chosen me, but it became a real burden to bear this burden. Earthquakes can be so devastating with a lot of loss of life and material goods.

As time went by the Lord spoke anew: "I want you to share this revelation publicly!"

"Is that for real, Lord?" I answered. "Who is going to believe me, and what if an earthquake does not take place? I will make myself look like a false prophet!"

"It is not about you but about My Word!" came the answer. Trying to argue about it with God was futile. God always pulls on the long end. When the sovereign Lord reveals His plan to His servants the prophets, they must overcome their inhibitions and obey. Whosoever is born of the Word of God overcomes the world.

Life with four little kids was eventful enough. To stay sane, my wife and I used to sing the following song to the tune of "Morning Has Broken" by Cat Stevens:

"Morning has broken . . . into a thousand pieces. . .

Babies are crawling . . . all over me . . .

Diapers are leaking, jam fingers menacing . . .

Piles of laundry are all I can see . . ."

On one of those broken mornings, the unexpected happened. Our baby Pauline was peacefully sleeping inside her baby bed. My wife and I were busy cleaning up in our bedroom when all of a sudden the shaking started. First subdued, but then more violent. An earthquake! My wife grabbed little Pauline and both of us bolted outside in search of our other three toddlers. They were playing outside in the garden, but when we got there they were gone. While we turned around, they all came running out of the house. An older brother who lived upstairs had chased them out again. At the first shaking they panicked and ran inside. To our great relief the earth shook only a short time. Later we found out that this earthquake was about six on the Richter scale. Only one person was killed by a falling wall.

"So are you still unwilling to make my warning known publicly by sharing it?" A quiet but stern voice spoke into my spirit.

"Yes, Lord, I got your message, and I will obey you no matter what!" I repented of my stubbornness.

In the local international fellowship, leaders of various ministries usually took turns to preach. My turn was soon to come so I prepared a message about prayer and intercession. That day the attendance was quite high, which increased my nervousness. In the middle of my message I told those present about the warning God had given me and my reluctance to share it.

"In about two years, an earthquake will occur in this city," I shared.

"However, God told me to challenge you all to intercede fervently so it will not happen. After all, when the Lord Jesus was still on Earth, he forewarned us about many natural disasters to come." Pouring with sweat—not just because of the high temperature in the building—I was relieved to end the message with people standing up to pray.

"There will be great earthquakes, famines and pestilences in various places, and fearful events and great signs from heaven." (Luke 21:11 NKJV)

After the meeting, a lady walked up to talk to me. She had just arrived back from England where she had attended church.

In that meeting, somebody she was not acquainted with had come to her with the following prophetic message:

"The place where you are going will be rocked by an earthquake but it can be thwarted by prayer."

Wow, was that ever a confirmation and encouragement! God heard the voice and intercession of His people. Two years passed by, and no earthquake took place. But fifteen years later, on October 8, 2005, a very destructive earthquake killed 87,000 people in Pakistan. By that time the local persecution of the Pakistani Christian minority had greatly increased. Could it be that God's patience had finally run out?

In answer to prayer, new leadership with a willingness to rebuild the ministry in Pakistan on the basis of worship, prayer and fasting was found. By November 1990 we were finally able to leave Pakistan to go on our long-deserved furlough to the Netherlands and the U.S. And, with that, our lives took a completely new and unexpected course. But that is a whole other story with its own set of challenges to be overcome!

THE TWO HARVESTS

This present world is going through a time of great shaking. This is God's doing, and it should not be a surprise. When shaking occurs, the real foundation you have built your life upon is revealed. Did you build on sand or on rock? Only the things that cannot be shaken will remain. Those born of God have received a kingdom that cannot be shaken. When you build your life on King Jesus the Rock of all Ages, you build your life on a solid, unshakable foundation.

"At that time his voice shook the earth, but now he has promised, 'Once more I will shake not only the earth but also the heavens.' The words 'once more' indicate the removing of what can be shaken—that is, created things—so that what cannot be shaken may remain. Therefore, since we are receiving a kingdom that cannot be shaken, let us be thankful, and so worship God acceptably with reverence and awe, for our God is a consuming fire." (Heb. 12:26–29 NKJV)

We still live in a time when God opens doors. This was our experience during all the years spent in Asia, and also now, living in Europe. He opens doors that no one can shut and closes doors that no one but He can open. Many believers seem not to be aware that God gave His children, those born of God, the same authority. They can also open or close doors at will. Men and women are the crown of His creation. Made in the likeness of God, they are destined to take responsibility for all He created. Mankind misused and corrupted this privilege by disobedience.

"Adam, where are you?!

This cry from our heavenly Father calling out to His wayward and lost sons and daughters still rings throughout all generations. Adam opened the door to the virus of sin, which spread and affected every man and woman and child from birth, resulting in death. Henceforth, the door to the Tree of Life was closed. Man did no longer rule over sin. Sin ruled over man.

> **"Therefore, just as sin entered the world
> through one man, and death through sin,
> and in this way death came to all people,
> because all sinned." (Rom. 5:12 NKJV)**

Thus, the first Adam and all mankind after him suffered.

> **"For if, by the trespass of the one man, death
> reigned through that one man, how much more
> will those who receive God's abundant provision
> of grace and of the gift of righteousness reign
> in life through the one man, Jesus Christ!"
> (Rom. 5:17 NKJV)**

Jesus, the "last Adam," reversed the whole situation. He is the Door through which mankind can return to the Tree of Eternal Life. His gift of righteousness enables man to be reunited with God, the heavenly Father, and once again reign in life with Him. God the Creator made us in His image and with a free will. Our Savior Jesus, while wrestling with the powers of hell and death, wished for this ordeal to pass. However, He submitted himself to God's will by saying:

> **"Father, if you are willing, take this cup from
> me; yet not my will, but yours be done."
> (Luke 22:42 NKJV)**

It all starts with taking responsibility for your own life first.

When you knock on doors of sin and wickedness and enter them, you fall into darkness and bondage. Each person exercises his own free will to make such a decision. Likewise, you can also choose to close such doors behind you. By repentance and faith in the name of Jesus you can then enter the Door of Life and overcome sin and darkness. Instead of being used as a tool of wickedness, you will be a tool of righteousness. Not doing your own will but obeying God's will is the way to overcome all life's challenges.

Today we are living in a time when wickedness and uncleanness are getting out of hand. In the last book of the Bible in Revelation 16, verse 13, the apostle John received a heavenly glimpse of what is happening in our days:

"Then I saw three impure spirits that looked like frogs; they came out of the mouth of the dragon, out of the mouth of the beast and out of the mouth of the false prophet."

Unspeakable, unclean things are being uttered, promoted and done openly and shamelessly. In open rebellion, people mock God and His Word seeking to destroy the foundations of our society. This calls for a whole new generation of overcomers: disciples of Christ who are willing to stand against and overcome this wave of wickedness. Those who have decided to repent and live holy lives. Those who have learned to overcome by unwavering faith in Jesus, the Son of God. In 1 John 2, the apostle John wrote to young men, encouraging them to stay strong because the word of God lives in them in order to overcome the evil one. Only when the word of God truly becomes a part of your life and lives in you will you be able to overcome.

"Let the one who does wrong continue to do wrong; let the vile person continue to be vile; let the one who does right continue to do right; and let the holy person continue to be holy." (Rev. 22:11 NKJV)

Wickedness causes man's heart to grow cold, cruel and merciless. Those born of God are called to stand firm and live the opposite way, their hearts filled with love, compassion and mercy. It takes simple disciples with such hearts for the gospel to be preached in the whole world. Many unreached people groups in various nations are still waiting to hear a testimony about Jesus. Only when the last people group has heard the gospel of the Kingdom, the end of this age will truly come.

"Because of the increase of wickedness, the love of most will grow cold, but the one who stands firm to the end will be saved. And this gospel of the kingdom will be preached in the whole world as a testimony to all nations, and then the end will come." (Matt. 24:12–14 NKJV)

Until Jesus returns in power and glory, the unregenerate world still lies under the dominion and power of sin and wickedness. This present end time will end with two harvests. A harvest of righteousness and a harvest of wickedness. For those alive today, there is a choice to be made. Do you want to be part of a harvest of righteousness unto eternal life, or are you going to be part of a harvest of wickedness unto eternal death? Do you choose to be part of those who will overcome or of those who will be overcome?

"I looked, and there before me was a white cloud, and seated on the cloud was one like a son of man with a crown of gold on his head and a sharp sickle in his hand. Then another angel came out of the temple and called in a loud voice to him who was sitting on the cloud, 'Take your sickle and reap, because the time to reap has come, for the harvest of the earth is ripe.' So he who was seated on the cloud swung his sickle over the earth, and the earth was harvested. Another angel came out of the temple in heaven, and he too had a sharp sickle. Still another angel,

who had charge of the fire, came from the altar
and called in a loud voice to him who had the
sharp sickle, 'Take your sharp sickle and gather
the clusters of grapes from the earth's vine,
because its grapes are ripe.' The angel swung his
sickle on the earth, gathered its grapes and threw
them into the great winepress of God's wrath."
(Rev. 14:14–19 NKJV)

There is no excuse for any Christian not to get involved in
the Great Commission in Matthew 28:18–20. All authority in
heaven and on earth has been given to Jesus. By that authority
He commands you to go, using His authority to make disciples
of all nations, baptizing them in the name of the Father and of
the Son and of the Holy Spirit. You are to teach them to obey
everything He has commanded you. And surely He will be with
you always, to the very end of the age.

There never have been so many unprecedented possibilities
to reach out to those unreached as in our present time. In their
days, the apostles Paul and Peter traveled slowly to other people
groups and nations sailing by boat or by walking, riding a horse
or a donkey. Traveling for missionaries stayed painstakingly slow
that way for twelve hundred years. Famous missionary Hudson
Taylor's first trip to China, by sea, took half a year! Only by the
first half of the eighteenth century the steamboat and the bicycle
were developed. The car and the airplane only came into the
picture about 150 years ago at the end of the nineteenth century. Since then, the time to travel long distances, or the ability
to reach out to people in faraway places has been drastically reduced. Telephone has only existed since 1876. The radio came
into use about 125 years ago. Television since 1927. January of
1983 is considered the official birthday of the internet, revolu-
tionizing communication. Since then the proclamation of the
eternal gospel to those who live on earth—to every nation, tribe,

language and people has been exploding! At the beginning of chapter 14 in Revelation, which describes the two harvests, an angel is flying in midair, proclaiming the gospel! Certainly God uses even the internet to overcome the logistical problems of reaching out to those who never heard the gospel.

"Then I saw another angel flying in midair, and he had the eternal gospel to proclaim to those who live on the earth—to every nation, tribe, language and people." (Rev. 14:6 NKJV)

God's plan for this world is made clear in John 3:16–17:

"God so loved the world that he gave his beloved only Son, that whoever believes in him shall not perish but have eternal life. For God did not send his Son into the world to condemn the world, but to save the world through him." (NKJV)

The costly price for the salvation of mankind has been paid already. Jesus, the Lamb of God, purchased with his blood for God persons from every tribe and language and people and nation. He has made them to be a kingdom and priests to serve our God, and they will reign on the earth. When the twenty-four elders in Revelation 5: 8–10 fell down before the Lamb, they were each holding a harp and golden bowls full of incense. Those bowls represent the worldwide prayers of the saints and the harps represent worldwide worship. Only through prayer and worship in the power of the Holy Spirit will the church be able to overcome and reign over this present darkness and set the captives free. When you are born of God, you are born to overcome by faith in Jesus Christ. Can you see the need to lay down your life and your own ambitions, bow down before the Lamb of God and say, "Yes Lord, here I am, send me!"?

"And when he had taken it, the four living creatures and the twenty-four elders fell down before the Lamb. Each one had a harp and they were holding golden bowls full of incense, which are the prayers of God's people. And they sang a new song, saying: 'You are worthy to take the scroll and to open its seals, because you were slain, and with your blood you purchased for God persons from every tribe and language and people and nation. You have made them to be a kingdom and priests to serve our God, and they will reign on the earth.'"
(Rev. 5: 8–10 NKJV)

EPILOGUE

FRUIT THAT REMAINS 1991–2024

"You did not choose me, but I chose you and appointed you so that you might go and bear fruit—fruit that will last—and so that whatever you ask in my name the Father will give you." (John 15:16 NKJV)

A GOLDEN BED

We were in a desperate situation when the phone rang at my brother's house in Houten, Netherlands. After leaving Pakistan we had spent two months in India to minister to the teams there. Then we left for Germany for three weeks to pick up a vehicle and drive on to the Netherlands for what was supposed to be a six-month furlough. Our home church in Rotterdam had arranged for a place to stay in a small town nearby. A family from our church gave us their home to stay in while they were on a three-week holiday in the U.S. This was nice and restful for us, especially since by that time in March 1991 Chris was five months pregnant. Jonathan was five, the twins Shekinah and Mark were three and Pauline was one-and-a-half years old—a lovely and lively bunch.

However, after the first week of rest, it slowly dawned on me that we would soon have to find another place to stay. As a father

I had the responsibility to look ahead and find a solution for my wife and family. I had already started to work in a jam factory so we could buy groceries. Our church graciously paid for a diaper service! Originally we had planned to stay only one or two months in the Netherlands and then visit the U.S. But flying with a highly pregnant wife was out of the question, so we knew we had to stay in the Netherlands until at least after the new baby was born.

Not finding a solution for a place to stay, I was getting a bit restless. The elders of our church had advised us to stay in the Netherlands and find a job for a living. This was not exactly what we felt the Lord would have us do. The Word of God had taught us that God's gifts and His call are irrevocable (Rom. 11: 29). We both knew that God had called and ordained us and had used us to bear fruit in Asia. Was this calling and ordination all of a sudden not valid anymore? This was quite a dilemma.

Instead of finally being able to take more rest, worries about how to find a way out of this dead-end street filled my mind. At the end of the three weeks my own brother, a medical doctor, and his wife suggested we come and stay at their home until we found a solution. They had four kids but they all moved over and made room for us all.

One day the phone kept on ringing. My brother answered the call.

"It's for you," he said and handed me the phone.

"Hello, are you Antoine van den Assem?" an unfamiliar, up-beat voice asked me.

"Yes I am," I answered.

"I am a businessman speaking to you from my mobile phone on my way on the highway. I heard you are looking for a place to stay?"

In the 1990s, mobile phones were very expensive, bulky devices and only available to a small group of people—like the one phoning me. Taken a bit by surprise I answered:

"Yes, you are right. My family desperately needs a place to stay!" Before I could explain our situation a bit more, he continued.

"I have a house available for you in Westmaas. A house with a golden bed!" Not aware where the city of Westmaas was located—and not sure whether we needed a golden bed—I quickly jotted down his phone number.

When we arrived in Westmaas to see the house offered to us, we found it the way it was described: apart from a kitchen, a completely empty row house. Upstairs in the master bedroom there stood a gold-painted double bed in all its glory. That was all, but not really a disappointment for an experienced, hardened missionary family. Soon, we moved in with our sparse belongings, happy to have finally found a place we could call our "own." Our family of seven slept peacefully in that one golden bed. One evening when I was out to join a prayer meeting at our home church in Rotterdam, the doorbell rang. Chris, who was alone at home with our four kids, answered the door.

A friendly looking elderly man introduced himself politely in Dutch.

"Good evening, I am a member of the local evangelical church. I heard you are a missionary family that has come to live in our town. Is there any way I could help you?"

Only later on we heard that this dear brother was quite unsure and a bit nervous about what to expect. He came to know that my wife was American, and he did not speak any English. He was very relieved to find out she was able to communicate with anybody. Okay, this time in broken Dutch, and with hands and feet . . .

And help us he did! In no time he had contacted a local ministry that provided us with all the furniture and clothes we needed. This dear brother was a horticulturist earning his living with growing cucumbers. He and his wife were prayer warriors as well and eventually became our most ardent supporters. For the past thirty-four years, they have been praying and supporting us financially. It wasn't until later we found out they supported many other missionaries from various organizations as well. They took their calling to pray and financially support the work of God's kingdom very seriously.

Another Dutch couple did the same. The wife was born of German nobility and had been married to a Dutch naval officer. During World War II, he died in a naval battle in the Pacific. She ended up in a horrible Japanese concentration camp where she almost starved to death. Together, with her new husband, this elderly couple was always present and praying for all the young people getting saved during the Jesus People revival in the Netherlands. This couple also decided to support our family monthly. They even kept on supporting us for two years after they died and went to heaven! In their last will, they had designated a portion of their inheritance for our monthly support. Both couples are great examples of laying up treasures in heaven. They overcame the natural human inclination to store up treasures on earth, choosing to bear eternal fruit that remains.

The baby was due in July, so the plan was for our family of seven to fly to the U.S. and visit relatives during the month of August 1991. In June, I reluctantly had to attend an important leadership meeting of the VFA mission in Germany. Chris was eight months pregnant and three of our kids were sick. During that meeting, important decisions were made about the future development of the mission. For strategic reasons, they decided to ask us to settle in Germany to develop and expand the fundraising and mission base there along with oversight of the ministry in Asia.

"Chris will never agree to this," I warned them.

"You call her and ask," they suggested. So as they all fervently prayed, I called Chris in the Netherlands. Amazingly, she was suddenly enveloped with great peace upon hearing this proposal to move to Germany. Yes, there was that Clear Voice again! On July 15, 1991, our youngest son Anthony was born in the Netherlands to the great joy of his parents and siblings. In the beginning of August, we all flew to the U.S. for a month of furlough. Poor baby Anthony was not amused by all this moving and commotion. In the beginning of September, we were back in the Netherlands to find a letter from our landlord of the golden bed. It informed us that by the beginning of October our electricity would be cut off. Bad news! Well, that shock was soon overcome. Since we now knew the direction was Germany, we decided that this was probably the Lord's way of telling us to get going even a little faster. Poor Jonathan had mastered some Dutch and was only one month in first grade at a Dutch school. Now he had to leave it all to go to a completely new country and start with another language. Such things do make missionary life extra hard on parents and their kids.

A MEDIEVAL CASTLE

We wrote a special newsletter explaining this new development. Living in Germany would be much more expensive, so we figured out what we needed for our monthly support. We put this before the Lord and our personal contacts in the Netherlands, the U.S. and Germany. Once 80% of this amount was pledged, we would take it as sign to go ahead with our move to Germany. This miracle happened and on October 1, 1991, we arrived in our new homeland. Did we have a place to stay there? Unfortunately, no! We had hoped to be able to settle in the city of Nuremberg where our VFA office was previously located.

Although we knew many people there, a door had not opened. In the last moment we were offered a temporary place to stay in a rundown castle in the village of Stein in the Oberpfalz (Upper Palatinate), a district in the east of Bavaria, Germany.

The Steiners, a noble family who built the castle in the twelfth century, once lived there. The latest owner, a friendly, talkative Christian lady, took us in, amazingly, as she misunderstood and thought we had twelve kids instead of five! Surrounded by a strong castle wall, we ended up staying two-and-a-half years in the gatehouse of that castle overlooking the river Pfreimd.

After settling in with our family and few belongings, we started the work of building up and expanding the VFA mission. For me, representing the ministry in and outside Germany, plus visiting and overseeing the teams in Asia meant a lot of travel. Being absent so much was quite hard on Chris who had to take care of our five kids while learning German and taking care of administration. Apart from the fact that our tiny apartment was also our mission office, an unexpected problem soon caused a lot more stress.

The son of our host, actually a friendly and helpful guy, turned out to be an alcoholic. When he was good; he was very good, but when he was drunk he was horrible. He was jobless and slept the whole day. In the evening he would go get drunk and became very aggressive. Late at night he returned to work making a racket in his workshop right underneath our apartment. This caused us sleepless nights and it became dangerous for me to leave Chris and the kids alone in the house. It all came to a head one evening. He was pounding on our door, shouting that he would go down and kill himself. We sensed he was really going to do it so we both fell on our knees crying out to God to intervene. After ten minutes, he was back at our door. With tears jumping out of his eyes, he shouted:

"I can't even kill myself!"

He had put a very powerful pneumatic rivet gun to his temple and pulled the trigger several times. Miraculously, each time he tried, the gun got stuck! I had to repent. I had haughtily thought to myself that living in Germany would be easy after all the challenges we had overcome in Asia. Humbled I asked for forgiveness. Surely the devil was not asleep in Germany. He was still working overtime trying to stop and discourage us.

The gatehouse apartment all seven of us lived in was romantic but a tiny 70 square meters (754 square feet). Actually, luxurious, after living so often in one room! While changing the diaper of our youngest daughter Pauline in our cramped quarters one morning, I cried out to God.

"Lord, please give us a much bigger place to stay; let it be cheap enough, and let it still be in our Oberpfalz district!"

At that time, the area we lived in was practically unreached with the gospel. A couple who was also connected to our mission had seen quite some revival while starting a new church in that area. Because of all the discouraging opposition, we concluded that the devil wanted us out of that district. All these past years in Asia we had been working hard to reach out to unreached people groups. Should we now give in and leave this hard place? Of course not. God answered our prayers. A pastor found a house for rent in the small town of Edelsfeld about a forty-five-minute drive away from our castle. We drove there to check it out to find a free-standing, empty, two-story house. It had a huge living room, a big kitchen, two toilets, two storerooms, a humungous bathroom and five roomy bedrooms. All together 200 square meters living space, which is approximately 2,152 square feet! The attic alone contained another 100 square meters. It was big, cheap and still in the Oberpfalz. For the next twenty-nine years this place became our family and mission base from where we continued to reach out to Asia.

REACHING THE UNREACHED

Often while looking out of the "window" in Asia, we could not see many others willing to come and help us reach the un-reached. This "10/40 Window" is the rectangular area of North Africa, the Middle East and Asia, between the 10° and 40° north latitudes. The 10/40 Window is often called "The Resistant Belt" and includes the majority of the world's Muslims, Hindus, Buddhists and Animists. More than half of the world's population and people groups live in the 10/40 Window. It is home to the majority of the world's least evangelized countries and unreached people groups. During mission conferences, altar calls are regularly made to encourage believers to obey and fulfill Jesus' Great Commission to go and make disciples of all nations. Thousands commit themselves to do exactly that. Unfortunately, very few of these commitments translate into more workers for the 10/40 Window. Sadly, instead of going to the most needy and hard-to-reach, unreached places, many choose to go to already reached, easy-to-reach places. We realized that this might be one of the main reasons why God wanted us in Germany.

With this challenge in mind, we decided to make the best of our time in Germany to focus on this need. God had already laid a foundation for our ministry in Germany through our activities there in the past. The first focus and indeed the best foundation for any remaining fruit had to be prayer. So, besides our daily Prayer Altar for the Nations, starting with a fax machine and twenty addresses, we began mobilizing Prayer for the Muslim world. This developed into a very large international prayer network. Later we developed two other networks, Prayer for the Hindu world, and then, as the Lord started to open doors for us to work in Buddhist countries, Prayer for the Buddhist world. In the meantime our ministry in Asia had expanded to Thailand where we hoped to build a missions training base for new workers. Previously we had used Sri Lanka for this purpose, but the political developments there had made it impossible to get visas.

In Germany we reorganized and streamlined the representation of our VFA mission organization in Europe to make it more effective and also started training new missionaries. An American couple, long-time missionaries with VFA, had returned to the U.S. to find a home church. They volunteered to take on the administrative work for VFA USA. In Germany, the Lord gave VFA GERMANY a team—a German couple was called by God to move to our town and help full-time with administration and prayer. Over the years, many others helped with the translation of our mission news and prayer mails into German and Dutch. Others kept our computers or secretarial work up to date or simply came and prayed.

We mobilized young German Christians to help organize our Vision for Asia mission conferences. The first one was named Reach Out '96. After that, two more Reach Out conferences took place in 1998 and 2001. All these interdenominational conferences aimed to convey four major themes:

1. The Church as Basis for Missions
2. Prayer Which Changes the World
3. Strategies to Reach the Unreached, and
4. Mission in the Power of the Holy Spirit.

These important subjects were based on our experiences living and overcoming as missionaries in Asia. There was much remaining fruit from these conferences. As a result, many were challenged and were sent out to unreached people groups. The participating mission organizations were motivated as well. Many decided to redirect their focus to the 10/40 Window.

There was lots of opposition to each of these conferences as Satan tried his best to thwart and discourage these endeavors. In 1996, my own father and the German pastor who had helped to get VFA started in Germany both died during the preparations of the first Reach Out conference. After that conference, one of the main pastors and his wife who worked together with us were even put into prison for a while. During the 1998 conference a high-speed train slammed into a bridge in a nearby town killing more than 100 people. After the last conference in 2001, all hell broke loose when some of our workers were taken hostage in Asia. All of this did not stop or deter us. The ministry in Asia kept expanding and many new workers were trained by VFA during the years after. They were supported and sent out to countries like Bhutan, Philippines, Cambodia, Mongolia, China, Israel, Kurdistan (Iraq), Jordan and Nepal.

From 2011 until today, we are experiencing an extraordinary phenomenon. Instead of having to go to the mission field, the mission field is coming to us. Scores of refugees from some of the most unreached people groups seeking shelter or employment started flooding Germany and Europe. For many it was a disturbing trend. For us it was a golden opportunity to reach them with the good news. Instead of us having to learn their language, they were required to learn our language. Iranians, Kurds, Arabs, Afghans and Jezidis to name a few. We came to know and befriended several religious subgroups we never heard about before. The Mandaean who believe in John the Baptist, and the followers of Yarshanism, with more than half-a-million adherents. Working together with the local church, more than eighty of these previously unreached people were discipled and baptized by VFA.

In 2020 in the U.S., and then in 2023 in Germany, young and energetic successors were found willing to take on responsibility and lead Vision for Asia into the next generation—wonderful answers to prayer! Through them, God immediately started opening even more new doors to unreached places.

THE DANDELION AND THE WIND OF THE SPIRIT

During our last Reach Out conference in 2001, the following beautiful revelation was passed on to those attending:

"Hey, we are all just like a dandelion blossom gone to seed!"

The young boy participating in the mission conference who spoke these words was only thirteen years old, but his message was truly prophetic. The Lord had shown him a picture of a dandelion blossom gone to seed. The wind of Spirit came and blew on it, scattering the little parachutes each with its precious cargo of seed to the ends of the earth. Yes, Lord, amen, so be it!

"And one of the elders saith unto me, Weep not; behold, the Lion that is of the tribe of Judah, the Root of David, hath overcome . . ."
(Rev. 5:5 ASV)

TO YOU WHO READ THIS BOOK:

Thanks for taking the time. You were born to overcome! We pray this book has been a blessing and an encouragement as you strive to overcome your challenges. May the seed of the Word of God fall into your heart and bring forth good fruit. May the seed of the lessons learned in this book germinate within you with hope and the power to overcome. May the seed of your life in Christ, which has died to itself but bears within the germ of Life, be blown upon by the wind of the Holy Spirit. May it be scattered wherever God wills, even unto the ends of the earth.

If you have any questions or comments, please feel free to contact the authors by email:
antoine@vfasien.org   chris@vfasien.org

On YouTube under "Antoine van den Assem, Message Nov 17, 2024" you can meet us personally and hear the message: Born to Overcome.

Vision for Asia – USA www.vfasia.org

Vision Für Asien – Germany www.vfasien.de